GAME PLAN

The 25 Secret Strategies of the Martial Arts and How to Use Them to Build a Great Life

Tony Higo

Also by Tony Higo:

Warrior Wisdom (Book and Audio)

Superkick

Copyright 2014 by Tony Higo.

All rights reserved. Printed in the USA. No part of this publication may be reproduced or transmitted in any form, by any means, electronic or mechanical, including photocopy, recording, or media information storage or retrieval systems now known, or to be invented, without written permission from the writer and publisher, except by a reviewer who wishes to quote brief passages in connection with a review written for inclusion in an educational publication or radio or TV broadcast.

ISBN: 978-1-291-72744-9

Published by:

AEGIS Publishing

http://www.nat-mac.co.uk

tonyhigo@gmail.com

This publication is designed to provide accurate and authoritative information in regard to the subject matter covered.

It is sold with the understanding that the publisher is not engaged in rendering legal, medical or other professional or personal services. If legal or medical advice or other expert assistance is required, the services of a competent professional person should be sought.

Dedication

I would like to dedicate this book to my Mum, Rita Margaret Higo, for her love, inspiration, leadership, support and courage throughout my life and her gift of one of the most powerful phrases I know…

'I don't care how well you do as long as you do your best.'

Thanks Mum

Foreword

Tony searched for many years in bookstores and on the Internet for the 'ultimate book on martial arts'; a book that is not about martial arts techniques, drills or tips, nor about some outdated obscure mystic philosophy that only the initiated can understand. Instead, he was looking for a book describing how martial arts wisdom encompasses all areas of our modern-day lives from managing our relationships to managing our money or our health. Eventually it became clear that he had only one choice: to write the book himself.

In **Game Plan**, he has crystallised his thoughts on how using martial arts strategies in all areas of our lives can help us reach our goals and make our lives more balanced and fulfilled by using well-structured plans and the application of time-proven strategies. After years of reading and studying, he has managed to clearly define the main strategies used throughout history, and to place them in different contexts so we can all understand how each main strategy works. From the Napoleonic Wars to Ancient China, from Columbo to Star Trek, he has used many varied examples to illustrate the fact that these game plans have always been present, and to show us how we are exposed to them every day.

As a practising martial artist myself (I have trained in martial arts for 19 years, first learning Judo with André Dalèle then learning the Aegis System with Tony Higo), I am grateful to see, at last, a book about martial arts that is both interesting to read and holistic. It has been a pleasure to support Tony and see the book come to fruition.

I hope the reader, whether or not they are a martial artist, enjoys **Game Plan** and takes pleasure in learning about well-worn expressions illustrating the strategies in question, as well as how to optimise each of them in different areas of our lives.

All the best,

Amaya Touchet-Higo

Contents

Foreword..v
Preface...ix

1 The Strategies of Focus 1
    The Strategy of Reaction 3
    The Strategy of Attraction 17
    The Strategy of Direction 31
    The Strategy of Function 45
    The Strategy of Faith 59

2 The Strategies of Leverage 73
    The Strategy of Energy 75
    The Strategy of Recruitment 89
    The Strategy of Isolation 101
    The Strategy of Alignment 115
    The Strategy of Pressure 131

3 The Strategies of Vulnerability 143
    The Strategy of Manoeuvre 145
    The Strategy of Exploitation 159
    The Strategy of Target 173
    The Strategy of Risk 187
    The Strategy of Example 203

4 The Strategies of Timing 217
    The Strategy of Patience 219
    The Strategy of Interruption 235
    The Strategy of Pace 251
    The Strategy of Opportunity 265
    The Strategy of Delay 279

5	**The Strategies Expectation**	**295**
	The Strategy of Duplicity	297
	The Strategy of Appearance	311
	The Strategy of Toughness	325
	The Strategy of Expectation	341
	The Strategy of Proximity	357
6	**Epilogue**	**371**
	Bibliography	373
	Acknowledgements	375

Preface

I take it for granted at this point, since you are reading this book, that you know what strategy means but you are curious to know more about it. If that is the case, then you are coming from the same place that motivated me to write the book.

Why I Wrote This Book

After studying martial arts for over 40 years and whilst in the process of refining the syllabus of the AEGIS system (the system of martial art that I teach), I began to think about the strategies that we use in the martial arts. I thought about fakes, feints, draws, spoiling, timing, distance, power, attack and defence and, whilst these are fairly common tactics in the martial arts, they are not really taught to any depth. Most martial arts syllabuses consist of techniques and sets of techniques, such as kata and combinations, but I have never seen a martial arts system that lists and quantifies the strategies that it uses. In fact, at least from my perspective, although the terms 'strategy' and 'tactics' are used on the mat, they are not taught in a way that a student can quantify and thereby learn easily.

Strategy in the Martial Arts

There is a song which goes: *'It ain't what you do it's the way that you do it'* and the way that we do it is strategy. Every martial artist uses strategy, but they are rarely taught what it is and how it works. For instance, in boxing, there are traditionally six punches; the jab, cross, 2 hooks and 2 uppercuts. The legal targets are anything above the belt on the front of the body. Then there are the rules. There are blocks, parries, smothers, dips, clinches and slips. This, basically, is boxing. But what makes boxing work? Boxing is much more than the sum of its rules and techniques, isn't it? The techniques are the content and the rules are the context, but where is the strategy? Where in boxing do you learn the strategies? How many strategies are there? How many distances? What are the rules of timing? When should one block and when should one parry? Every boxing gym in the world will give you an answer of some sort but many will contradict each other and I doubt that more than 10% will have them written down in a form that a student can study.

Or take karate as another example. I've studied the works of Gichin Funakoshi in some depth and, as far as I can see, Karate-Do consists of a syllabus of katas which were passed down through oral tradition until Gichin Funakoshi wrote them down and had the techniques photographed for his book Karate-Do Kyohan, known as the master text. The book covers some of the history, Funakoshi's philosophy and then a breakdown of all the katas. In all this, with all its range of kicks, strikes and blocks, where is the strategy detailed? Each kata is a practice strategy designed to master a series of techniques, but they are not applicable fighting strategies that one could use in combat. What does each kata teach us about strategy? About proximity, timing, mis-direction, surprise, duplicity, or drawing an opponent?

I've used boxing and karate as my examples because I have studied them at depth, but the observations I make could be applied to just about any martial art in the world. To my knowledge, none of them actually teach strategy in any complete form and most in only the very basic of terms.

I'm sure that most martial artists reading this will, by now, be heartily disagreeing with me, but to them I would say: "Name 5 strategies off the top of your head without referring to any that I have already mentioned above." I would wager that 99% of martial artists would be struggling to name more than 2 or 3, if they could name any at all.

My issue with this is that the martial arts virtually invented strategy and yet most of the martial arts styles and systems of the world today, whilst they use strategy (everybody does), could barely name 4 or 5 actual true strategies or how to use them in more than 1 or 2 ways. Strategy, therefore, is the best kept secret in the martial arts, and this should not be the case. Every black belt in the world should be at least proficient in understanding and applying strategy, and that knowledge should not be confined to just combat. Nor should it be an instinctive application of strategy – like a cat uses its own strategy to stalk and catch a bird. If you are a master of martial arts, shouldn't you know your strategies like a chemist knows the periodic table? Yet martial artists don't know what strategies they are using or the rules and laws that those strategies correspond to. As I see it, no-one can claim to be a martial artist if they are lacking a deep, thorough and quantifiable knowledge of strategy.

This was a starting point for this book and, when I started refining my AEGIS system syllabus, I realised my own shortcomings when it came to strategy. This is why I decided to study and learn it at the deepest level I could, so that I could not only improve my system, but also improve myself, my life and the lives of my students.

What is Strategy?

It might seem a little late for this question after all I've just said about strategy, but my starting point for this book was just this question. It's in my nature to need to break everything down to the smallest component I can cope with, so that I can see how the thing is put together and understand how it connects and works; at that point I feel I know enough to use it.

So what is strategy? The word 'strategy' comes from the Greek 'strategos' meaning 'general', so right from the outset, we can see that strategy was based in the martial arts. The word 'martial' itself derives from 'Mars' the Roman god of war, therefore martial arts are the study of war.

Today, strategy is any way we attempt to achieve an outcome or goal. When we walk down the street we are using a strategy, when we eat a meal we are using strategy, so every action we take is the use of strategy. In short, strategy is how we achieve our goals from the most simple, like driving a car or jogging, to the most complex, like planning a trip to the moon.

Why Do We Need Strategy?

We all strive to understand our lives and to create meaning and purpose that makes life joyful and gives us a sense of progression and worth. Yet, most people are travelling blindly without real goals, or perhaps even the knowledge that they have ultimate control of their destiny. A small group of people have learned that they are in control, have set goals and are implementing them to better themselves and their lives. A very, very small minority have a deep understanding of strategy and these people are the most powerful people on the planet.

To understand strategy is to understand life, how it works, and how to use that knowledge to make it work better, which is what this book is about.

How Strategy Works

I wrote **Warrior Wisdom** a few years ago as a study to find the laws that martial arts are governed by, and, in so doing, discovered that what governs martial arts also governs everything else in life. What I call the AEGIS laws of combat underlie everything we do, from our attitudes and expectations to our strategies, how we implement them and how we study our results to review the success of the process before we begin it again. The 25 AEGIS laws are the building blocks of everything we do; they are the constants that are always present, which is why I termed them 'laws'. Game Plan, the term I use to describe strategy, is how we use these elemental laws to achieve our goals, making the laws work for us in our lives.

In my search for the laws of combat, I strove to break down the keys to success in life to their most basic elements and in order to understand strategy, I had to do the same thing. Most books on strategy, and there are many, do not do anything but offer solutions to individual challenges without addressing how the strategy itself will work. This suggests that they are only concerned with offering solutions to problems that they know the answer to, but at no point do they break the strategies down in such a way as to suggest they really understand how it works. Maybe it is because they don't care about or haven't asked the question, 'how does strategy work?' If we understand how it works, instead of just how to use it, then we can use it so much better and getter bigger results.

For me, this idea of using strategy like sets of techniques, as most books and experts do, is not a sufficient enough understanding of strategy and is more like a doctor who prescribes drugs without fully knowing what the drug does. A doctor who does this is likely to make a disastrous mistake and a strategist has the same chance. Using strategy well demands a thorough understanding of it and that means knowing it at its most elemental level, with a knowledge of each component of each strategy. A strategy is like a recipe for a meal and each individual stratagem within it represents each ingredient. The difference between a cook and a great chef is that the cook knows which ingredients to put in by following a recipe, but not what effect and consequence each ingredient will have on the outcome of the meal. A true chef, like a true strategist, understands exactly how each ingredient works: he creates the recipes instead of following other people's and, in doing this, he creates the biggest results possible. The problem is that there are not enough chefs in strategy which is where Game Plan comes into the picture.

Constructing a Game Plan

The ancient Chinese were very advanced when it came to strategy and for centuries they studied the workings of strategy. Sun Tzu wrote his classic work the 'Art of War' over 2000 years ago and it is still a book highly valued by business executives and military personnel alike. In addition and possibly even before Sun Tzu, the ancient Chinese also had their 36 strategies of war to draw upon for almost every occasion. These 36 strategies have been used for centuries by Chinese military, business and diplomatic corps and are truly comprehensive in their spectrum. I have provided examples throughout this book, demonstrating how the 36 strategies apply in relation to Game Plan.

The 36 strategies are a mixture of true stratagems and strategy sets and, whilst they are valuable and powerful, they still don't get to the core of strategy. They give the user a way to achieve success without a true understanding of how he achieved it, but they have still been invaluable in helping me to understand strategy from the ground up.

After several years of study, testing and re-testing the various strategies I could find from as many sources as I could find, I finally identified 25 individual stratagems which are at the core of every strategy that has been used throughout history. I found that these strategies are controlled by the elemental laws that I identified and specifically categorised into 5 of the AEGIS laws: Focus, Leverage, Vulnerability, Timing and Expectation. When added together, they make up any strategy that we use to get what we want. The strategies fall into 5 individual categories governed by 5 of the AEGIS laws of combat and these are:

1. The Law of Focus – the strategies based on managing focus and concentration
2. The Law of Leverage – those based on creating and managing power
3. The Law of Vulnerability – those focused on managing weakness and strength
4. The Law of Timing – those based on managing the timing of events
5. The Law of Expectation – those managing the predictability of actions and events

We will look at all of these in detail in the course of this book and at how the 25 individual stratagems work in our lives and how they have worked in the past, both in war and traditions.

How to Use this Book

Strategy is a powerful but subtle study which is testament to the fact that so few people know how many strategies exist or how to use them. For this reason I have set out each chapter into sections which will help to give the reader both a global and specific understanding. To achieve this I have given each stratagem a definition and, to demonstrate that all strategies cut both ways, both positive and negative, I have outlined both the yin and yang of each term together with examples of each strategy in 10 key life examples which are:

1. Overview
2. In Tradition
3. In Warfare
4. In Combat
5. In Relationships
6. In Personal life
7. In Health
8. In Wealth
9. Personal Growth
10. Summary

By the end of each chapter the reader should have a thorough grasp of the strategic concept detailed and be able to recognise how it has probably been used in the past, how it has been used against us and how to begin using it deliberately to start getting the results we desire, to create an amazing life, or at least one that makes more sense that it does right now.

The 5 key strategy types of Focus, Leverage, Vulnerability (changed to Invulnerability for reasons that will soon become apparent), Timing and Expectation form an acrostic to aid memory which is F.L.I.T.E. (which has formed part of the working title of this book: 'Fight or FLITE' for many months before it became Game Plan). This is intended to demonstrate once again the duality of the strategies by linking them to the biological response of 'Fight or Flight', i.e. the two choices we have in every decision.

If you are serious about taking control of your life in a positive way, the Game Plan strategies of FLITE will give you the edge you are looking for, whether you are intent on world domination or simply want to get a better handle on why your life is how it is. I have tried to make this book entertaining as well as helpful and informative, and, if you want to get the best out of it, I would advise you to carry this book with you, study it at length and dip into it regularly as you form your own Game Plans to bring personal success.

I hope you find **Game Plan** as useful and interesting to read as I have found it to write.

Good luck,

Tony Higo

FOCUS STRATEGIES

'What You Focus on Becomes Your Reality' The AEGIS Law of Focus

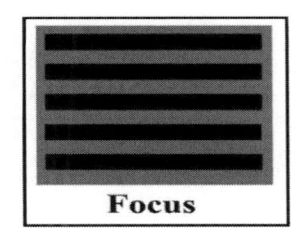

The strategies of Focus are so named because they seek to control our focus; that is, the direction of our commitment and concentration. The AEGIS Law of Focus states: *'What we focus on becomes our reality.'* So, to be effective, our use of the strategies must be believable to the target, drawing his focus away from the true direction that he should be focusing on and toward a false direction that we have created.

The 5 strategies of Focus are:

1. *Reaction* – to create under-reactions and over-reactions
2. *Attraction* – to draw a reaction toward ourselves
3. *Direction* – to send our target in the wrong or right direction
4. *Function* – to enable or disable our target's physical or mental focus
5. *Faith* – to make our target focus internally

In self-defence and sport combat, the Focus strategies are amongst the most useable and practical. Combine them together in your martial arts study, practice and application.

STRATEGY NO. 1

The Focus Strategy of Reaction

Definition: Fight or Flight

Overview of Reaction

Reactions are emotional: we either fight or we fly. The real skill in Reaction lies in knowing when to fly or fight. At times, our emotions can get the best of us. We can become angry or stressed which is the wrong reaction to have in that moment. Sometimes, on the contrary, we are not emotional enough and we fail to show concern or take action where it is needed. Over-reacting and under-reacting are both potential dangers in strategy. It is important to focus on what matters and what is real if we want to manage our reactions for effective results.

We can train ourselves, both consciously and unconsciously, to react in certain ways at certain times – this is called conditioning. Conscious conditioning is very useful when we know a thing might happen and we want to make sure we respond in the best way possible to meet that situation. Unconscious conditioning must be identified and examined, so that we can eliminate reactions that are not serving us.

'It is not stress that kills us; it is our reaction to it.'
Victor Hugo

The Yin and Yang of Reaction

The Yang
respond
oppose
answer
explode
over-react

The Yin
unresponsive
lack of answer
lack of opposition
inaction
ignore
under-react

The Reaction Strategy in Tradition

Going Off Half Cocked

In the days when guns were muskets, the weapon had to be primed and charged manually and the hammer cocked to a ready position to ignite the charge precisely. Loading a gun could take 20 or 30 seconds, during which time the gunner was at his most vulnerable. Sometimes, in the heat of battle and under pressure (see Pressure strategy), the musketeer would not properly cock his gun causing it to misfire. This was known as 'going off half cocked' meaning not being fully prepared for action. It was the novice who committed this mistake, usually owing to his battle reactions being either too high or not high enough.

'People make fast moves around me, I react. I can't help it.'
Lawrence Tierney

The Reaction Strategy in Warfare

Like a Red Rag to a Bull

The goal in warfare is to make your opponent react to your action when he should not and to not react when he should. We have only two responses in Reaction: go or stay, react or ignore. The key to these two responses is emotion. The AEGIS Law of Emotion states 'Emotion is the fuel that drives motion' and so we use anger and fear to create reaction or we remove any apparent danger to create inaction. Either response must be the wrong one for our opponent and the right one for us. Once we have the response we desire, our opponent has fallen for our Reaction strategy.

Gandhi's Passive Resistance

India gained independence from Great Britain in 1947 after 100s of years of being ruled by it. It was a long struggle and the key player in India's accession to freedom was led by Mohandas K. Gandhi. He developed a system of fighting without fighting using the Reaction strategy. Today we know his method as 'Passive Resistance', but Gandhi himself referred to it as Satyagraha or 'Truth Force'. Gandhi knew he could not hope to face the British and win on a battlefield. But, he had learned during his time in South Africa that an effective way to get what he wanted was to be downright stubborn. Standing his ground on his principles but never lifting a finger to strike back, he made masterful use of the Yin side of Reaction. He would not allow his own people to react with violence of any kind and the British had no way to fight back at him. They were prepared for warfare but Gandhi would not fight them using their weapons, only his own – which was to politely resist. If they knocked him down, he got back up and started again, never ever using violence. In the end he got his way. His strategy did not allow his armed foe to use their weapons efficiently and, instead, he used reasoned arguments, gaining worldwide acceptance and support for his struggle. Eventually, the pressure (see Pressure and Energy) and power of his followers gave the British no alternative (see Isolation) but to grant India its independence.

Nelson Mandela used a similar tactic in overcoming the Apartheid system which gave the minority whites far more rights than the black population of South Africa. Gaining gradual worldwide support (see Recruitment) he became the world's most famous political prisoner. When he gained early release, he held the future of South Africa in his hands. After 27 years in prison, he might have vented his anger and remorse at the whites. If he had said the word, he could have launched a civil war costing the lives of millions, but instead he chose the Yin side of Reaction and spoke to all South Africans, including everyone in his discussions. He laid no blame at anyone's door and brought the nation together as a whole. The transition from the unfair and racist Apartheid system followed peacefully. There was civil unrest and violence but civil war was avoided by using non-reaction instead of emotionally-led reaction.

Chinese Strategy No.13 – Beat the Grass to Surprise the Snake

This strategy turns on creating an uncalculated, instinctive and emotional response. Over-reactions come through fear, anger or surprise. Under-reactions result from a lack of sensitivity to the potential danger posed by a situation.

Make your enemy fearful of your actions. Make him react to everything you do. In combat we call this the 'feint'. We attack and make the opponent defend then, when we attack again and when he responds, we pull short our attack drawing his defence too far forwards and exposing the intended target (see Target). Or we reverse our action by appearing to be no threat – too slow, too weak – so that feeling over-confident, he drops his guard and becomes careless in his defence once again uncovering his vulnerability (see Target).

We can make our enemy react by insulting him and goading him about his family, his financial situation, his intelligence, his looks or some other area where he might respond emotionally without thinking. When he reacts (see Attraction) he creates openings for us to attack. The feint is designed to trick an opponent into reacting either too much or not enough. In over-reaction he acts emotionally with anger or fear and so, hopefully, forgets his original plan or is unable to complete it. Conversely, when he fails to see the threat, he doesn't show enough emotion and, therefore, fails to raise his defences.

> **'A life of reaction is a life of slavery...
> one must fight for a life of action not reaction.'**
> Rita Mae Brown

The Reaction Strategy in Combat

Like a Cat on Hot Bricks

Make your opponent nervous or make him careless. Attack, withdraw and, when he reacts to your feinted attacks, attack the opening he has created by his over-reaction. Hit him hard to make him nervous, hit him light to make him careless, so that he attacks you with more confidence (see Faith) as you set him up for your counter-attack. Strike at him but pull your punch short (see Proximity), so that he extends his guard too far, thereby uncovering a target.

Make threatening moves (see Pressure, Toughness and Appearance) to make him jumpy and nervous, so that he doesn't know whether to respond or not. If you can make him react to your feints, he becomes a slave to his fear and, each time he reacts, he falls further into your trap, becoming an easier target to hit. His confidence will wane (see Faith). He will be filled with doubt and might even surrender early – and an early surrender results in less risk for both sides of the conflict.

> *'Insult his children and insult his parents –*
> *it will anger him and bring about rash acts.'*
>
> Sun Tzu

The Reaction Strategy in Relationships

Fire and Ice

If you want to get the worst out of someone, over-react or under-react. Over-reaction, such as flying into a rage, can make your partner nervous and it can even signal the onset of bullying or intimidation; neither of which could be part of a good relationship.

Take an interest in what your partner and friends do. If it is important to them and if you care for them, it should also be important to you. It may not always be interesting to you, but if you want to have a good partner, then you have to *be* a good partner which means being the type of partner you would want to have.

Don't take your relationships for granted. There may come a time when you need allies (see Recruitment and Alignment) and you can frighten people away with your inappropriate reactions. The phrase 'a friend in need is a friend indeed' works both ways and, whilst good friends will always try to be there for you, you should not take advantage of their care. Listen to your partner, your children, your friends. Don't be guilty of reacting too much or too little and be prepared to apologise when you get the balance wrong (see Alignment).

Creating conflict is easy with people we know very well and sometimes we have to tread carefully when emotions are close to the surface – and even when they're not, they can soon rise to the surface if a comment, action or look is taken for disrespect or disapproval. It is often the people nearest to us that are the easiest to upset; perhaps because with them we share a longer history, one that has seen more ups and downs, more tempers and more hurts. But our relationships are important parts of our lives, so we should try not to react too rashly ourselves. When those close to us react badly, we should be prepared to stay calm, being neither fire nor ice.

> *'In politics... never retreat, never retract... never admit a mistake.'*
>
> Napoleon Bonaparte

The Reaction Strategy in Friendship

Keep a Cool Head, Not a Hot One

Friends, family and allies may sometimes fall prey to their emotions: getting upset when things go wrong, taking things to heart and lashing out with blame and hurtful comments. There are times when a hot head can serve us – especially when our head is not as hot as it appears (see Toughness) – but real anger can make us do or say things that may hurt, and once said cannot be taken back. Conversely, too cool a head can be seen as lack of care or interest. At the right time, both ends of this spectrum are valuable but at the wrong time, they also both act as weapons against us. Remember that emotion is the enemy of strategy and the weapon of the strategist.

Guide friends away from reacting emotionally and from 'going off half cocked'. Decisions made in anger are rarely good ones. Better to sleep on it and face the challenge with a clearer and cooler head. Certain situations make us more susceptible to this kind of reaction, especially where family and close relationships are involved. So, counsel your friends to stay calm at this time, and to consider the consequences of their actions.

At other times a friend or ally might not be rising sufficiently to a challenge: perhaps they are not paying their bills on time or fulfilling their obligations towards other friends, workmates or customers. At this time, you can give them the proverbial 'kick up the backside' to make them aware that they should be taking action soon in order to avoid more severe consequences.

'Revenge is a dish that people of taste prefer to eat cold.'
Louis Mazzini from 'Kind Hearts and Coronets'

The Reaction Strategy Personally

Hit a Nerve

Anger, fear, hurt and apathy are emotions that are rarely useful in any situation, unless they are part of your strategy. Be conscious of the fact that anger and hurt might be easy reactions but that, in hindsight, we are rarely proud of ourselves afterwards. Work on being able to keep your cool without appearing too distant or unconcerned. Remember that any situation that seems like a crisis now will not seem so for very long, and after even a few weeks might be just a distant memory. The key is not to invest too much emotion into events whose importance will soon fade.

Sometimes people try to hurt our feelings and they might succeed too. They say painful things and we react with anger or hurt silence. Perhaps they have hit a nerve; they know where we are vulnerable and use that knowledge to harm us. However, it is they who have the problem. They are the ones who are angry and feel the need to lash out; we are just a nearby target. Keep in mind that whatever they do or say will only hurt us if we let it.

Take responsibility for your actions and emotions. You don't have to react by kicking back. You can instead choose to respond in a better way and one of the best ways to act is calmly. The answer to the Reaction strategy is very often to not react at all and keep going. Sometimes we want to lash out. Anger can be enjoyable because it means we are right (or at least think we are) but we must counsel ourselves with the thought: 'Would I rather be right or would I rather be effective?' Anger might feel good now but, in the long term, it will serve our purposes little, if at all.

Conversely, do respond to important demands. Recognise what needs to be attended to: send birthday cards, messages, pay bills on time, look after the important demands on your time, and give proper time to friends and family. Don't get involved in feuds and long-term disputes without good reason, forgive people for their foibles and outbursts – bear in mind that they may not be able to manage their emotions as well as you do, and that even the most even-tempered person can resort to unreasonable anger at times.

'How people treat you is their karma; how you react is yours.'
Wayne Dyer

The Reaction Strategy in Health

Adverse Reactions

Use your emotions to motivate your personal health regime. Watch, listen and read inspirational material to psych yourself up to training regularly and eating healthily. You may have 80 or 90 years in that body of yours, so it makes good sense to keep it in the best order so that it doesn't let you down when you might need it most.

Positive emotion toward health and fitness is the key to good health and longevity. So, manage your emotions through exercise, meditation and study. As Tony Robbins, the personal performance coach says 'stand guard at the doorway to your mind' by eliminating negative influences and instead focusing on the positive. Learn to manage your stress and remember that your biggest stress today will barely be a memory tomorrow. Problems that seem insurmountable right now are often, in hindsight, seen as blessings in disguise. How often have we lamented a setback that prevents or blocks a course of action that we really want, only to look back later and thank our lucky stars that it did?

When it comes to health, there are many challenges that have to be managed, often small but adverse reactions that constantly occur. These are those little voices that say: 'Don't train today, do it tomorrow instead' or: 'One cheeseburger and fries won't hurt' and: 'Why not rest today and do double tomorrow?' These mini adverse reactions happen almost every day as we strive to build and maintain our health. Sometimes we will respond to them and take a day off from our healthy lifestyle but mostly, if we are serious about our health, we won't. We'll refuse to listen to these little voices. If we exert discipline, we'll be rewarded later by the 'after workout high' or simply the satisfaction of a target weight achieved as we step on the scales. This can only be done by learning to react adequately to our emotions.

> **'It's not what happens to you,
> but how you react to it that matters.'**
> *Epictetus*

The Reaction Strategy in Wealth

Buy in Haste, Repent at Leisure

I've adapted this old adage from 'marry in haste, repent at leisure' to describe those 'must-have' emotional purchases and investments. Don't react by buying 'stuff' that you don't need. Instead, take a long view of where you want to be financially and discipline yourself to achieve it.

If you want to build wealth you have to resist impulsive buying of things that don't help you: toys, gadgets, games, the latest phones, I-pads and the like. These purchases are often just a Band-Aid for some deeper issue. Perhaps, as a child, you were deprived of material possessions such as toys, new clothes or even having your own room? Maybe you felt deprived of love and affection from your parents and family? Or it might be because a feeling of boredom, that you are not enough, so you chase happiness through the acquisition of things that make you feel better or more worthy? Your feelings of lack motivate you to react to the pain you feel inside, to these unexamined needs, by buying things you don't really need to help you feel better. What is called these days 'retail therapy'.

If you are the kind of person who constantly needs to buy like this, then there are two reasons why you need to fix the problem. The first reason is that impulse buying will hamper your wealth building. Also, if you do manage to build wealth, you can easily end up losing it again if your need to buy grows like your wealth, with bigger and bigger purchases. The second reason is that your reaction to the pain you feel inside needs to be dealt with or it will eventually sabotage more than just your wealth building.

When we employ the Reaction strategy against someone else we seek to make them over-react or under-react; that is to either, act too much, or not enough. Reaction works by making our target act in a way that's not within their control; a way that we can manipulate to our own ends. Circumstances can create the same scenarios for us, like impulse purchases for instance; not with conscious intention, but it can have the same effect as if we did it intentionally. As we've seen, we can create the adverse reactions unconsciously by falling prey to our emotions. Emotions are necessary but they must be controlled if they're not to get out of hand. To combat the negative reactions caused by out of control emotions, we have to know how they arise and how to fix them. Here are two key ways which can help and work in more than just wealth building:

a) ***If you do not know what action to take*** – if you don't have wealth, don't know anyone who does and don't come from a wealthy background then the high chance is that you don't know what it takes to build wealth. In this case, your reactions in financial decisions will be 'anti-wealth', in others words, the wrong decisions. The fix for this is to get a wealth education by studying the many books and courses available on wealth accumulation. Frankly, this is a must; otherwise you won't know when to act, react or not act when planning and implementing your wealth strategies. Of course, reading books won't change you overnight, you must also put into practice what you learn and gradually condition your wealth skill-sets.

b) ***If you keep taking the wrong action through unexamined conditioning*** – as we discussed above, our conditioning since childhood dictates much in the way we react to different situations. Our core beliefs about religion, race, money, etc are mainly acquired in childhood and if nothing major comes along to challenge or change those beliefs, they will stay the same. If you have unexamined beliefs that are contrary to wealth building then you will continually sabotage yourself and your wealth. To prevent this, you must examine your beliefs about wealth and eradicate any which are in conflict with your desire to become financially free. This takes effort and study, and then building new habits to overcome your old ones – like the ones that make you want to spend when you should be saving instead for instance.

Learn to recognise and manage your reactions and inactions when it comes to wealth by first knowing what your conditioned reactions are and how they fit with the reactions you need to have.

'The possibilities are numerous once we decide to act and not react.'
George Bernard Shaw

The Reaction Strategy in Growth

Jumping to Conclusions

Over-reaction is not always pretty, and not always helpful. Under-reaction can make you appear cold and callous, and that is not always a useful state to be in either. Don't let emotions run your life, but enjoy the pleasant ones that come with personal growth. Take pride in what you achieve but don't allow egotism to take over. Remember to take joy in the success of those around you too; just because they have it doesn't mean you've lost it.

By now you've probably understood that, in order to use the strategy of Reaction as part of your personal growth strategy, you have to keep yourself under control, neither reacting too much nor too little, applying strong self-discipline to your projects and goals. Emotion is necessary, but it should be seen in the motivated attitude toward your projects. Remember the Law of Attitude: 'It's your attitude, not your aptitude that determines your altitude' – which means we must manage our attitudes. Both emotion and discipline are attitudes; the skill is in keeping these two attitudes in the right balance. Focus your efforts on your goal. Apply your discipline and motivation. Recognise when you are under-reacting or over-reacting, working to keep your reactions in balance so that you use the strategy of Reaction – instead of it using you.

'People react to criticism in different ways, and my way is definitely to come out fighting.'
David Beckham

Summary

We've seen and examined how reactions must be managed to get the best out of life. Over-reaction and under-reaction are both poor responses unless they are managed responses. Use them as weapons when necessary but, in the main, be wary of them and manage them as well as you can. Be conscious of how you react in any situation; remove bad reactions and develop good ones.

Reaction Strategy in Brief

1. Don't 'go off half cocked' – get your reactions right.
2. Set your opponent up to react badly.
3. Make your opponent nervous so he doesn't know how to react.
4. Don't be guilty of not reacting when you should.
5. Help friends to react or stay when they should – be their guide.
6. Anger or apathy are usually regretted later – manage your reactions.
7. Create healthy reactions to bad health situations.
8. Educate yourself to build great wealth reactions in your life.
9. Don't let your ego rule your reactions – get a grip on yourself.
10. Work to get the best reactions in all your relationships.

STRATEGY NO. 2

The Focus Strategy of Attraction

Definition: Bait the Hook

Overview of Attraction

We move toward what is attractive, and away from what is not. We are either: attracted or repelled, attractive or repulsive. Draw your target toward you by making yourself irresistible to him, or by creating an attraction to draw him in. Another way to use the Attraction strategy is through its opposite (or Yin side): revulsion – a situation which repels and repulses one's target, which pushes him away.

When you can't find an opening, because your opponent's defence is too strong, for example, create one and draw his attack to you. When your opponent moves to attack, he reveals openings in his defence which you can exploit. You can then lure him in like a flower lures a bee.

'Progress is the attraction that moves humanity.'
Marcus Garvey

The Yin and Yang of Attraction

The Yang

draw
attract
lure
entice
offer
sell
market

The Yin

repulse
repel
detract
deter
put off
ugliness

The Attraction Strategy in Tradition

Beware of Greeks Bearing Gifts

This is a well-known phrase dating back to the most famous use of the Attraction strategy: the legend of the Trojan Horse. According to the legend, the Greek army had besieged the city of Troy for 10 years, with no advantage (see Exploitation) gained on either side. Until, according to legend, the hero Odysseus came up with the idea of building a wooden horse big enough to hold warriors within its belly.

The Greeks built that huge wooden horse, and, during the night, they left it outside the gates of Troy. They then retreated from their position of siege outside the city walls and in the morning the Trojans awoke to find the Greeks gone and only the wooden horse remaining. The Trojans saw this as a victory, and the horse as a gift; a sign of respect from the retreating Greeks, as acknowledgment of their defeat. However, when the Trojans brought the horse inside the city, the warriors within leaped out and opened the gates allowing the Greek army which had been hiding nearby to charge in and sack the city. This gave rise to the famous expression: 'Beware of Greeks bearing gifts'.

'We shall draw from the heart of suffering itself the means of inspiration and survival.'
Winston Churchill

The Attraction Strategy in Warfare

Stick Your Neck Out

In warfare there are times when we must make ourselves an attractive target to our enemy. This happens when we cannot find where their vulnerability lies (see Target). In this case, we fake our own vulnerability so that they are persuaded to attack us, and in doing so, reveal a chink in their armour which we can exploit.

Chinese Strategy No. 15 – Lure the Tiger from the Mountain

The ancient Chinese knew the value of the Attraction strategy, as the colourful name above suggests, and every good general throughout history has used Attraction and its variations. The name of this strategy gives a good description of how it works, which we'll examine below in more detail.

Attraction strategies work especially well when combined with feints and fakes (see also Reaction and Direction). Attraction, Reaction and Direction fit together as the 'trinity' of both single combat and warfare and you should apply yourself to learning them well.

There are two basic types of draw strategy:

a) *The passive draw* is where we make ourselves the target, offering a vulnerable spot; lowering our defences, whilst pretending that we don't realise our apparent mistake. We wait (see Patience) for our opponent to take the bait, and when he does, we deliver the effective counter-attack making use of the opening we have just created.

b) *The aggressive draw* is where we hit first to get our opponent to react – like a taunt or tease to make him retaliate, seeking his revenge. As with the passive draw, when he makes his move, he creates an opening which we can take advantage of.

The draw strategy is a simple and effective one, which, like Reaction and Direction, preys on our opponent's emotions to make him react without thinking. Or, if he can think, we want him to believe that our strategy is genuine and that his reaction is the best course of action.

Deception is at the core of all competitive strategies and it's important to see the deceptive nature that is inherent to the first 3 Game Plan Strategies of Reaction, Attraction and Direction.

We have seen the two types of draw strategy, now let us examine how they work with Direction. The direction (see Direction) of the draw is important, and there are three types of draw:

a) *The draw in* - where we draw the opponent toward us.

b) *The draw out* - where we draw the opponent out of his own safety area like the Trojan Horse.

c) *The draw away* - where we draw the enemy away from something or someone we wish to protect, luring the opponent away from the target.

The Pied Piper of Hamelin

The legend of the Pied Piper of Hamelin is an example of the 3rd kind of draw: the draw away. The piper was commissioned by the townspeople of Hamelin to rid them of a plague of rats which had brought disease and despair to the town. The Pied Piper played his pipe and the rats were drawn to his hypnotic tune. They followed him away from the town and he led them into the river where they drowned, with one exception. One rat escaped and so the mayor of Hamelin refused to pay the piper the promised fee. Swearing revenge, the Pied Piper returned to Hamelin while the townspeople were in church. Playing his pipe again, he lured the children away with his magical music and neither he, nor the children, were ever seen again. We hear reference today of this tale when we are advised that we must 'pay the piper'.

'Pretend inferiority and encourage his arrogance.'

Sun Tzu

The Attraction Strategy in Combat

An Offer They Can't Refuse

Let's see examples of how the Attraction Strategy works in close combat. It's not uncommon to find an opponent whose defence you can't breach. When you find yourself unable to gain an advantage, you can initiate the draw strategy.

Self-defence can range from facing one opponent to several, and it could also be your own actions that have attracted your attacker toward you. Perhaps you are in the wrong place, saying the wrong things or doing the wrong things – shouting offensive remarks, being too aggressive, too passive, or too different. A great deal of trouble can be avoided if we remember that there are people around us who are just waiting to take advantage of our situation. This being the case, we should think twice about how vulnerable we appear, especially if we are in a strange place and alone. Think of it this way: our vulnerability can make us attractive to people who want our money, goods, or to do us harm. Our actions can make us into an unintentional draw, i.e. attractive to a potential attacker, so we must remain conscious of when we are more likely to put ourselves at risk (see Risk).

The Attraction strategy is designed to lure an opponent into our trap and when it is used well, it is used with deliberate intent. But, as we have just seen, it can also be used unintentionally, giving us a result that we don't want. If you are faced with an attacker and have time to respond, then using the draw can still work effectively in your favour in the same way as we saw above in warfare. No matter how well protected and guarded your opponent is, his defences are compromised when he makes a move to attack. If he attacks your head with a punch for example, he uncovers his body; when he attacks your body, he uncovers his head. The key is to know what he will attack with if you can and to be ready with your own response when he commits himself. Once he does, you cannot delay as the opportunity (see Opportunity) won't last long and your tactic might not work a second time.

Remember though that if you don't put yourself at risk in the first place, you can avoid having to use the draw strategy, either intentionally, or otherwise.

'*We only get one chance to make a good first impression.*'

Anonymous

The Attraction Strategy in Relationships

Something for Nothing

All positive relationships begin with attraction of some kind, and every person who seeks to find themselves a romantic partner will use the draw strategy to make themselves a target – that is, to make themselves attractive to another person or group.

Every weekend across the world, people are preparing themselves to go out on the town, in the hope of finding a mate, and the entire fashion and cosmetic industry exists to provide products to make us more attractive to our prospective or existing partners.

In business relationships, we have dress codes which we observe, so that we fit the expected persona for our chosen market: smart suits, shirts, ties, briefcase, behaviour and even the language we use are all ways to make ourselves appear (see Appearance) attractive to the right partner in business. To dress too casually in a business environment might make it look like we are not taking the situation seriously, or that we have such inexperience in business, that we don't know the social mores for the situation. Only those at the very top of their industry can dress down for meetings, and only to those partners whom they outrank, either financially or through reputation. If we want to fit with a certain crowd and be accepted as a serious player, we must make ourselves an attractive prospect. We must align (see Alignment) with our target at every level we can if we are to get the opportunities we desire. We must consider carefully what is expected (see Expectation) of our appearance so that we give ourselves the best chance we can have.

> **'The philosophy behind much advertising is based on the old observation that every man is really two men – the man he is and the man he wants to be.'**
> William Feather

GAME PLAN

The Attraction Strategy in Friendship

Like Attracts Like

Most of our friendships involve appearing attractive to each other – not only sexually attractive but certainly attractive in some way including: our looks, fashions, backgrounds, interests, hobbies or jobs...

However, we can't always be attractive to everyone we meet. If we are socially awkward, look different or odd, it can be very difficult to make friends within certain circles. If that initial attraction is missing and we don't know how to overcome it, we can be left lonely and isolated. In some circumstances, this lack of attraction to others can be so intense that the rejection turns into bullying, where someone is so emotionally repelled that they find the other person's presence a reason to make verbal and physical assaults. Some people suffer horribly for being different, having their entire lives blighted by being bullied. It's important to remember that most of our communication is how we look and sound: roughly 55% of our communication is through our body language, with another 35% being how we sound and only around 10% conveyed by the words we use. That means 90% of the way we engage with others is physical, so it's easy to see how important the strategy of Attraction in friendships can be.

Once we have become established friends, then how they look, or how we look, is no longer important. In lasting friendships, looks become less and less important as our personal qualities take precedence over our appearance. But in order to create the relationship at first, there must be something to draw us together. If you have a friend whose appearance or shyness makes it hard for him to make new friends, then you can help him by introducing him to a wider circle of people, who through your introduction, will see past any initial awkwardness and become attracted to the real person and his real qualities.

'Barriers tend to intensify romance. It's called the 'Romeo and Juliet effect.' I call it 'frustration attraction.''
Helen Fisher

The Attraction Strategy Personally

Draw Their Attention

Is there a situation where you don't fit but would like to? Is it business, relationships or opportunities that you seek? Then you must make yourself an attractive proposition to your target.

Attraction at its worst can be incredibly trivial. Consider the fashion industry for instance: nothing about it is as important as they would have us believe. But at its core is a basic human need to fit in. We are biologically programmed to try to fit into a group for our human survival. We are pack animals at heart and we all want to fit in with some type of group. In order to do so, we must make ourselves attractive to that pack. If we don't, we can actually become so unattractive as to repel the pack we would like to join. Consider your target, study it, find their hot buttons and draw them toward you by being exactly what they are looking for.

In business and commerce, this is known as marketing and every business uses it to attract customers with advertising campaigns, branding, logos, web sites, Facebook and other social media pages. Everything a business does is to make itself attractive to their potential and existing customers – from the way their staff dresses to their mission statement, which expresses their core values. In life, if you want to attract interest from the right people, then you must market yourself in the same way a business does.

'No matter what anybody says, relationships are based on physical attraction. The first time I saw my wife, it was pure animal whatever.'

Denis Leary

The Attraction Strategy in Health

Careful What You Wish For...

Our health is one of the most important things we can ever focus our strategy on. We have no idea of how long we might be on this earth and how much of our longevity is decided by our genetics, lifestyle, conditioning or expectations. What we do know though is that a bad lifestyle and a negative attitude can have a serious effect on our health, and ultimately the quality and length of our life. However, although we don't know what effects our heredity will have overall, we can tweak and manage how long we live, and the general level of our life quality, by using the strategy of Attraction. Our thoughts and actions attract to us what we focus on. Focus on health and you become healthy; focus on alcohol or drug consumption and you attract ill health. If you focus on exercise, then you attract strength; focus on good nutrition and you repel ill-health.

Successful strategists are different from ordinary people because they consider all their options before they make a move. They do this so often and have so many strategies already prepared, that they can devise a new strategy in the blink of an eye. Whilst ordinary people are wondering what to do, strategists are already doing it. Strategists consider the present, past, near future, distant and very distant future. In health, as in most areas of our lives, we must become natural strategists and consider all five of these time frames. Look after your health today and you attract a longer life tomorrow. This is the opposite of what unhealthy people do. They take their pleasure today and let tomorrow look after itself. This is ok for today; however, it's a recipe for a short life, of which the last few years will be spent in painful ill-health.

Not much in life that is worthwhile in the long term comes with taking the easy road in the short term. Make yourself a target to attract a long and healthy life so you can live to appreciate what you have achieved for as long as possible.

'Whatsoever a man soweth, that shall he also reap.'
Galatians VI

The Attraction Strategy in Wealth

The Law of Attraction

There has been much written over recent years about the law of attraction and many people have discovered their first self-improvement book in Rhonda Byrne's **The Secret** which popularised an already well known concept within the realm of personal development.

The law of attraction itself also repels many pragmatists who see it as an 'airy fairy' new age style concept which they cannot believe in because it is not based on any logical system of acquisition. However, the law of attraction does exist and is not based on any 'airy fairy' concepts; it is instead a very practical way of bringing your dreams into reality. The law of attraction requires a full study and examination in itself, and we have little space here to cover it in any detail. What I will cover is that getting what we want – including wealth or health – is about creating flow in our thoughts and our actions, which means allowing things to happen and not trying to control everything. We must examine our beliefs and make them congruent with our desires. For instance, if you want to build wealth and set your goals to do so, you must examine your beliefs to see that they are not blocking you. Many people have been conditioned to believe that money is evil or wrong, without having any real credence or truth. Unfortunately, many beliefs that we hold as adults originate in childhood; some are still valid and useful but others have lost their usefulness, if they ever had any. Yet they remain within us as unexamined rules that still dictate our adult attitudes and actions. If these beliefs are not re-examined they will stand in the way and sabotage our efforts to build a happy future (wealth, happy relationship, positive body image, etc...).

The law of attraction can only work when one's beliefs are in alignment, (see Alignment). For instance, if you want to become wealthy then your core beliefs about money, time management and success must be in alignment with this desire. Otherwise it's like trying to run a marathon while wearing a ball and chain, while you're pulling one way, it's pulling the other way. Any progress you make forwards is painful and slow as the weight of the ball and chain tries to drag you back. If you really want to build wealth and grow as a person you must lose your ball and chain, i.e. your conflicting beliefs. Only then will you attract wealth into your life.

'All that we are is a result of what we have thought.'
Buddha

The Attraction Strategy in Growth

A Magnetic Personality

There are many books and courses available based solely on the strategy of attraction (under its other name of 'the law of attraction') because it is a fascinating strategy to use to get what you want in life.

Unfortunately, some people are attracted to the law of attraction because it seems like a passive way to get what you want. However, though it has its passive element as all good strategy has, you must put in the ground work if you want to build high achievements. The strength of the strategy of Attraction is its ability to create a situation where you become a magnet for what you want, where you attract what you want to you, so that it comes to you, instead of you going to it. How do you do this? By deciding precisely what you want and where you can find it and then putting yourself out there, making yourself attractive to those who can provide what you desire. Whether it is wealth, or personal growth in the form of educational or spiritual growth, you must advertise that you want it, make yourself attractive to it, and put yourself in front of it.

During a marketing campaign for a new film, the producers create something very specific, designed for a market place that they know exists. They then tell everyone about the film to draw in viewers. They create interest in their project, offering snippets of it to tempt their audience. They invite their critics to review the film, meet with the actors in person, sweet talking them and providing lunches, banquets and galas so that their reviews will be more positive, since a positive review can pull in a still larger audience. Everything the producers do is designed to pull in the size of paying audience they need to make their venture a financial success.

Your personal success is the same process; put yourself in the way of the type of success you desire. If you are a writer, put yourself in the way of readers and if you are a singer, put yourself in the way of listeners. Whatever it is you have to offer, put yourself in front of people who want what you have.

'I tried to look presentable for a show, but not for sexual attraction. It was strictly for show business.'
Little Richard

Summary

We draw towards us what our thoughts and actions create. If we study we draw education, and if we fail to study we draw ignorance. The study of the martial arts draws towards us good health, safety and leadership. In business we attract customers through marketing which really means to let potential customers know that we have something they want. On the opposite side of attraction we repel things and people, by taking actions that offend them, either through not knowing what it takes to attract them or deliberately to scare them away. Study the strategy of attraction well as it exists in so much of what we do and can therefore often be taken too lightly.

Attraction Strategy in Brief

1. We move toward what is attractive, and away from what is not. We are either: attracted or repelled, attractive or repulsive.
2. There are times when we cannot find an enemy's vulnerability and so we make ourselves appear vulnerable, luring him to attack us. His attack reveals a chink in his armour which we can exploit.
3. Attraction strategies work especially well when combined with feints and fakes (see Reaction and Direction). They fit together as the 'trinity' of both single combat and warfare.
4. It could be your own actions that have attracted your attacker toward you. Perhaps you are in the wrong place, saying the wrong things or doing the wrong things; saying offensive remarks, being too aggressive or too passive, etc.
5. All positive relationships begin with attraction of some kind, and every person who seeks to find themselves a romantic partner will use the draw strategy to make themselves a target; that is, to become attractive to another person or group.
6. Most of our friendships involve being attractive to each other, not necessarily sexually attractive but certainly attractive in some way, including our looks, fashions, backgrounds, interests, hobbies or jobs.

7. Is there a situation where you don't fit but would like to? Is it business, relationships or opportunities that you seek? Then you must make yourself an attractive proposition to your target.
8. Make yourself a target to attract a long and healthy life so you can live to appreciate what you have achieved for as long as possible.
9. If you really want to build wealth and grow as a person you must lose your ball and chain, your conflicting belief. Only then can you attract wealth into your life.
10. The strength of the strategy of Attraction is its ability to create a situation where you become a magnet for what you want, where you attract what you want to you, so that it comes to you instead of you going to it.

STRATEGY NO. 3

The Focus Strategy of Direction

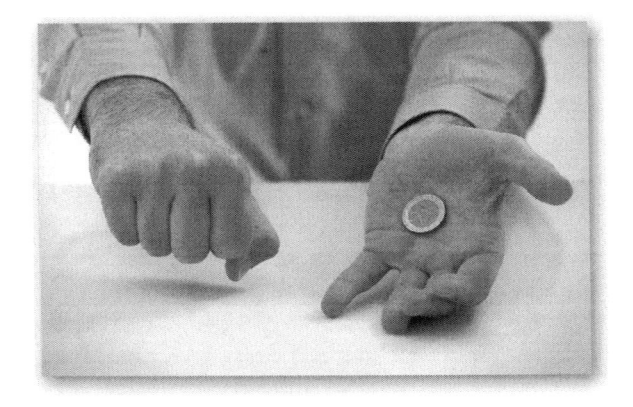

Definition: Barking Up the Wrong Tree

Overview of Direction

Having direction gives us a sense of purpose and motivation. But going in the wrong direction can frustrate our efforts, lead us into danger and waste our time. When we lose our direction we always find ourselves lost. Stay alert to your true path and recognise distractions early. In combat, mis-direct your enemy's focus and in friendship, help them to achieve the right direction and look out for times when you yourself might have no direction.

'Time moves in one direction, memory in another.'
William Gibson

The Yin & Yang of Direction

The Yang

way
course
line
road
track
bearing
route
path

The Yin

misdirection
wrong way
deviation
misleading
diversion
distraction

The Direction Strategy in Tradition

Barking up the Wrong Tree

This phrase, meaning 'to be going in the wrong direction' or 'to have misread the situation', dates back to the early 19th Century USA and to hunters stalking raccoons. Raccoon hunters operated at night using dogs, and whenever a raccoon was chased up a tree, the dogs would bark at the tree to alert the huntsmen to the location of their prey. The hunters would then climb the tree to catch the raccoon. In the event that there was no raccoon to be found, the hunter would declare that the dogs were 'barking up the wrong tree'.

> *'The secret of life is honesty and fair dealing.
> If you can fake that, you've got it made.'*
> Groucho Marx

The Direction Strategy in Warfare

Which Way to Turn

In warfare, fake your enemy, send him the wrong way. Send him left when he should go right, up when he should go down and right when he should go left. Your adversary must believe your deception if it is to be effective. He must at least commit to the way you send him, so that even when and if he realises he has been duped, it is too late for him to alter course in time to prevent you landing the decisive blow.

In combat and sport, we call this the fake. A boxer might launch a punch to his opponent's head and when his opponent raises his defences, switch the blow to his now exposed body. A footballer pretends to move left to draw his opponent's defence in order to dupe him into committing to the wrong direction as the faker slips past him on his other side.

Chinese Strategy No. 6 – Be Heard in the East, Attack from the West

The formidable Chinese warlord Ts'ao Ts'ao's headquarters were attacked by Yuan Shao with his army of 100,000 men while Ts'ao was away with his army. At first, he decided to take his own army to free his HQ but one of his advisers suggested another tactic. On his advice, Ts'ao Ts'ao sent his army toward his HQ, intending to outflank his enemy to the west, but this action was a fake. In response Yuan Shao sent half his force to intercept Ts'ao Ts'ao flanking manoeuvre. Ts'ao quickly turned his army around and attacked Yuan Shao's remaining force occupying Ts'ao's HQ and, catching them weakened and unawares, successfully routed them. His use of mis-drection regained him his headquarters.

Chinese Strategy No. 8 – Secret Escape Through Chen Tsang

The victory gained through the secret escape through Chen Tsang led to the establishment of the Han dynasty in ancient China. The ploy used by Liu Bang involved repairing roads that he had earlier destroyed in his retreat from Guanzhong. He did this in full view of his enemy, Xiang Yu, who knew that the repairs would take years and so didn't take the threat seriously. However, whilst the Liu Bang openly repaired the roads he was secretly moving his troops through the small town of Chen Tsang toward his target of Guanzhong where Xiang Yu was encamped. Liu Bang's secret approach took his enemy by surprise which gave him victory.

The key to this strategy is creating a situation where your enemy does not react to what you are doing because he sees no threat (see Reaction) whilst you are actually sneaking from behind him.

Chinese Strategy No. 31 – The Strategy of the Beautiful Woman

In ancient China, one of the 36 strategies of war involved using a beautiful concubine to lure a general away from thoughts of war. During the Spring and Autumn period in China, Chu Chien ruler of Yueh suffered a humiliation at the hands of Fu Ch'a and determined to wreak his revenge. Whilst strengthening his forces, he searched the land and found the most beautiful girl he could find. He spent 3 years having her turned from a simple girl into a sophisticated woman who could dance, sing, and recite poetry and paint. He arranged an audience for her with Fu Ch'a. Fu Ch'a was immediately besotted by Hsi Shih; he spent all his time with her and completely neglected the government of his kingdom. Whilst he was so distracted and in the arms of the beautiful concubine, Chu launched his attack and thoroughly destroyed Fu Ch'a using the strategy of the beautiful woman.

> *'Fake it until you make it.'*
> Steven Tyler

The Direction Strategy in Combat

Lead Up the Garden Path

Use the strategy of Direction to fake attacks to your opponent; attacks that send him the wrong way to divert him from uncovering your real targets which lie in a different direction. Send him left so you can go right and up so that you can go low. As long as he falls for your fakes, you can make effective attacks to his vulnerable targets. Remember your fakes are only true fakes when they are believable, which is where the real skill lies. Practise your fakes in combat so that your opponent, literally, doesn't know which way to turn.

Attack his head to uncover his body, attack his body to uncover his head, attack his left side to uncover his right and right side to uncover his left. Throw punches high so that he forgets about protecting his legs and attack his legs so he forgets to protect his body and head. Circle right to attack left and left to attack right, attack his nose to uncover his ear. Everything you do is to make him commit too far in any direction so that he can't recover in time to protect the target (see Vulnerability) you have created by sending him the wrong way.

If you can focus your adversary away from your real intent, and have him believe your fakes, you will compound his errors, creating confusion (see Function) and making your attacks doubly effective. The secret of all effective combat is deception. Strategy has developed over the millennia so that we don't have to match strength for strength – and the inherent injury for injury that comes with it. Instead, we use deceptive strategies which reduce our risks of injury and defeat. The strategy of Direction is one of the most valuable tactics we can use in all combat and competitive sports.

'Efforts and courage are not enough without purpose and direction.'

John F. Kennedy

The Direction Strategy in Relationships

When You Come to a Fork in the Road, Take It

Don't allow work, hobbies, TV or other trivial habits to lure you away from those who matter. Whilst the nature of balance is such that we must constantly compromise it in order to learn, grow and move forward, never let any distraction seem more important than your family and friends. Remember: no one ever lay on their deathbed saying 'I wish I'd spent more time at work' but many have wished they'd spent more time with their loved ones.

In business relationships, the Direction strategy can work against you too, if you are not careful, by directing you away from your business – especially when times are hard and business is suffering. It is sometimes easy to take solace in drugs, alcohol or a hobby that directs you away from the pain of your suffering enterprise. It's a biological reaction (see Reaction) that, in times of danger, we will 'fight or fly'- but sometimes we fight when we should fly and fly when we should fight. The point is that, unlike a life or death threat, a money or business problem (however painful) is not likely to kill us. Yet, our biological response cannot tell the difference, so we react as if the danger were life threatening. We avoid the problems that surround us by diverting ourselves into unimportant activities – like designing a new advert when we should be phoning customers to book appointments for instance.

Problems will not go away if we avoid them, we must deal with them. We must sit down and really look at the problem. Sometimes we have to bite the bullet and attack it face on, and sometimes we have to call it a day and recognise that the venture is over. Either way, we must not allow ourselves to be mis-directed away from important issues; we must re-focus our priorities. Only then will we have our best chance to get back on track.

> **'I can't change the direction of the wind, but I can adjust my sails to always reach my destination.'**
> Jimmy Dean

The Direction Strategy in Friendship

Wild Goose Chase

Help your friends to stay on track, not to be side-tracked by unimportant issues and trivialities. Help them stay focused on their priorities.

Often, as a friend or ally, you have a better view of what is happening than the person experiencing the difficulties. You are not as close to the problem as your friend is and he might be unable to see 'the wood for the trees'. Often the stress of certain situations can blind us to the real issues and we send ourselves 'on a wild goose chase', wasting time and energy (see Pressure) on a problem that does not need solving.

Conversely, it is sometimes us requiring help and our trusted friends who come to our aid. A good friend knows us well and understands our foibles and eccentricities; they can often see things more clearly than we can ourselves. They can help guide us in the right direction. Obviously it's up to us to make the final decision on what to do, but listening to a friend's opinion and not just our own helps us to make the right choice and avoid wasting time and energy on a wild goose chase.

A difficult time in our life such as a bereavement or break up can distract us so much that we forget to look after those who need us most (including ourselves!) We dwell too deeply and too long on our loss. This is when a friend can help us see things more clearly, get our life back on track (or simply get back to work) and regain a sense of normality.

Sometimes, it could be a friend who is seduced away from his job, friends or family by another person with whom they become infatuated, or it could be the lure of drugs, alcohol, work or fame. In helping them to recognise their true priorities, it's important to remember that 'you can lead a horse to water but you can't make him drink'. You can advise, counsel, guide your friend and point them in the right direction but, in the end, they must be the one to take action.

'If you don't know where you're going then any road will take you there.'

Chinese proverb

The Direction Strategy Personally

Follow Your Nose

Remind yourself often of your goals and priorities. Balance the various facets of your life – heart, mind, body and spirit – as equally as you can. Recognise that a part of each day of the week must be set aside for yourself, your family, your health, eating the right foods and completing the tasks you need to do to earn your living or look after those who rely upon you.

At work or in relationships beware of those who draw too much on your time. What are their motives? Are they deliberately misleading you or are their distractions innocent? At work, we might find that we have competitors who seek to re-direct us from our true goals and literally have us barking up the wrong tree. Even those who act innocently can be such a distraction and, whilst we are often keen to help, remember that those who demand the most help sometimes do so because they won't take responsibility for their own actions or stand on their own two feet. Be ready to guard against diversions which appear minor, such as the work colleague who stands in your office doorway chatting distracting you from your work, or a TV programme that draws you in when you should be spending quality time with your family. Also, be aware when you should create diversions for your family and friends (which don't have to be deceitful or mercenary in nature) that will help to keep lines that will help to keep lines of communication open.

Here is an example of a popular Direction tactic, intended to keep a dialogue flowing so you don't lose control of a conversation. It is often used in selling and politics but is equally useful in other circumstances too. This tactic is used in response to a question that you don't want to answer directly, because to do so may compromise your discussion. For example, this is used to re-direct a difficult direct question, such as a brand new customer asking you: 'How much is it?' To give an answer as direct as the question might not help you or your customer. Perhaps the price alone might divert the customer from considering other more important qualities of your product. To avoid replying with the price directly, you can use a diversion tactic like this one: 'We have a full range of prices to meet your budget, perhaps you'd like to try the product first to see which model suits you best?' What you have just done is answer a question with another question. This technique keeps the dialogue open whereas, if you simply gave a price, the door to the sale might be closed and both you and your customer could lose out. Not every question can be answered directly and some direct questions are 'leading' questions, designed to lure (see Attraction) you into saying the wrong thing. This will allow you not to let yourself be manoeuvred – whether in your position as a business person or as a customer – into a position you do not want to find yourself into.

Stay alert to your true direction and the intent of others, so that you can recognise when a situation is true, or simply a diversion – whether intentional or not – designed to distract you from your goal. This takes a high degree of vigilance to maintain, so you shouldn't expect to always get it right.

> **'You can't fake quality any more than you can fake a good meal.'**
> William S. Burroughs

The Direction Strategy in Health

Eyes on the Prize

Be wary of new fads in diet and exercise until you have studied them carefully. Marketers will have us believe that their products are entirely new and different and that we must have them if we are to progress. We can easily be mis-directed away from what is tried and tested, such as fresh fruit, vegetables, natural proteins, carbohydrates, fats, vitamins and minerals. Diet shakes are not real food nor are protein bars or snack bars; these are chemical concoctions often made from waste materials like whey, or packed full of the wrong kind of sugars and offering no nutritional value. Good food is basic and has not changed since the dawn of time so don't be lured into fads and fashions that seek to divert you away from this simple fact.

With exercise, remember that there are 168 hours in a week and some of that time should be spent caring for the vehicle that you live in: your body. It makes no sense to live a long life if your lifestyle has left you a virtual invalid. Modern drugs may keep you alive – but at what quality of life? TV, computer games, internet, the pub etc., will all steal our time away from the extra effort and discipline needed to pull on our training kit and go the gym or the dojo. Also, the effects of good diet and regular exercise are important not only for our physical fitness but also our mental fitness. It's so easy to be diverted toward relaxing rather than training hard, but the effects of taking it easy for too long and too often will have their negative effects, just as regular exercise and good diet will have positive effects over the long term. The key is to focus on the right direction.

*'Go confidently in the direction of your dreams.
Live the life you have imagined.'*
Henry David Thoreau

The Direction Strategy in Wealth

Go Against the Grain

If you are sucked into living your life to the limit of your income, you are forgetting that changes such as health issues accidents and loss of a job could leave you vulnerable. It has been estimated that most families are only 3 pay cheques away from homelessness, which means most people are leaving themselves very vulnerable (see Vulnerability) to sudden and negative changes in their circumstances. Put money aside each week and month into savings, live well within your means, make well-planned investments that will secure your future for when you are too old to work or if you are no longer able. Don't be distracted away from a secure future by the latest model of car, bigger houses and the whims of fashions. Even the squirrel has the sense to put nuts away for times when food is scarce, so we should do no less.

Read books on wealth creation and money management. Learn the difference between savings and investments and how to manage risk (see Risk). The majority of people will never achieve wealth because they are mis-directed away from its importance by clever marketers who convince them to buy, buy, buy instead of saving and investing for their family and their future. Don't follow the trends that everyone else is following or you'll find yourself being faked out, mis-directed away from a wealthy future. To achieve wealth, and that seemingly magical financial freedom, one must 'go against the grain' to go toward wisdom.

'If our condition were truly happy, we would not seek diversion from it in order to make ourselves happy.'

Blaise Pascal

The Direction Strategy in Growth

Carve Your Own Path

Educate yourself to a high standard and remember you are your biggest asset. Be the expert; don't rely on a company to provide your income, moving up a corporate ladder that doesn't appreciate or compensate you for your true talents and worth. Big companies only serve themselves and only the very smallest minority at the very top of the corporate ladder achieve great wealth – and that often at the cost of their health and relationships. We are not here to work all our lives simply to put wealth in someone else's pockets; we are here to achieve our own destiny, to do what we feel is important on issues that matter to us, and the corporate route means you go their way and not your way.

If you're in a job (which often stands for '**Just Over Broke**'), you'll find as you get older that replacing your job if you have to, can become much harder to do. So make provision to bring in passive income, develop income-earning hobbies, become the industry expert. Don't be faked out by corporate promises unless you are the one making them. Be able to stand on your own two feet if your company cannot. Develop yourself spiritually. Learn to relax and take time for yourself so that when you finally retire, or even before, you learn how to be at peace and not sent hither and thither by new trends and inessential periphery. Maintain a direction that serves you in the long term. Follow your destiny, not a pay cheque. Soon, you'll find that the passion you have for what is most important to you will reveal a new and profitable future that allows you to follow your own path – and not to be mis-directed into a life of employed drudgery, dreading every Monday morning and longing for every weekend.

> *'The direction in which education starts a man will determine his future in life.'*
> Plato

Summary

The strategy of Direction is a useful tactic in combat, sport and conflict but, whilst we can send our opponent the wrong way, we too can be sent the wrong way. Sometimes, it is not a person who distracts us; it can be a glittering object, a beautiful person or thing or even our own lack of purpose that allows us to be mis-directed. The defence against mis-direction is to remain vigilant and focused on the real prize.

Direction Strategy in Brief

1. Having direction gives us a sense of purpose and motivation, but the wrong direction can frustrate our efforts, lead us into danger and waste our time.
2. In warfare, fake your enemy, send him the wrong way. Send him left when he should go right, up when he should go down and right when he should go left.
3. Remember your fakes are only true fakes when they are believable, and this is where the real skill lies. Practise your fakes in combat, so that your opponent, literally, doesn't know which way to turn.
4. We must not allow ourselves to be mis-directed away from important issues. They won't go away on their own, so we must re-focus our priorities, and then we will have our best chance to get back on track.
5. Often the stress of certain situations can blind us to the real issues and we send ourselves 'on a wild goose chase', wasting time and energy on a problem that does not need solving.
6. Stay alert to your true direction and the intent of others, so that you can recognise when a situation is real, or whether it is a diversion, designed to distract you from your goal.
7. Good food is basic and has not changed since the dawn of time so don't be lured into fads and fashions that seek to divert you away from this simple fact.
8. Don't follow the trends that everyone else is following or you'll find yourself being faked out, mis-directed away from a wealthy future.
9. Follow your destiny, not a pay cheque, and you'll find that the passion you have for what is most important to you will reveal a new and profitable future that allows you to follow your own path in life.
10. Consider all sides of Direction and what is a direction, mis-direction, distraction, diversion, illusion, fantasy, and learn to know when you're on the right path and to recognise quickly when you're not.

STRATEGY NO.4

The Focus Strategy of Function

Definition: Tied Up in Knots

Overview of Function

When we can function freely, we have choice. Without choice, we are trapped: Being tied up is the physical inability to function, confusion is the mental inability to function. Create mental or physical confusion in your enemy and you stifle his actions, making him an easy target. But beware that you don't do it to yourself. In cooperation and friendship, help friends and colleagues to be free of confusion so that they can function efficiently.

'All things are subject to interpretation. Whichever interpretation prevails at a given time is a function of power and not truth.'

Friedrich Nietzsche

The Yin and Yang of Function

The Yang

capacity
purpose
use
role
ability
operation
doing
action

The Yin

malfunction
confusion
inability
dysfunction
inaction
inactivity
inertia

The Function Strategy in Tradition

From Pillar to Post

In the Middle Ages, every village had its own crime control and places of punishment. Some had a pillory or stocks where an offender could be placed as a punishment and sometimes pelted with rotten fruit or vegetables. For more serious offences, the wrongdoer could be placed first in the pillory and then led to the whipping post for further punishment. On his way to the whipping post, the accused would be jostled, harassed and generally abused by the mob. Which is where the phrase to be knocked 'from pillory to whipping post' came into being. It has since been shortened to 'from pillar to post', meaning to be a victim of frustration and in a state of flux, unable to function properly.

> *'I've been the queen of dysfunction and made every mistake one can make.'*
>
> Janice Dickinson

The Function Strategy in Warfare

Tied Up in Knots

When an opponent can move freely he has more options and choices and is, therefore, more of a danger. But if he cannot move freely, he is an easy target. Work to prevent your enemy from having either the choice or ability to move and you can secure an easy victory.

Chinese Strategy No. 35 – The Strategy of Links

This strategy, one of the 36 ancient strategies of the martial arts, concerns the famous battle of the Red Cliffs. The Chinese warlord Cao Cao (also written as Ts'ao Ts'ao) had his ships docked on the Yangtze River, tied together to prevent them moving too much, as many of his soldiers were not used to being aboard ships and were suffering sea sickness. The enemy forces of Liu Bei and Sun Quan capitalised on this immovability by sending fire ships disguised initially as forces wishing to surrender to Cao Cao. Once close enough, the ships were set alight and the wind carried them straight into Cao Cao's armada. Because his ships were tied together they could not be mobilised and were destroyed, giving Lui Bei and Sun Quan the advantage, which they took to win the day.

Chinese Strategy No. 20 – Disturb the Water, Catch the Fish

This is another famous Chinese strategy which focuses on creating confusion in one's enemy so that he cannot think or function properly. By confusing his thinking, one stifles any action he can take, as he cannot decide what to do or which way to turn, leaving him open to attack. We are most dangerous when we can think clearly and most vulnerable when we cannot think at all.

Giving an enemy too many decisions to make by, say, attacking from many directions at once, creates a situation of physical and mental overwhelm. In this situation he cannot think clearly, prioritise or act effectively and becomes easier to defeat.

'I used to go away for weeks in a state of confusion.'
Albert Einstein

The Function Strategy in Combat

Pull the Wool Over His Eyes

In sport martial arts, such as points fighting, there is a tactic called the 'blitz', which I will mention again later as it uses several of the FLITE strategies. The 'Blitz' consists of very quickly and suddenly attacking one's opponent. The blitz uses the strategies of Expectation, Pace and Pressure to create a mis-function in our opponent, acting so quickly that he cannot react because the speed of attack prevents him from thinking clearly.

Another example of the Function stratagem can often be seen when we are faced with a much superior opponent. If we cannot score, and he constantly scores against us, we become like a rabbit in the headlights of a car, unable to move for fear of doing the wrong thing (see Faith). Our frustration leads to confusion, and confusion leads to mis-function or failure to function at all (which is effectively the same thing). He beats us to the punch with superior speed and agility (see Pace and Manoeuvre) and when we try to fight back with our own attacks, we find he is not there anymore by the time we do. Or, even worse, he hits us every time we try.

In other martial arts, such as boxing, we spoil and foil our opponent's punches before he can launch them properly. We push and pull him to spoil his mental equilibrium and physical balance; clinching and spoiling his technique once again creates frustration making our opponent unable to function and therefore unable to fight. In grappling we apply locks, holds and strangles to prevent him from moving at all, getting him to surrender by tapping out because he is entirely unable to fight back.

Mis-function is both physical and mental; mental mis-function creates physical mis-function and vice versa. The key is to make an opponent not know what to do. If he does know what to do then we need to prevent him from being physically able to do it. Kicks and strikes can cause this to happen through knockouts or compounded injuries, locks and holds by making an opponent unable to move or escape. In a boxing ring, we can corner our opponent so that he has insufficient space to move (see Manoeuvre) and is thereby unable to function. In a mixed martial arts fight, we achieve this by choking, submitting or sitting on his chest and pounding him into submission.

An opponent who can't think of what he should do next, or who can think what to do but is physically unable to do it, is prevented from functioning. The Function strategy in combat removes choice. A martial artist must consider all sides of the Function strategy as it is crucial in combat, and it must be studied at different ranges (see Proximity), angles (see Alignment) and height levels. For instance in unarmed combat there are 5 standing levels:

1. ***Standing***
2. ***Crouching***
3. ***Kneeling***
4. ***Lying on top*** of an opponent
5. ***Lying beneath*** an opponent

The position that gives the greatest choice of movement is 'standing' because this position permits us to easily adopt all the other positions and thereby manoeuvre (see Manoeuvre) fully. The worst position to be in is position 5 which is underneath our opponent as this gives us the least ability to manoeuvre and thereby function.

However, some systems, such as Brazilian Ju Jitsu, specialise in using this bottom position very effectively, luring an opponent into a lock or choke like a fly in a spider's web. Yet, this effectiveness is immediately lost if you are faced with two opponents at once because whilst one is tied up with the first attacker, the second is free to attack as he wishes. This type of Function based on levels also works in distances (see Proximity) where the further one is from one's opponent, the more choice one has to function and the closer one is. For instance, in a clinch, one has the least ability to move and thereby function. This is why any serious martial artist (and thereby strategist) must study Function in depth.

In short, the key to the Function strategy is to prevent your opponent from being able to function whilst improving your own ability to function, creating a disadvantage (see Exploitation) for him – which becomes an advantage for you.

'When a man's knowledge is not in order, the more of it he has the greater will be his confusion.'
Herbert Spencer

The Function Strategy in Relationships

The Old Ball and Chain

A relationship is, at some level, a partnership – whether it be in business or marriage or friendship. Each side must fulfil their part to maintain the balance of the relationship.

If one side constantly needs support or is unable or unwilling to function on an equal level, then the partnership falls into imbalance. The law of balance states that 'with balance we can achieve almost everything but without it we can achieve nothing that lasts'. A relationship must maintain balance if it wants to survive. In the old days, a husband would go out to work and the wife would manage the home, which kept the marriage balanced by allocating specific functions to each member of the pair. Nowadays, often husband and wife both work, so the daily tasks must be divided between the two equally so that neither one is doing too much. Otherwise, the partner with the most to do will become tired and resentful of the one who is not doing enough. Both partners must function equally, supporting each other, working together on what they are capable of doing and supporting the other when their relative skill-sets are uneven.

If one partner is doing all the work and the other is doing nothing, the imbalance will stifle their joint success, in effect spoiling their function. Any successful relationship must be moving forward in some way, which it might still do in this situation, but it can be like walking with one foot nailed to the floor; forward progress is made difficult and painful. If this happens and continues happening, it can mean the end of the relationship.

We must develop strategies in our relationships to recognise and deal effectively with these mismatches before they are allowed to grow so large that they become insurmountable and the relationship crashes.

> '*The test of a first-rate intelligence is the ability to hold two opposed ideas in mind at the same time and still retain the ability to function.*'
>
> F. Scott Fitzgerald

The Function Strategy in Friendship

Don't Know Which Way to Turn

High emotions, such as fear, stress, loss and anger, make us vulnerable to acting rashly or not acting all. Imagine a friend in this situation, perhaps so upset by a relationship break up, bereavement or financial crisis that they do know what to do. In the face of such stress they become confused, not knowing which way to turn.

We can be there to advise, guide and lead our friend out of their troubles. Running errands, standing by their side at important meetings, sitting down with them and helping them to formulate plans and initiate those plans so that their level of confusion is reduced to the point where they can begin to function again.

There is an old saying: 'Give a man a fish and you feed him for a day. Teach him how to fish and you feed him for life'. This reminds us that, whenever we help and guide our friends, we must eventually step back and let them decide and act on their own. It is like teaching a child to ride a bike; initially we can hold them upright whilst they get to grips with how to balance, steer and pedal and, gradually, we need to take less and less part in the action until they can ride without our assistance.

My point is that, in order to help others, we must help them to help themselves: to be independent, to stand on their own two feet as it were, even though in the early days they may have to lean on us completely.

'What we can or cannot do, what we consider possible or impossible, is rarely a function of our true capability. It is more likely a function of our beliefs about who we are.'
Tony Robbins

The Function Strategy Personally

Backed Into a Corner

We must be able to recognise when we are unable to function mentally or physically, just in case we don't have anyone to help us to resolve the issues we have.

At times we will all suffer great stress which will prevent us from thinking clearly. Perhaps we might find that circumstances have backed us so far into a corner that we cannot move. Experience in solving problems will help us to understand and develop strategies that we can draw upon, which will often work in problem situations that seem to be entirely new. For instance, the Law of Study states 'the more we know the easier it is to know more'. This also means: the more problems we face, the more easily we will be able to solve them (since we have experienced them often.)

There is a useful attitude which explains that if we are facing new problems all the time, then we are growing. Obviously we must reflect on how we feel about these problems and consider: 'Are these problems really problems or are they opportunities (see Opportunity)?' A problem is generally only as big as we think it is, which comes down to our perception, so it is wise to ask ourselves: 'How can I deal with this? What is the worst that can happen? And then what?' We cannot avoid problems, but we can think differently about them.

We must also be aware of whether we are facing the same problems over and over, i.e. if we are falling into the negative side of the Law of Predictability which states 'If you keep on doing what you do, you'll keep on getting what you get'. People who achieve little in life constantly answer the same problems with the same solutions and end up getting the same results. They end up in a vicious circle of same problem, same answer and remain there until they come up with a new solution. So beware of doing the same thing over and over and expecting a different result, as this is how you build for yourself a cage that will prevent you from functioning and, therefore, from progressing.

'The superior man is distressed by the limitations of his ability; he is not distressed by the fact that men do not recognize the ability that he has.'

Confucius

The Function Strategy in Health

Between a Rock and a Hard Place

We hear a lot these days about the effects of stress and overwork, where people become unable to function effectively as a result of being overwhelmed by how much they have to do and the time and resulting pressure to get it done well enough.

We work to constant deadlines and have to achieve certain results but there is an optimum workload that each of us can handle. When that workload becomes so large that we cannot at any point complete it, the resultant stress can turn into ill-health which can lead to collapse and, consequently, the inability to function. The effects of stress can be a killer and so we must work to maintain 'work/ life balance' so that we are always able to function.

To function also means to move physically, as in taking regular exercise, which helps to reduce stress and build physical health. If we are prepared to create smaller positive stresses now, such as taking a few hours of exercise each week, we will keep the body strong and the mind free of confusion, so that we are later able to manage more stress, both physically and mentally. The nature of exercise, whether it is physical or mental, is to increase our ability to manage stress. We stress our minds with positive stress (or eustress) learning and training more so that we raise the bar on the amount of distress it takes to cause us to mis-function and collapse.

'Intelligence is the ability to adapt to change.'
Stephen Hawking

The Function Strategy in Wealth

Financial Freedom

Financial stress is obviously linked to many of the life stresses we face daily. It is, therefore, a wise thing to build more money than we need so that we always have access to enough to deal with meeting our daily needs, even into old age.

I use the term 'access to enough' purposefully, because some of the stress we face (see Pressure) is created by us accessing cash through borrowing on loans and credit cards. In the short term, this can solve our cash issue today but problems can occur in the longer term, since, every time we borrow, we reduce the amount we have available in our cash flow by the amount we have to repay each month. If we constantly solve our financial issues by borrowing, we may find ourselves unable to function financially – this is what we call 'bankruptcy'.

If we manage our money by planning, earning, saving and investing, we raise the bar, as in Health above, on the amount of financial stress we can cope with before we become unable to function.

The key function of money is as a unit of exchange; a value for value swap of goods or services, however money has the added value that it can be stored up and loaned to others. Or it can buy things that others want, such as a house, and be leased to someone at a profit. At some point money starts to function quite differently in that, instead of you working for it, it starts working for you. Most people's function is to work for money; they become controlled by their need for it. As a result, their days are spent making enough money to live on, which controls their mental and physical functioning eight hours each day and five days each week. When money starts to work for you through leveraging (see Recruitment) its power, you cease to be controlled by it and start to be the controller of it, which creates much less stress on your time both psychologically and practically. The financial stress caused by having your days controlled by earning money is a major cause of mental stress which causes mis-function. We live in a society that needs money to make it function, so stay ahead of the game by building your own reserves of money and leverage it by investment, so that you stay ahead of your needs and inflation by always having more than you need and spending less than you earn. Make sure that money functions for you, rather than having you functioning for it.

> **'Form follows function – that has been misunderstood. Form and function should be one, joined in a spiritual union.'**
>
> Frank Lloyd Wright

The Function Strategy in Growth

Freedom of Choice

I mentioned earlier the importance of attitude, and it's worth reminding ourselves of the Law of Attitude which is at the very core of everything that we do: 'It's our attitude, not our aptitude that determines our altitude'.

Confusion is a state of mind, and if we know this we can use that knowledge to free ourselves when confusion strikes us. This means that dis-function and function are also simply states of mind. A state of mind is an attitude, and an attitude is also a stance or position. The amount of stress it takes to either make us function or stop us functioning, is dictated by our attitude. This knowledge gives us great power over our lives, because it means that we have the ability to control how we respond, and so gives us a choice in every situation; choice is freedom, and freedom is the ability to function.

Personal growth begins with the attitude that we can live a better life by becoming a better person, and this open attitude creates the space for great things to happen. However, on the other side of the coin, if we close our minds to growth, we put ourselves into a cage or chains which restrict our movement in both thought and action. We can so easily limit ourselves by how we think and we only have to look around us to see people doing this all the time, placing emphasis on the unimportant – such as fashion, phones, TV, and trawling the internet for things that have no real value. The size of your TV or bank balance is not more important that the size of your circle of quality friends or your contribution to society. What film stars are wearing, doing or saying, as portrayed in trashy magazines, will have no effect on your life unless you make it a focus.

To grow personally and spiritually, one must face constant challenges, resolve them and move forward. However, if we fear challenge, we fear growth and progress, so we must condition ourselves and educate ourselves constantly. This way, we can remain conscious enough to recognise when we are moving forward, which means functioning optimally, and when we are trapped, which means not functioning at all. At times we will come to a full stop, unable to solve an issue, but we must simply step back, take time and re-think. The answer will come from within ourselves or through the experience of others that we can draw upon.

There is no problem in the world that someone else hasn't faced and published their solution to somewhere. Knowing this is another way to maintain our ability to function.

'Minds are like parachutes – they only function when open.'
Thomas Dewar

Summary

The Function strategy is key to all our success or failure. When we are able to function we are able to progress and, when we cannot function, our progress is frustrated. We must recognise that we are never truly stifled; we always have a choice no matter how trapped we may feel. It may be disguised as a decision we don't want to make (cancelling a holiday, selling your 2nd car, paying for extra tuition when necessary), but it is still a choice. Manage your attitude well and you will always be able to function.

Function Strategy in Brief

1. In warfare: create a situation where your opponent cannot function. If he can't function, he can't fight.
2. In combat: clinch, turn, trap, lock and hold your opponent. Remove his ability to function.
3. High pressure can create mis-function, low pressure, and inaction. Find the optimum point where your ability to function thrives.
4. In relationships, all partners must have their function, otherwise there is an imbalance which can lead to a failure of the partnership.
5. We can help others to function, but we can't function for them.
6. A closed mind is already failing to function. Keep an open mind instead.
7. The ability to function is the ability to change.
8. We always have a choice, even when it seems we have no choice. The answer to a problem is not always the one we want but there is always at least one way out of any problem.
9. Don't tie yourself down, except to the things or people you value most.
10. Use your attitude to free yourself from unnecessary stress, frustration and confusion.

STRATEGY NO. 5

The Focus Strategy of Faith

Definition: Faith Can Move Mountains

Overview of Faith

We all have doubts and fears and so too do we have faith and trust. Confidence is the measure of both ends of this spectrum. We need to learn to build confidence where it's lacking for no good reason and avoid doubt turning into paranoia. When we can create misplaced doubt and confidence in our opponent, he becomes vulnerable as his focus fails him. Doubt is necessary in the right circumstances, but in the wrong circumstances it is a killer. You must learn how to create doubt for enemies and faith for friends and for yourself.

'You gain strength, courage and confidence by every experience in which you really stop and look fear in the face.'
Eleanor Roosevelt

The Yin and Yang of Faith

The Yang	The Yin
assurance	doubt
self-confidence	faithless
sureness	diffidence
authority	distrust
certainty	disbelief
faith	mistrust
belief	misgiving

The Faith Strategy in Tradition

Or I'm a Dutchman

In the 1600s England was constantly involved in both trade and war with the Dutch and the two sides became highly competitive. From England's point of view, the Dutch became everything that the English despised, with the result that many phrases came into the language showing disdain for the Dutch: Dutch courage, going Dutch, Double Dutch, and so on. To be Dutch was something that every Englishman would think abhorrent and the opposite of what an Englishman expected to be. The phrase 'Or I'm a Dutchman' added after a statement implies absolute confidence in our foregoing assertion – so a sentence such as 'It will rain tomorrow, or I'm a Dutchman' means it will definitely rain for instance. Used less today, the phrase still expresses absolute certainty about fact or statement.

'A man of courage is also full of faith.'
Marcus Tullius Cicero

The Faith Strategy in Warfare

Sow the Seeds of Doubt

Many strategies involve direct conflict and action, but the Faith strategy happens in the mind of our adversary first. Where he is certain, we must create doubt: doubt in himself, his allies and his soldiers. He must even doubt his enemy. His confidence must be crushed, because this will take away his will to win. If he thinks he can't win, then he won't be as motivated to fight so hard. This means an easier fight for you.

Chinese Strategy No. 33 – Create a Rift

This ancient Chinese strategy undermines the confidence between allies, creating doubt where faith and trust once reigned. Spread gossip, divide the group (see Alignment and Isolation), get them to turn on each other, create dissension in the ranks, and sow the seeds of confusion, inaction and wrong action. This is the strategy of divide and conquer; an enemy is weaker when he is alone (see Isolation) and even weaker when, as well as being alone, he knows others are out to get him too.

Everyone has a degree of confidence or doubt within them, on any subject, but that faith or doubt is always vulnerable in the right circumstances. When your enemy is too strong or powerful, create doubt where there should be confidence and confidence where there should be doubt. In extreme circumstances it can be necessary to point to someone and call them a thief, liar or cheat in order to create doubts in those nearby, making them think that this person is untrustworthy. Mud sticks, so throw it at your enemy. Tell those he relies on of his failings, especially his cheating ways (even if he doesn't have any). Provide proof where you can and fabricate it when you cannot. Smear his name so those he relies on lose their confidence in him.

Alternatively feed him sugared words, tell him he looks good when in fact he looks foolish, furnish him with proof that his action will win the day, when, in fact, he is heading for a fall. Gain his trust and then lead him like a lamb to the slaughter.

Lord Haw Haw

In 1939 Nazi Germany used its radio programme 'Germany Calling' to broadcast anti-British propaganda to the British nation. Lord Haw Haw was the broadcaster whose English-accented tirades detailed the futility of the British war effort. Most famously, the voice of Lord Haw Haw was that of William Joyce, an American born fascist supporter who was recruited by the Nazis because of his English accent. Throughout the war, Joyce tried his best to demoralise the British people through his broadcasts designed to break their will and unleash fear and doubt on them. In the end, Joyce was caught and tried for his crimes against Britain's war effort.

The early days of the World War II were a dark time for Britain, unprepared as it was for the Nazi war machine. Churchill knew that Hitler would not stop until he gained world domination. He had broken the treaties and alliances he had made (see Alignment) without a thought and crushed anyone who stood in his way. His rule was one of bullying and intimidation and Churchill knew he had to be stopped, and for that, he needed the USA to help. The USA though was under no threat and had no need to join in a costly war against an enemy who could not reach their shores to be a threat. Churchill did his best to bring the Americans into the war with his speeches and visits; he told President Roosevelt that Hitler would not stop and that, if he achieved victory in Europe, it would be the ideal launch point for an offensive against the US. Churchill also warned that the subjugated peoples of Europe would be forced to become the soldiers of the Nazis and made to move across the Atlantic to invade the US. Roosevelt was weakening in his resolve, Churchill's message was creating the doubt he needed to convince the US to stop Hitler before he could build momentum (see Energy and Pressure). There was actually no proof of this and Hitler never showed any inclination to move out of Europe. Eventually, the Japanese attack on Pearl Harbour played into Churchill's hands and convinced Roosevelt that he must join the war to block (see Interruption) Hitler's progress and give Britain the support it desperately needed.

'The most vital quality a soldier can possess is self-confidence.'
George S. Patton

The Faith Strategy in Combat

Treat Those Two Imposters Just the Same

In combat, use your tactics to psych your opponent out and break his faith in himself. Build him up, knock him down, rattle his confidence and develop his doubts.

When he does not know which way to go, he will likely go the wrong way or simply freeze (see Function). Don't believe his strategies against you either; beware of his smiles and friendly words. If he makes you feel good, doubt him. If he makes you feel bad, doubt that too. Base your actions on solid strategies, on what you know through careful study of the situation and a thorough knowledge of the 25 strategies of **Game Plan**.

If you don't feel confidence, you have to fake it so that your opponent doesn't see your fear. If he sees your fear, it will give him confidence and that can add renewed vigour to his attack, believing that your fear indicates your pain or that you are close to defeat. Conversely, if your opponent sees only your confidence, he might believe you have something up your sleeve or that his blows have not, or cannot, hurt you.

A key part of this strategy is understanding that feelings are not the whole picture; just because we feel confidence, fear or doubt does not mean that we cannot win or cannot lose. Many people in the grip of fear have still achieved success, still won through; just as many who had faith that they could not lose have then lost.

What does this tell us about faith and doubt? It tells us that despite feeling either emotion, they do not necessarily signify the truth; the truth lies in the end result. So never be too confident, nor too doubtful; simply take a balanced view and see what happens.

'Modest doubt is called the beacon of the wise.'
William Shakespeare

The Faith Strategy in Relationships

Easier to Give Birth Than to Raise the Dead

Good relationships require confidence and trust; bad relationships lack these two elements and that is often why they fail. We are often led to think that 'the grass is always greener on the other side of the fence'. But is it? How far do we try to make a relationship work before we start looking elsewhere? Or how long do we stick with a relationship hoping it will get better? The difference between faith and doubt is (as always between two opposites) a balancing act. We must give time and effort to a relationship. To get the balance right we must have trust, which involves having faith in ourselves and our partner and in our own decisions and judgement.

Within the relationship we must also give our trust and receive others' trust. In order to get trust we must also give trust, or we will create an imbalance in the relationship. We must accept our friends and partners without doubting them, but by also knowing what they are capable of achieving. We might trust them to do their best on a task, but not trust that they have the skills necessary to do the task right. The general rule is to put our faith in others first, but we must not do so too blindly, either. We must keep our guards up, without being for both our good and our partner's, and recognise when we are trying to raise a dead relationship, when, instead, we should be giving birth to a new one.

> *'Trust in God, but keep your powder dry.'*
> Oliver Cromwell

The Faith Strategy in Friendship

Get the Balance Right

Our friends, family and allies can suffer from a crisis of confidence in themselves, their abilities or their skills. Even their life direction, and progress through it, can be called into question when things are going badly and times are hard. Help them to see the reality of their situation; that their doubt is just a blip on their way to success. Remind them of the successes they've had in the past, re-build their confidence in themselves. Just the fact that one of their friends would go to such lengths can give them the confidence that they are worthy. Be patient, listen and guide them to accept a short term failure and see it as what it is really is: a temporary setback. Give them examples of others or yourself who faced similar problems but came back stronger and better.

At other times, be their counsel and guide when they are over-confident and threaten to take too big a risk without due diligence, knowledge or previous experience. Perhaps at work or in business or even relationships, help them to see clearly what the situation really is without totally deflating them. Often it is harder to calm someone's over-confidence than to build their confidence up, as your efforts could be seen as jealousy or envy. In that case, give them evidence if you can to support what you say, so that your advice doesn't look like jealousy at their potential success.

'Faith is not something to grasp, it is a state to grow into.'
Mahatma Gandhi

The Faith Strategy Personally

Faith Can Move Mountains

Doubt and Faith are the two sides of the same coin, and we travel a fine line between them throughout our lives. The problem is that sometimes we have to be our own counsellor, and remind ourselves to take a balanced view of our situation.

Set standards for yourself in new ventures; you should have feelings of trepidation – it is a sign that you are taking things seriously – but don't let these doubts delay your action (see Delay). If you have taken the advice of qualified experts, studied and researched for yourself and are not risking all you have on the venture (see Risk), then it has the best chance it can have.

Remember that even good tries can fail and that some of the greatest achievers in history failed at first. But, at each attempt, they learned from the experience, and went forward again with better qualifications (and maybe a few scars too). Also recognise that to have doubts is natural and, if we take notice of them, it helps us to take balanced action, based on good knowledge of our subject.

The balance with the Faith strategy is always neither too much doubt nor too much faith. If you have too much faith in your enterprise, you will advance blindly and carelessly, but too much doubt will cripple you and stop you from taking the necessary action. You must steer a middle path between the two, and if at times you are edging more one way than the other, don't worry. Remember that every step we take must, of necessity, compromise our balance. That will often be a cause for worry but recognise that it is a necessary and integral part of growth.

If you can achieve this understanding then you're definitely on the right path.

> *'Be faithful in small things because it is in them that your strength lies.'*
> Mother Teresa

The Faith Strategy in Health

Nothing New Under the Sun

Confidence in our health comes to us through experience and a good attitude. We maintain our faith through adhering to a healthy lifestyle of exercise, nutrition and clear mental outlook.

We are all born inheriting the genetics of our forefathers, and this can play its part in our health plans, but we must not doubt that there are ways to help and improve our condition.

If you suffer from poor health, then have faith that you can improve, if not your condition, but at least how you think about it. A healthy attitude can do wonders for our physical and mental condition. I'm not talking about miracle cures (and not ruling them out either) but we have all seen people in good health who constantly complain and seen people with serious conditions who are bright and cheerful. The difference is their positive mind set. Conversely, we see people who abuse their bodies, full of faith that disease and illness will never happen to them, or that they will be able to change their ways at the 11th hour, and avoid any chronic conditions. We should have faith in our future health based on our present actions, our diet and exercise regime. It's not rocket science that our lifestyle affects our health, so treat your body well if you want it to be still in good condition in old age. Middle age and old age will last a lot longer than your youth, and the damage you do to your body in your youth will likely be felt for longer as you grow older. It will often become the cause of illnesses, pain and medicated conditions that could have been avoided with a little care and prevention.

Don't doubt that smoking, drinking, poor diet and lack of exercise will bring down the strongest of us eventually. Whilst people are living longer than ever before, many spend their final years as invalids, suffering chronic pain and discomfort. This may be genetically or accidentally unavoidable, but some of it could also be avoided with a good health regime. Put your faith in this tried and tested method if you want a long and healthy life: Good nutrition, regular exercise, positive mind set.

'We are twice armed if we fight with faith.'
Plato

The Faith Strategy in Wealth

Who Do You Trust?

Many people have put their faith in their advisors and investment companies to look after them in retirement and ill-health, only to find things change for the worse: their planning being insufficient to bring the returns they need for a good retirement fund, advisors that can't be trusted or investment managers who get their investment decisions wrong for instance.

There are many poor unfortunates who placed their faith in a company's reputation to provide for their future, and quite a few of these found out too late that their expected fund was either gone, or too small, to provide for what they needed to live on in retirement. Unfortunately, because investment companies protect themselves against being held responsible if their funds don't perform well enough, most of these people have no recourse when this happens. We should be cautious about placing our financial futures in the hands of others; taking a passive role in our own wealth creation can be a risky course of action and most wealthy people wouldn't dream of it. In white water rafting the instructor will tell you that, if you fall out of the boat, 'you must take part in your own rescue'. Putting our future in the hands of our advisors is one thing, but prudence cautions us to check their progress regularly. True wealth comes from managing your own affairs. Donald Trump has hundreds of employees and many advisors on whom his wealth depends, but I'll put money on it that he never fails to check their numbers! It's not that he distrusts them – he wouldn't employ them if he did – it's just that the mid-point between confidence and doubt is prudence, what investors call 'due diligence'. In short, don't put too much trust in your advisors; they don't have the same incentive to look after your finances as you do, and if you don't trust them, then you should fire them.

If you don't trust anyone, then your faith is out of balance, possibly without good reason, and you must question this mind set. We have to trust people, it's just a wise move to measure their character and their competence and not just have blind faith, but neither should you have an attitude that means you will not trust anyone. Put your faith in people gradually, let them earn your trust through their actions, and never trust blindly, as even the best of us can make mistakes. Manage your own money, and use advisors when you need them, but check their work too, for safety's sake. Learn the basic skills you need to understand how to manage your money and put your faith these skills.

'Rashness belongs to youth; prudence to old age.'
Marcus Tullius Cicero

The Faith Strategy in Growth

Fake It Till You Make It

There is a saying in personal development circles: 'You have to fake it till you make it'. This means you must pretend to have a confidence that you don't actually feel, in order to attempt things that need an experience you don't have.

Confidence, as another saying goes, 'is always borrowed and never owned'. This is because confidence is not a constant and you only need extra confidence when you don't have it; when you already have it, you don't have the need for it. Confidence is a moving feast; there is always a point at which we lack it, at least in something, and a point at which it will fail us.

As children, we often put our faith in how things will change, when we are 'big'. But when we get bigger, we find that our confidence is not often as strong as we had hoped it would be. We are confident in what we have proven we were good at, but there are always things that we are not good at, or which we have no experience of, and at this point our confidence is suddenly lacking. In our twenties and thirties, our confidence peaks as we reach our prime physical health. With the onset of middle age however, that physical confidence starts to wane as our physical strength decreases. Yet, at the same time, the confidence gained through our experience comes into its own, and we cease to carry the worries and doubts that might have plagued us when we were young. So you see how fickle confidence, faith and doubt can be? Yet, we need them, they are like barometers which tell us when and how to act, and when and how not to. The skill is in finding where you lack either, and in fixing them.

Faith is gained through action, as is doubt. Faith comes from successful action and doubt from failure, but we must manage our faith and doubt, irrespective of how they arise, to ensure we are not being too optimistic or too pessimistic. This takes practice, judgement and study of the results. It's easy to look back on the past or towards the future with an unrealistic view, and this comes through not examining our past successes and failures realistically.

Study both your skill areas and your desires, but most of all study YOU, because success and failure are merely your perceptions of past events.

To see success or failure in a truer light we should ask two powerful questions first:

a) What is the worst thing that can happen if I fail?
b) What is the best thing that can happen if I succeed?

If you fail: How bad will it be? Will you fail completely? Or will you achieve part of what you wanted? In which case how big a failure was your try? Has the attempt left you dead or are you alive enough to try again? Are you ruined, or just a little burned by the experience?

If you succeed: Will your achievement last forever? Or will you look back in a few months and years and think little of it? Will it change your life forever? Will you be made and never have to try to do anything ever again? Will it mean you'll never have to go shopping, do the laundry or go to the toilet ever again? Or will the reward for your success be temporary, a stepping stone toward future goals?

The reality of any attempt is found in answering these two key questions honestly, because the difference between success and failure is often very small, yet our perception of the effect of either will be a major part of whether we attempt the goal at all. Examine your attitudes, so that you have neither too much confidence nor too much doubt; don't let your emotions rule your goal plans and actions without first taking the time to study the REAL reality of your success or failure in a situation.

Faith and Doubt, like winning and losing, are mental concepts; they don't really exist except in how we allow them to affect us. They are not physical like our bodies; they can't be touched or seen, only their effects can. They have no colour or weight, except the weight we give them, but they exist in our minds and they do affect our actions. So if faith and doubt only exist in our minds, what weight should we give them in controlling our actions? The answer depends on the size of the goal and our preparation for it. If we haven't prepared properly, then we should have doubt. If we have prepared properly, then we should have faith. Yet often our conditioned emotions will get in the way. We must recognise and acknowledge that we feel doubt or confidence in any course of action, but that these feelings have little to do with the final outcome.

In your journey of personal growth, be constantly aware of the effects of faith and doubt. Use them when they push you forward and listen to them when they try to hold you back, but remember that the final outcome in any situation is only revealed through the actions you take.

> **'If you can meet with triumph and disaster and treat those two imposters just the same.'**
> Rudyard Kipling

Summary

The strategy of Faith is complex and ever-present. It is something we deal with every day on some issue. Our confidence is borne out when it works out and turns to doubt when it cops out. In conflict, work to create doubt in your enemy and build confidence and faith in your friends. Keep your guard up for when the strategy is being used against you and be alert to situations to recognise if it is a factor in negotiations. Don't be over-confident to the point of arrogance or doubtful to the point of paranoia.

Faith Strategy in Brief

1. We all have doubts and fears and so too do we have faith and trust, it's what we do with them that makes the difference.
2. In war, create doubt where faith and trust once reigned.
3. In combat, psych your opponent out and break his self-confidence.
4. Good relationships need faith and trust; bad relationships lack these two elements, which is why they fail.
5. Our friends can suffer from a crisis of faith in themselves, their abilities and skills: be their support and guide.
6. Have faith in the tried-and-tested and a healthy scepticism of the new and untested.
7. Doubt and faith are two sides of the same coin, keep them in the right balance.
8. Trust your advisers, but check their work regularly. Their character may match their competence, but sometimes it might not.
9. Be aware of the effects of faith and doubt. Use faith to drive you forward and doubt to hold you back when necessary.
10. Remember: Faith can move mountains.

LEVERAGE STRATEGIES

'Create More With Less' The AEGIS Law of Leverage

Leverage

Leverage strategies seek to optimise and maximise the power and leverage that we can command and use to achieve our expectations. All strategy is about leveraging our resources, from our ability to communicate better or worse with others to increasing our physical and mental strength. Leverage is the creation of power, strength and energy.

The 5 strategies of Leverage are:

1. *Energy* – increasing and decreasing power
2. *Recruitment* – the use and misuse of resources
3. *Isolation* – the removal and separation from others
4. *Alignment* – connecting with others
5. *Pressure* – the application and use of power

Leverage is both local and global in its use; local in that it can involve our personal leverage and global in the use of external leverage, such as people, apparatus, conditions and money. Leverage strategies are visible and useable in all the other strategies.

STRATEGY NO. 6

The Leverage Strategy of Energy

Definition: A Tired Man is a Weak One

Overview of Energy

Energy is power; it is strength, money, stamina, resources and leverage. We all have access to energy; the energy we can exert physically is finite but the power we can harness through other people and things can be almost limitless. Use your enemy's power against him; your friend's power in his favour and your own power wisely. Use up your opponent's energy so he tires and cannot continue the fight; let him waste his time, money and resources so he is left with no power.

In friendship, with allies and with oneself, build your energy, save it and conserve it. Recognise what is your energy and leverage it to make your life easy, better and full of worthy achievements.

> **'All the forces in the world are not so powerful as an idea whose time has come.'**
>
> Victor Hugo

The Yin and Yang of Energy

The Yang
power
strength
force
energy
might
stamina
endurance

The Yin
impotence
powerlessness
weakness
frailty
fatigue
tiredness

The Energy Strategy in Tradition

As Fit as a Fiddle

This phrase developed in medieval times and has been slightly corrupted over time. It was originally 'as fit as a fiddler' and referred to how a fiddler at banquets would keep going as long as the revellers kept going – which could be very late into the night. As the guests danced and drank through the evening, gradually getting slower, sleepier and drunker, the fiddler kept on playing. He was himself expected to play and to dance at the same time and must have had considerable skill as well as stamina. Over time, the phrase 'as fit as a fiddler' lost its last letter and became what it is today: 'as fit as a fiddle', meaning to be excessively fit and energetic.

'The greater the power, the more dangerous the abuse.'
Edmund Burke

The Energy Strategy in Warfare

Wear Them Down

Energy is power. It represents force and momentum and the advantage (see Exploitation) goes to the army with the greatest numbers and most powerful weapons. However, to rely on force and strength alone is a fool's strategy; better to remove the energy of your opponent by deception, making him weaker, less able to fight back and therefore, less of a threat.

The Battle of Asculum 279 BC

King Pyrrhus of Epirus gained victory over the Romans in 279 BC at the battle of Asculum in Apulia. The battle was fought between Pyrrhus's army and the Romans, commanded by Consul Publius Decius Mus. Pyrrhus's forces, though they won the battle, suffered severe losses of the elite of their army. From this victory at such a high cost, we take the phrase 'Pyrrhic Victory' meaning 'victory at high cost'. Because so much was lost in order to secure a win, a Pyrrhic victory is only a half victory; where the losses are sometimes far greater than the achievement itself. Whenever possible, avoid fighting strength against strength unless you have the superior strategy and remember that progress is not only measured by achieving your outcome, but also by how you managed your energy to get there.

David and Goliath

The Biblical story of the future King David of Israel tells of the youthful shepherd, David, challenging the giant Goliath and how, instead of matching power for power, he stayed at a distance (see Proximity) and brought Goliath down with his slingshot. He could not have hoped to match Goliath's strength or weight, and neither did he have the skill with weapons. All he had were his accuracy (see Target) with his slingshot and his own common sense in playing to his strengths, and not being drawn into fighting a conventional combat. David stayed out of range of his giant opponent and leveraged the energy of a well-targeted rock to down him. Once Goliath fell, David was able to deliver the killing blow, winning the day for the Israelite army.

Chinese Strategy No. 4 – Await His Tired Steps at Your Leisure

This ancient Chinese strategy works by encouraging your opponent to use up his own energy; pushing too hard, fighting too hard, wasting his money and resources in his war with you. If you can get him to do this, then you can save your own energy and can step in for the final blow when he is exhausted.

How do we do this? One way is to anger him through insults and taunts (see Reaction): insulting his family or finding his emotional hot button and deriding what he cares about (see Target). Get him to chase you or attack you when he can make no progress. The term 'Stonewall' means to put up such a good defence that your opponent cannot make any impression on it, just as castles and fortresses provide actual stone walls to protect its inhabitants by being stronger than the enemy's power.

However, no stonewall is impregnable and if you have the power to bring down the walls or use a tactic to draw your opponent out from behind them (see Attraction as in the strategy of the Trojan Horse) then you can weaken his power and gain victory.

The secret of using energy in offence is only to fight head on when you have the greater power, never when you have merely equal power. Consider also that your knowledge of strategy is power as much as your physical strength, mental attitude and motivation.

Chinese Strategy No. 19 – Pull the Fire From the Kettle

Around the year 200 CE the famous Chinese warlord Ts'ao Ts'ao was successful in uniting almost the whole of Northern China under his rule against another powerful warlord Yuan Shao. The battle of Guan Do saw Ts'ao Ts'ao's forces of around 20,000 strong pitted against Yuan Shao's army of over 100,000. Ts'ao Ts'ao was a formidable general and had, in the past, defeated larger armies but nothing of the size of Yuan Shao's current force. He knew he could not face such an army on an open battlefield. So, with the help of his generals, he decided to use the strategy of Energy. Instead of targeting the army directly, Ts'ao Ts'ao decided to target their energy. There is an old saying, attributed to Napoleon Bonaparte, that 'an army marches on its stomach' meaning that much of an army's motivation comes from being well-fed. Similarly, Ts'ao Ts'ao targeted his first attack on Yuan Shao's supplies; by burning them entirely, he effectively destroyed the army's energy. Yuan Shao's army fell into disarray, motivation waned through lack of supplies and Ts'ao Ts'ao won the battle of Guan Do by removing their supplies – and therefore sabotaging their energy source.

> **'Man's greatness lies in his power of thought.'**
> Blaise Pascal

The Energy Strategy in Combat

Rope a Dope

The trench warfare of the First World War was the cause of hundreds of thousands of deaths. The foolish generals matched strength for strength and man for man against the new German machine guns, exhibiting extraordinary stupidity in their strategy. In competitive martial arts, we often see fighters whose only strategy is their physical strength and stature. Often, when they come up against a clever opponent they are soon bested. In the famous boxing match billed 'the Rumble in the Jungle', Muhammad Ali defeated the mighty George Foreman; not by matching strength for strength but by outwitting his foe with his now famous 'rope a dope' tactic, which sapped his opponent's energy. Foreman was bigger, heavier, stronger and could hit harder. Foreman was also younger and very motivated. Ali knew he couldn't stand toe to toe – and, in any case, that wasn't his style. Ali knew that whenever you cannot match your opponent for strength, speed or endurance, you must beat him with superior strategy, as that is the only way you can win against a stronger opponent. Ali avoided and evaded, hit and ran (see Proximity and Manoeuvre), foiled and spoiled (see Function and Interruption,) taunted and flaunted. He drew, feinted and faked (see Reaction and Direction) and, finally, he kept Foreman in the fight for longer than he had ever fought before, sapping both his energy and his confidence (see Faith) until Foreman was finally exhausted and fell to Ali's final onslaught (see Pressure).

This fight is a classic of strategy and is probably the most cleverly-planned and executed boxing match of modern times – which is testament to the catalogue of strategies I have listed during its description. Many strategies were used, but the key strategy was to tire Foreman out, sap his energy before moving in for the fatal blow.

> **'Make the best use of what is in your power,
> and take the rest as it happens.'**
> Epictetus

The Energy Strategy in Relationships

The Balance of Power

Power in relationships does not mean to have the upper hand, but to have an even hand. Friendships, partnerships, marriages and families are not situations where you should be seeking the upper hand or to exert your power, except if it is in aid of the relationship itself.

When we argue, we can fall prey to our emotions and lash out verbally or even physically. This is a misuse of power; it is a form of bullying and intimidation which has no place in healthy relationships (see Pressure and Toughness). We must learn to use our power to control our emotional outbursts and be strong enough to admit our failures and failings. If we have a partner or friend who will use this against us later, then we may have to review that relationship and remember that we have the power to quit any relationship in which we are unfairly treated.

Another aspect to consider is the energy of the relationship itself, the power and force that keeps it together. A relationship cannot maintain this by itself, nor can one partner alone keep the relationship together without undue stress on their part. The energy in a relationship comes from all the partners involved; which is how the relationship becomes stronger than the sum of its parts. When partners pull away from each other, the power that they could once exert is lost. One should always consider the long term goals of any relationship whether it be a romantic one or otherwise and when necessary re-focus (see Direction) and re-affirm (see Recruitment) the reasons for the relationship, so that one has a clear reminder of the strength it brings to everyone involved and the potential loss that breaking the relationship could have. A true partnership or friendship is strong because it combines the powers, skills and knowledge of all its parts (see Recruitment and Alignment). Unless we find ourselves in situations that cannot be avoided (such as illness or injury), we should strive to only remain in relationships where we all benefit equally.

'The most common way people give up their power is by thinking they don't have any.'
Alice Walker

The Energy Strategy in Friendship

Keep Your Strength Up

'A fool and his energy are soon parted'. Money, time, strength, attitude, property are all sources of energy that are finite; that is, they are limited in their availability. Friendship can be a source of strength or a drain on our energy; it must be carefully managed if we want to get the best out of it. We must invest our energy into our friends in order to be a good friend but we must also recognise when that investment is being mis-placed, and is therefore a waste of energy.

Some people we call friends are a drain on our energy and abuse of our time, emotions, finance, kindness or reputation. At times, these people may be good friends and their drain on your energy may be just temporary – when they are in need of some extra help as they are going through a difficult phase for example. At other times, the person that is a drain is always a drain and these people are not often real friends; at the very least, they accept your friendship but don't return it when you need it and they are rarely there for you when it is your turn to need a little extra support. Friendship is about care and attention, which must come from both sides, or the relationship will fall out of balance.

Too much emotion in a situation can lead us to take action that we are not qualified to take, whether through lack of education, preparation or calculation. Investing carelessly, lending in the same way, working too long or too hard or both, all of these situations will drain our power, unless we can align (see Alignment) or recruit others to our cause (see Recruitment). You can be the recruit of your friend and guide them to the best decision. Help them if you can, fund them if you must, but do this without depleting your own resources.

When helping a friend, remember what the air steward advises in the pre-flight instructions when you catch an aeroplane: 'In the event of a loss of cabin pressure, please put on your own oxygen mask first'. If you fail to look after yourself, you will have no energy to help anyone else.

Friendship is power (see Alignment and Recruitment) but don't abuse that power or allow yourself to be abused by it. Friendship can be used as a tool; but to do so on a constant basis is to misuse the energy of this friendship.

> *'Nearly all men can stand adversity, but if you want to test a man's character, give him power.'*
> Abraham Lincoln

The Energy Strategy Personally

Knowledge is Power

Recognise the power you possess personally. We are seldom powerless except when we are completely unable to function (see Function). Energy deals with both our strength and our weakness and extends to our physical strength, stamina, finances, education, availability of time, character, knowledge, emotion and intelligence.

Our greatest power lies in the application of our intelligence. Studying the 25 FLITE strategies will aid you in using that intelligence. The ideas you can bring to mind is only limited by your imagination. But since your imagination is fed by your education, you can create enormous power in your life through constantly studying, examining, reading, listening and reviewing what knowledge you have. As the AEGIS Law of Study states: 'The more you know, the easier it is to know more'. It is important to grasp this idea as it gives us unlimited power. Money, property, businesses, our physical strength and our looks and youth can all come and go but while we have our intelligence, we have access to power. Many entrepreneurs have made and then lost their fortunes only to regain even greater success through the power of their intelligence and acquiring extra strength gained through experience.

Worry, stress and fear will erode your personal power and, like all power, must be managed to ensure it is used well, if at all. There are some things that we have the power to control and some that we have the power to change but tomorrow is something we can do nothing about. Where does the energy of our mind come from? Mainly, our attitude is the source of our energy. The Law of Attitude states: 'It's our attitude, not our aptitude, that determines our altitude'. This phrase was first coined by the great Zig Ziglar, whose whole career was based on the power of attitude. No matter how high your IQ, or how many letters you have after your name, or how many degrees you have, or where you studied, or your blue-blooded pedigree, none of it will have the power on your life that your attitude has.

Our attitudes can be affected by many things, mainly our perceptions and expectations. These are the judgements we make about our lives, and no amount of IQ can give us the right attitude. Attitude is something we can choose and that gives us great power and energy in our lives, yet most people are unaware that their attitude is their choice. Once we realise that we can choose the attitude we have then our life is ready to take a whole new direction.

We lose personal power when we lose our attitude and we must guard our attitudes closely so that we are not dragged down by faulty careers, relationships, jobs and worrying about world events or bad news in the media which we can do nothing about. Whatever our situation, we can always choose our attitude towards it. It is normal for things outside our control to stress our attitudes, making it difficult to focus on our positives. Let's face it, thinking that the world is a terrible place based on the bad news that hits us daily from every angle (internet, TV, radio, newspapers, social media and gossip) is just adding worry and stress to your life. Stress, worry and fear are all concerned with our hypothetical future. The rule is: 'If you can't do anything about it, then don't worry about it.' This is not to give into fatalism. It is in realism where your power begins and ends. Recognise where you are powerful and use that power wisely; build your attitude, protect it, nurture it and enjoy the energy it brings to your life. Similarly, recognise that there are things you can do nothing about, so avoid wasting energy on unnecessary guilt or worry.

'Power is like being a lady...
if you have to tell people you are, you aren't.'
Margaret Thatcher

The Energy Strategy in Health

Power Down

Youth, physical strength, endurance and innocence are all powers that we can use to our benefit but, like all physical gifts, they fade over time. As we get older, our strength wanes and likewise does our motivation.

We have all seen fighters who have seen their best day make comebacks that fail. Age has crept up on them, gradually wearing down their physical strength, but at an imperceptible rate. They think they can still do what they could when they were young. But there is a very short space between our prime and being past it and there is no flag that suddenly pops up to tell us we are getting old. Young people can't imagine the feeling of not being able to do the things they once could and, consequently, they over-estimate the importance of physicality and under-estimate the importance of mentality. The power that we have physically is nothing compared to the power of our intellects.

Our health is a main source of our energy and that energy comes as a whole package: heart, mind, body and spirit. Vibrant health is about balancing those four energies so that they support each other. Intellect alone is not health, nor is pure emotion or physicality or spirituality; total energy comes through total health. It's no good having great physical fitness without also mental fitness. Neither can we be healthy if we live only on our emotions as we then become the victim of a rollercoaster ride of ups and downs. Nor can we be purely spiritual because we also have to be practical, earning a living, paying bills, cooking, cleaning etc. To lean too far in any direction makes us lose our life harmony, our life balance. Good health, providing us with good energy, is only achieved through harmonising all the different parts of our lives. The key, therefore, to energy in health is to balance your four energies of heart, mind, body and spirit. Without balance, we are like a car that has lost a wheel or a ship that leaks, we are going nowhere fast.

If we look after our strength, power and energy in heart, mind, body and spirit and balance this nurturing so that we attend to each intelligence as equally as we can, then we can reach a ripe old age without serious regrets. Eat well, train well, think well, love well and balance well and you won't go far wrong.

> *'What it lies in our power to do,
> it lies in our power not to do.'*
>
> Aristotle

The Energy Strategy in Wealth

On the Treadmill

Knowledge is power and so is wealth. Wealth is not just money, but also friendships, agreements, property, family. Financially, you can create great things with wealth and it is everybody's potential and responsibility to look after themselves and their family financially. We live in a society that, rightly or wrongly, runs on cash to provide our shelter food and comfort, and there's no getting away from that.

With a good plan, you can accumulate enough to look after you and your family without ever being a burden on the state or charity. Those who fear wealth will never have any and, whilst there are more important things in life, wealth does help you to focus on those important things. Wealth won't make you happy, but, equally, it won't stop you being so either. Of course we've all seen rich people portrayed as unhappy, but that is the individual who is unhappy; the money has nothing to do with it. Wealth gives you the power of choice, the power to help yourself, the energy to achieve the things you want and the ability to help others to do the same. If you have a problem with wealth, such as feeling that it's wrong to have a lot of money or that you only get rich by taking from the poor for instance, then you need to get over it. Wealth is a strategic tool, so make the most of it and, if you don't have it, then use strategies to create it. Money is neither good nor evil. It is simply a way to provide comfort for ourselves and those we love: food, a roof over our heads, stuff we enjoy and that entertain us, education, leisure.

Wealth can give you the life of your dreams and opportunities for yourself, your family and your friends. Wealth offers us the power to step out of the rat race and off the treadmill of drudgery. It can give us the option to live a life that is more fulfilling and giving. What would you do with your time if you didn't have to go to work?

**'Human kindness has never weakened the stamina
or softened the fibre of a free people.
A nation does not have to be cruel to be tough.'**

Franklin D. Roosevelt

The Energy Strategy in Growth

Power Play

The search for personal growth is the search for personal power. Recognise the power you have available and the power you lack (see Vulnerability strategies). Study the strategy of power; how it has been used in the past and how you can use it in your future.

The Law of Game Plan states that 'Proper planning prevents poor performance'. The 25 Game Plan strategies are your power to get whatever you desire from life but you must also draw upon your own power such as your attitude, your focus, your ability to stay balanced, to judge and to recognise both challenges and opportunities. Our lives are controlled by the AEGIS Laws of Life – study them so that you understand how life works, what is important in life, and then apply them strategically in your favour to create the life you want in the short term and also for the distant future (see **Warrior Wisdom** – the 25 Elemental Laws that Govern Life and War by the author). One of the greatest powers we have is choice. The ignorant closes the door on choice through fear of change, but the true leader, who is working to grow, desires change because change is the doorway to choice and choice is freedom (and freedom is power). Seek constant change and constant improvement as these together give us power over our lives and our futures.

> *'If you realized how powerful your thoughts are, you would never think a negative thought.'*
> Peace Pilgrim

Summary

Energy is power, so use what you're learning in this book to build your power and remove your powerlessness. Recognise your power and the power of others, where it starts and where it ends, and learn how to create more energy and use it as a force for good. The Law of Vulnerability says: 'To know your enemy's weakness is strength, to know your own is wisdom'. Keep this in mind as you decide on your next course of action and decide on the best way to spend your energy on.

Energy Strategy in Brief

1. Identify what energy is: power, time, health, character, strength, knowledge, resources… Learn how to use yours wisely.
2. Beware of Pyrrhic victories. They will sap your energy and cost more than the rewards they bring.
3. A stronger opponent can be beaten by a stronger intelligence.
4. Power in relationships is not to have the upper hand, but an even hand.
5. With friends, help them if you can, fund them if you must, but do so without depleting your own resources.
6. Our greatest strength is the application of our mental power over our physical power.
7. Wealth offers us the power to step out of the rat race and the choice of how to spend our time.
8. The most common way people give up their power is by thinking they don't have any.
9. Good health is one of our main sources of energy. Strive to maintain the right balance in the development of your heart, mind, body and spirit.
10. If you realized how powerful your thoughts were, you would never think a negative thought.

STRATEGY NO. 7

The Leverage Strategy of Recruitment

Definition: Many Hands Make Light Work

Overview of Recruitment

We cannot do everything alone; at times we need to recruit others to help us. At other times we must let go of those who should help but don't or those whose help becomes unnecessary or too expensive. Recruit others to your cause against a larger enemy or a bigger goal. Recruit also: money, time, skills and education. Find the people who want to do what you don't or who can do what you can't. Recruit people who believe in what you want to achieve, lead and support them. Shape them into your loyal army.

'Men are moved by two levers only: fear and self-interest.'
Napoleon Bonaparte

The Yin and Yang of Recruitment

The Yang	The Yin
enlisting	firing
employment	dismissal
enrolment	sacking
gathering	de-mobilisation
delegation	unemployment
mobilisation	removal

The Recruitment Strategy in Tradition

Sling Your Hook

This phrase meaning to go away or 'get lost' is thought to be an old nautical phrase from the days of the great sailing ships of the British and Merchant navies, the hook being the anchor which keeps a ship moored in place when it is at rest and the sling the apparatus that holds the anchor in place. 'To sling one's hook' therefore is to wind up the ship's anchor and set sail again.

The phrase is thought to have been less insulting and more descriptive in its earlier forms, but eventually became more of an insulting instruction to someone who has outstayed their welcome; hence, 'sling your hook' being the opposite Yin side of recruitment.

> **'Do not hire a man who does your work for money, but him who does it for the love of it.'**
> Henry David Thoreau

The Recruitment Strategy in Warfare

Many Hands Make Light Work

If you can outnumber your foe, you can stretch his resources by sending him in too many directions at once; spread his resources thinly or simply overpower and overwhelm him (see Pressure) with your sheer force of numbers.

Recruit, train, lead and support your army to your cause, releasing yourself from having to get your hands dirty. Remember that Recruitment leverage extends also to more than just people; it also extends to money, energy and resources. Set traps that will over-extend your enemy's energy and finances. Get him to waste his money in trying to defeat you or let him wear himself thin or burn himself out (see Energy). If your adversary has more power than you, don't face him directly or you will find yourself outmatched. Manage your own recruits, money, soldiers and helpers so that you remain stronger.

Look after your troops and see if you can lure away (see Attraction) your enemy's troops to your side. Never forget how much more you can achieve with a group working for you than you can ever achieve alone. Be the general of your own army.

Chinese Strategy No. 3 – Borrow a Sword to Make Your Kill

When you have built an army, you will have recruited soldiers and officers, some who have proven their worth and some who are an unknown quantity. If you are asking your soldiers to risk their lives on your behalf and are relying heavily on their commitment to your cause, then you need to know whether they are up to the task. Will they stand and fight, following your instructions and the strategy you have put in place? Or will they cut and run at the first sign of trouble? The strategy of 'Borrow a sword to make your kill' is therefore a way to test the mettle of your troops to examine how they will fight for you since it will be your soldier and his sword executing your kill.

When you recruit soldiers (or staff, partners or supporters) to your cause therefore, it is wise to test their loyalty before you send them into battle. Train them well in what you want them to do. Supervise them and give them smaller tasks to see how they perform before you let them loose in battle or put them in front of important customers. Give them tasks and get them to report back soon, assigning increasingly bigger tasks each time, advising, counselling, training and testing them constantly until they are fully able to replace you. You must be able to fully trust both their loyalty and their competence if they are to be valuable employees.

There are 5 levels of initiative that every good leader must recognise in his team, so that he knows what stage they are at and which level of responsibility they are ready for. These are:

1. *Waits to be told what to do.*
2. *Asks what needs to be done.*
3. *Offers to do what needs to be done*
4. *Does what needs to be done and reports back frequently*
5. *Does what needs to be done and reports back infrequently*

The measure of a good team member is one who seeks responsibility early and endeavours to complete the task well. The difficulty for many leaders is to release the reins of responsibility. They often feel that no one else can perform the jobs as well as they can and, initially at least, that's probably true. But unless you gradually release your tasks by delegating responsibilities, you can never move forward, growing your army. Let's face it, you can't do everything, and anyone that thinks they can is just making things difficult for themselves.

Chinese Strategy No. 14 – Borrow the Corpse, Revive Its Soul

This ancient Chinese strategy works by utilising another's name or reputation, riding on the back of another's energy, time or influence. If you have little personal influence, you might be able to utilise the influence and reputation of someone who has or had influence.

We can see examples of this in the film industry where a director with a small budget recruits a star whose popularity is in decline. They can recruit the old star cheaply and hope to gain a wider audience to their production through using the old star's name. Having this key actor might also help the producers to attract more financing to their production.

Wherever you can, ride the wave of popularity by attaching or aligning yourself to it (see Alignment) like a surfer using the energy of the wave to get his thrill in the ride, back towards the beach.

'If you go looking for a friend, you're going to find they're very scarce. If you go out to be a friend, you'll find them everywhere.'

Zig Ziglar

The Recruitment Strategy in Combat

Two Heads Are Better Than One

Don't go head to head with an enemy who is stronger than you. Recruit allies if you can, and recruit your own body and mind, too, as your greatest ally.

Be fitter, stronger, better educated, better informed than your opponent. Use your personal leverage, your striking power, speed, movement and strategy to increase the force you can exert. Look for ways to recruit your enemy's troops, energy or resources and recruit his other enemies to your cause, fighting together, as in 'the enemy of my enemy is my friend'.

Recruit your own resources and the resources of others. If you look very strong and well-supported, he may not wish to engage with you anyway, which means you use less energy to get your win.

In street defence, recruit friends or bystanders to your cause and, if you expect trouble, avoid quiet places where there will be no one to assist you. Recruit your senses to your cause by staying alert to signs of danger, aggression, or simply bad vibes that you sometimes pick up in certain situations.

If you are faced with an aggressor, recruit your wits and all your energies and commit yourself to never giving in and to seeing yourself safe no matter what the cost or the fear. Remember what assets you already possess and recruit them to your cause.

> *'A team is where a boy can prove his courage on his own.*
> *A gang is where a coward goes to hide.'*
>
> Mickey Mantle

The Recruitment Strategy in Relationships

There is no 'I' in Team

Be a recruit and an ally (see Alignment) to your partners. Help others, and others will help you. Be loyal, accepting, patient (see Patience).

The way to recruit friends is also the way to recruit a partner. Two heads are better than one and many of us work well in the right relationship. Just remember that your partner is not your opposition unless you take a completely opposite stance. Often we see husbands and wives in complete opposition to each other, back biting, disagreeing on small issues as well as large. If you cannot live with your partner, then have the courage to make the split. Don't stay together because you fear being alone. Being alone is not a curse; in fact it suits many people. It's also not a failure; it's not necessary to be in a relationship to be happy. Being in a relationship takes work, compromise, patience, loyalty and understanding of the other person's needs and not only your own. Be the partner you would like to have. Share their interests, make time together, and take notice and heed of what they say without simply 'kowtowing for a quiet life'.

Partnerships are like armies; they must be nurtured and cared for to get the best out of them. Recognise the power that comes from working together and the power that comes through being part of a supportive team. So much can be achieved by recruiting the skills, attitudes and drives of others. Each team member, though, must bring their special skill to the relationship; this can mean technical skill, management, special knowledge, sales, invention, spare time or even cash. Your recruits must also share your dream, and in the early days of a partnership you may all have to work just for the love of it, as there is often little cash available in new start-ups.

Beware also of partnerships where the partners don't have different skills or resources to bring to the table, as you could end up in a situation of 'too many chiefs and not enough Indians'. If partners all have the same skills as each other, then what benefit do they offer? Without recruiting the skills you lack, whether it be force of numbers or of relevant skills then the partnership will be lacking the cohesion needed to help move things forward.

'We all need each other.'
Leo Buscaglia

The Recruitment Strategy in Friendship

Recruit Allies

When a friend needs help, after biting off more than they can chew for instance, you can assist them by being their recruit. They may be overwhelmed (see Pressure) by a task or emotionally stressed through a bereavement, illness or break up. Help them to focus and bring your own resources to the task. Time, money, people, advice,... all of these can help to get your friends back on their feet or to achieve the task that may seem too big for them. Show them that they cannot do everything on their own and that it is not a weakness to ask for help. Every successful achiever throughout history became so by enlisting the help of others to their cause.

By being a good and loyal friend, you will encourage others to your friendship even though not all of them will be as loyal as you are, or as committed. However, that is not the point, as you will find that a small but loyal band who will be worth their weight in gold. Avoid gossiping and speaking ill of others behind their backs. Instead, offer impartial advice and try to be supportive of all who make up your circle of friends.

Our friends will not always have our understanding of life, of its laws and strategies, so seek to help and support those who will listen and protect those who cannot.

> '*Finding good players is easy. Getting them to play as a team is another story.*'
> Casey Stengel

The Recruitment Strategy Personally

Delegate Responsibilities

Recognise when you need help and don't be too proud to ask for it. Nobody can achieve success alone – unless their goal is to be alone (see Isolation).

If you are self-employed and working on your own account, you will soon find that you are responsible for a lot of things and the growth of your business will be held back if you insist on doing everything yourself. Sometimes we hold onto tasks that we should delegate because we feel no one can do them like we can or that help is too expensive. The truth is that some people can do certain tasks better than we can do them ourselves, and those who cannot initially can be trained to do so eventually. The skill in building a team is to accept that, at first, your employee may make a mess of things, and that this can happen to anyone. None of us are totally competent from the outset. But if you train your people well, show them exactly what you expect, and do not expect too much at first, they can take a great load off your back in time. Although it takes time to do this, that time is passing anyway so the earlier you start the sooner they'll be trained.

Those of us who cannot release tasks to others to perform end up trapped by our own workload. Whereas, if we could gradually relinquish our less important tasks, we could quite quickly find ourselves free of all tasks, except those of most importance or simply those that we enjoy doing the most.

To be able to step back and see things more clearly, take the time to think, study and plan. This is the way to realise your dreams and, in the process, you will give employment to others, who can share in your dream themselves and perhaps one day take over the reins when you retire (see Proximity).

In short, recruit others to your cause and train them well (do not skimp on training), give your loyalty to earn theirs (see Expectation) and also learn how to fire those who will not or cannot fulfil their tasks – but make sure first to give them the best chance. People who see how you have supported and nurtured them are the most loyal. Do not be greedy with money either; pay people well for good work. Buy their loyalty through your loyalty and reward their loyalty and work ethics well.

'Soldiers generally win battles; generals get credit for them.'
Napoleon Bonaparte

The Recruitment Strategy in Health

Marshal Your Resources

To live long and happily is a worthy goal and we must work consistently to maintain our health in heart, mind, body and spirit. Use the strategy of Recruitment as part of this goal by realising that no one thing will make and keep us happy or healthy.

True health needs all four of the heart, mind, body and spirit intelligences to be activated, working together with the 5th intelligence of balance in order to keep them all in flow. Too much of any one of these intelligences will leave us out of balance. Too much emotion will leave us at the mercy of anger, sorrow, over-excitement and the like. We will experience all of these emotions in our lives; this does not mean we must become a victim to them. We must use our mind and body to lift ourselves out of depression or other dark thoughts and, eventually, as we gain control over our intelligences, we can find our true path and our spiritual nature.

The opposite of recruitment is to de-recruit, which is to remove, fire, or sack; to let go or make redundant. We do this with employees whose usefulness has ended and we should also do it with the habits and conditioning that are holding us back. Find those habits that are not serving you and get rid of them. Unfortunately, like removing an employee whose service is no longer required, this can be very challenging. Letting an employee go can be difficult emotionally; they have family, commitments and feelings, so it can be painful to let even the most useless employee go. With bad health habits, it will be a different sort of pain, but a pain nonetheless that needs eradicating.

A good way to sack those bad habits is to either recruit new ones in their place, or to wean yourself off the habit gradually. In short, recruit all your intelligences for a long and healthy life and make your bad habits redundant.

'I am convinced that nothing we do is more important than hiring and developing people. At the end of the day you bet on people, not on strategies.'

Lawrence Bossidy

The Recruitment Strategy in Wealth

A Fool and His Money

The accumulation of wealth relies on the recruitment strategy. Wealth in itself is the recruitment of income and capital, just like the recruitment of employees or soldiers, who must be enlisted, trained, motivated and cared for. Money must be treated the same way if you want it to grow and support you, to provide for yourself and your family.

Take time to study your financial goals and manage your finances, recruit knowledge about how money works. The great thing about money is that it is not something magical and, like anything else in life, you can acquire it through education and hard work. Just like any other skill, you must study and practise.

Manage your money deliberately since, like your business, it cannot manage itself. Many are the would-be millionaires who made a fortune only to lose it through poor management. Recruit trusted advisors and accountants, bookkeepers, solicitors and investment advisors. You have to be an expert in many fields if you want to do it all yourself, and it is often a mistake to try. Instead, acquire a basic knowledge of how each field works, set yourself in a position to oversee what is happening and be on top of it.

Don't wait too long between checking on your progress. Three months is a good time frame. Also, when it comes to paying bills, banking cash or checking your accounts, do it very regularly, on a daily basis if possible. Every well-run household, as well as every business, knows that 'cash is king' and having good cash flow is important to everyone who lives in a modern day society.

Learn the difference between assets, liabilities, income and expenditure, the four keys to managing money which make up every balance sheet in business. They are not the boring or meaningless phrases that they appear to be. They are useful tools and once you understand how they work and what they can do for you, they can become exciting and meaningful. If you learn how to manage them well, you will have the power to recruit financial wealth in abundance.

> **'Never hire someone who knows less than you do about what he's hired to do.'**
>
> Malcolm Forbes

The Recruitment Strategy in Growth

Education, Education, Education

You can probably see now how the strategy of Recruitment can help you grow your business, organisation, wealth and employees. Depending upon your personal growth area, you must recognise where you need to recruit outside help. Education, study time, learning from the mistakes of others, all serve as part of our recruitment strategy. There is nothing you can experience that has not been experienced before, so draw upon the knowledge and skills of others so you don't have to suffer the pain of being a pioneer in everything you do.

What is the key to Recruitment in Growth? Education, education, education. Learn about yourself through the experience of others by means of books, EBooks, audio books, courses, seminars and groups. Use the internet, which is an enormous resource of knowledge – both free or to buy – so find your area of interest and educate yourself with the skills you need to move forward in your chosen direction.

'But I don't like reading', or 'I find it difficult to read!' this attitude will get you nowhere, except keep you where you already are. Take responsibility for your own education and remember that 'It's your attitude, not your aptitude that determines your altitude'. This is the key to all success, the cornerstone and foundation of your future, but no one else can give you the right attitude, it must come from you, from within. You must recognise that your attitude is your greatest resource and it is up to you to recruit yourself to your cause. If you are unhappy with your life, dissatisfied with your life, uncomfortable with your life, then you must use that pain to spur you on toward a better life. However, you can only change what you have if you decide that you are entirely responsible for the life you already have. If you want more from life you must also be prepared to do more. Part of the price to pay is to accept that you are where you are because you've done what you've done with the knowledge that you had. If you want to move forward into a different life, then you have to have new knowledge to support your new direction and that knowledge is found in education. If you want to know something you've never known before, then you have to learn something you've never learned before.

Recruit all your energy and intelligences and add to that your continued education and motivation and you will begin on a terrifically rewarding journey.

> **'Walking with a friend in the dark is better than walking alone in the light.'**
> Helen Keller

Summary

Recruitment is a key leverage strategy and one that you must focus your energies on. We can't do everything ourselves and only a fool would try to. It's quite hard for some of us to delegate our tasks to others, but you can be sure that you will never achieve great success alone or by doing everything yourself. You have skills – you are your own VP – so why waste your skill on also cleaning the office toilets? Delegate less important tasks and watch your organisation grow.

Recruitment Strategy in Brief

1. We cannot do everything alone; at times we need to recruit others to help us.
2. Recruit, train, lead and support your army to your cause, releasing yourself from having to get your hands dirty.
3. Utilise another's name or reputation; ride on the back of another's energy, time or influence by association or manipulation.
4. Recruit allies if you can, and also recruit your own body and mind as your greatest ally.
5. Be a friend to your friends. Help others and others will help you.
6. If a friend bites off more than they can chew, you can assist them by recruiting yourself to their cause.
7. Recognise when you need help and don't be too proud to ask for it.
8. Recruit to your cause education, study time, and learn from the mistakes of others.
9. Delegate less important tasks and watch your organisation grow.
10. Never hire someone who knows less than you do about what he's hired to do.

STRATEGY NO. 8

The Leverage Strategy of Isolation

Definition: Cut Them from the Herd

Overview of Isolation

Few people want to be alone, isolated or cut off from the group. Without the support of the group, we lack leverage and power. We lose confidence in our abilities and question the decisions we make. We are herd animals at our core, and our success as a species is the result of our working together. Therefore, when we are rejected or cut off from the group, we feel lonely, without support, advice and encouragement. In conflict, cut your enemy off from his allies, his money and his resources; make him doubt himself and his supporters too. In cooperation, do the opposite: bring friends back into the fold, provide them with resources and assuage their doubts.

'Too much of what is called 'education' is little more than an expensive isolation from reality.'

Thomas Sowell

The Yin and Yang of Isolation

The Yang
loneliness
segregation
marooned
sequestered
set apart
shun

The Yin
accumulated
gathered
together
included
ally
befriend

The Isolation Strategy in Tradition

Sent to Coventry

This phrase is an excellent example of the Isolation strategy and dates back to the English Civil War of the early 1600s. Coventry was strongly loyal to the Parliamentarian forces and the King's soldiers who had been captured in battles around the Midlands were kept in Coventry. The citizens would refuse to offer help, food or communication to the Royalist prisoners. The prisoners were virtually marooned, with no money, no friends and no support. Getting away from Coventry was not an easy task, owing to the poor roads and danger of being picked up again, so the prisoners had no choice but to endure the misery of being 'sent to Coventry'.

'I used to think the worst thing in life was to end up all alone, it's not. The worst thing in life is to end up with people that make you feel alone.'
Robin Williams

The Isolation Strategy in Warfare

Cut Off Their Retreat

Whereas Recruitment and Alignment allow us to create energy and apply Pressure (see Energy and Pressure), Isolation is the removal of someone's leverage. Every warlord or general needs to lead his army, marshal his resources and supplies because without all this he is alone, deprived of his power.

Chinese Strategy No. 28 – Remove the Ladder When He's on the Roof

This ancient Chinese strategy works by cutting off the retreat of an enemy. The key element is to isolate our enemy. After luring our enemy into our reach (see Attraction), we spring our trap (see Function) to bar his escape so that we can have him isolated from his main force or his reinforcements. This strategy can be used against an entire army or against a targeted individual (see Target). Your main objective is to remove the enemy from the leverage of his allies because, if he is alone or small in number, his power (see Energy) is proportionally reduced. The more alone he is, the better. When he is cut off, not only from his allies and their weapons but also their advice and support, doubt and uncertainty (see Faith) will start to kick in and your enemy will become even more vulnerable, both physically and mentally.

Chinese Strategy No. 22 – Bar the Doors to Catch the Thief

The wisdom of this ancient strategy is based on Sun Tzu's advice to never fight the same enemy twice, meaning that if you can isolate and totally destroy your enemy in one setting, you will never to have to fight him again. This has obvious benefits, and, throughout history, many armies have used this tactic to remove their opposition entirely.

This strategy, whilst being totally ruthless, can also act as an example (see Example) to other potential enemies who, knowing your 'no prisoner' reputation, will become less likely to want to engage with your forces. Another way to apply this strategy works by demonstrating that you have the power to massacre the enemy without actually using it; that you could exploit and annihilate him but instead, let him off the hook. In so doing, you will hopefully gain his respect and even recruit him as an ally (see Recruitment) as a result.

Combat is a strange type of communication which occurs once verbal agreement has broken down and anger, hurt and ego become the only way to communicate. When an opponent is totally beaten, he will do one of two things: either fight all the harder because he has nothing to lose, or totally submit (like a dog rolling on its back in submission). If your opponent fights back with all the energy that desperation gives him as he can see that he is losing, he may still be capable of pulling off a lucky shot and even making a complete comeback to win the fight. On the other hand, if you have him beat, but show him respect by not pushing your victory too far, letting him save face and keeping his dignity, then he will view you in a completely different light.

The key to this strategy in warfare therefore cuts in two ways:

a) *Isolate an enemy entirely and destroy him*, meaning you never have to fight him again. This is fine if you have sufficient resources to destroy him totally.

b) *Isolate an enemy entirely but let him off the hook* at the last moment, because you haven't enough resources to destroy him, particularly if he fights back desperately.

Both sides of the strategy involve isolating one's opponent but with a different outcome.

> **'We don't function well as human beings when we're in isolation.'**
> Robert Zemeckis

The Isolation Strategy in Combat

Go it Alone

In one-on-one combat, whether it be in sport or elsewhere, one is always alone at some level. For instance, in full-contact competition, you train with your partners and coaches to get ready for the fight, but, as the big day approaches, you are the one with the nerves, the doubt and the worry of how the fight will go. It is your reputation and safety that are on the line.

Before the fight, when you are warming up in the dressing room, you are the one preparing your mind, settling your nerves and visualising positive outcomes. Your name is called and your team lead you to the ring with the crowd shouting and cheering; some shout encouragement and some bay for blood as you climb into the ring. Your team do their best to keep you positive and fill you with advice. Those last moments before the bell goes seem to last an eternity and you just want to get this thing over with, just to do what you've trained for. As the bell sounds, a quiet calm washes over you; there is no more to fear - this is it! Your team and supporters scream their advice and support, but there is only you in there, and your opponent, and you are both alone.

Single combat, that is, to fight risking your safety and possibly your life, makes you entirely responsible for the outcome, with no one to lean on or help. You are totally accountable for the result, completely isolated, which can be both scary and empowering, if you can see past the fear. Recognition of the fact that, in the final analysis, we are all alone and no one can feel what we feel or live what we live is an important step toward acknowledging either fear or our acceptance of it. Acceptance is a powerful ally because it makes you independent, self-reliant and gives you a sense of peace. You're holding nobody up and letting no one down. This is the true mind of the warrior.

We should consider how else the Isolation strategy can be applied in combat, not only by isolating your opponent from his allies or even his weapons, but also by isolating specific targets on his body (see Target) or looking for the vulnerable spot to attack. Alignment of the relevant joints in the arm, shoulder, hip and leg helps to define and isolate the key components of a technique in order to create greater speed and power (see Pace and Energy) in our movements. With proper recognition and isolation of movement, we can create greater leverage which means that even if we are lighter and smaller than our opponent, we can potentially match his power. Knowing and training the correct muscles and joints independently allows us to maximise our body weight when applied in technique, cutting out any unnecessary movement which might waste our time, focus and energy. If you watch an experienced runner matched against a novice, you can see that the expert moves more efficiently and therefore gains greater speed with less effort. The same applies in martial arts; the martial artist trains for years to create more efficient movement through practice and study, so that even light blows can carry massive power with seemingly little effort.

In summary, Isolation in combat is not always a bad thing and does not always mean we are alone or even at a disadvantage. If we understand how to apply the strategy of Isolation, we can turn it into an advantage that we can exploit.

**'If isolation tempers the strong,
it is the stumbling-block of the uncertain.'**
Paul Cézanne

The Isolation Strategy in Relationships

Private Lives

Relationships thrive on anything but isolation, but there may be occasions when people feel isolated in a relationship. How does this happen? When the partners cease to align and start to diverge in interests and expectations. This can be something that occurs gradually or it can be a misalignment that existed from the very beginning but was covered up by the infatuation often felt at the start of new relationships. Whichever way it occurs, the sense of isolation can spell the end of the relationship.

Bad behaviour in a group relationship can result in being temporarily sent to Coventry at best and being completely expelled at worst, separated from the group completely, cut off and left alone. Without the group, we feel alone, friendless, cut off and powerless. This is the strength of isolation when it is used as a weapon, since everyone is vulnerable to it, if not emotionally at least practically.

Bullying and intimidation are the dark side of isolation and are included here because they can often happen in the privacy of a relationship. Bullying is a private activity; while outsiders would decry it, those inside are party to it. Even if they don't like it, if they are a witness to it and do nothing about it they become a party to it, even when it is against their own wish (because they may be too small or weak to do anything about it). Often, witnesses who don't stand up for the victim are too afraid to do so because they fear becoming the victim themselves if they say anything against the bully. This is the power of bullying: the victim is isolated, physically, mentally or emotionally which makes the bully more powerful. The bully couldn't bully if the victim was in the open; the bully's leverage relies on the victim's isolation from the support of others. This is why most bullying takes place in private, small groups. Although, there are some cases when bullying takes place within large groups such as in institutional bullying, where a whole organisation is based upon and supports the bullying of its members.

If you're in the situation of being bullied, you should consider how you are being isolated and what leverage your bully has over you. Is it your job or your safety? Who can you recruit to help, or can you deal with this alone? Do you think going it alone is the only way or perhaps you think being bullied is your fault? If you are bullied, you must take action, don't allow yourself to be targeted, don't take the blame and don't suffer in silence.

'Even if you are a minority of one, the truth is the truth.'
Mahatma Gandhi

The Isolation Strategy in Friendship

A Friend in Need

Comic actor W.C. Fields famously coined the adage: 'A friend in need is a pain, get rid of him', which could quite accurately describe one use of the isolation strategy.

'A friend in need is a friend indeed' is a more laudable use of the benevolent side of Isolation and certainly more of what one would expect from one good friend to another (see Alignment and Recruitment). At times of high stress and emotion caused by a sense of failure or loss, it is easy to be left in a state of isolation. Humans are basically pack animals, so we thrive on being part of the pack and despise being faced with separation from it. Of course, there are always times when we desire to be alone, but that is done by choice. Being alone is not the same as being isolated. Because isolation is forced upon us, we are left with no choice – or at least that's usually the way we feel at the time.

When our friends feel cut off and alone, we can be their support with comfort and advice, a physical demonstration that they are not isolated. We can make the conscious effort to reach out to them and keep them in the loop, even if it means that we are always the ones making the first move for a while. We can call, email, and send a text, even when we don't get an answer back immediately. Sometimes, it is important to give just for the sake of giving. It can take time and a great deal of patience to help your friends stay connected when they're going through a difficult patch. Yet, you must try your best to provide comfort and inspiration to help get them back on an even keel. The same goes for when you're feeling low. The essence of being and having friends is the very opposite of isolation, at least physically. Emotionally though, we can be in the midst of our closest friends and still feel isolated and alone. Yet, knowing that we have family and friends who love us and care for us can bring us great solace, if not immediately, then eventually.

It is sometimes easier to isolate yourself and stop calling on your friends. And it can be difficult for your friends to help get you out of your depression if you refuse their support and block their communication.

'Loneliness and the feeling of being unwanted is the most terrible poverty.'
Mother Teresa

The Isolation Strategy Personally

Separation Anxiety

At some level we are always isolated; no one can experience what we are experiencing in any given moment and even the most sensitive and empathetic of us are denied this.

If we are at one with ourselves (see Alignment), we can reduce the need to feel emotionally connected to others specifically because we are at peace spiritually and therefore feel connected to everything. This type of personal examination goes very deep and for most people who deny spirituality, it can seem like pie in the sky. But those of us, who seek to understand ourselves more deeply than we might have before, have already glimpsed the enormity of our spiritual selves. This is a big subject and philosophers have discussed it at length for millennia. But it is important to understand that the more we connect spiritually – that is, we understand ourselves, our fears, needs and desires – the less we find we need the comfort of others based on our doubts and failings, and the more we can stand alone.

Once we attain this level of spirituality through study and meditation, we can truly appreciate those around us for who they are, and not for what they can do for us emotionally or because they fill some sense of lack or fear of being alone.

> *'First they ignore you, then they laugh at you, then they fight you, then you win.'*
> Mahatma Gandhi

The Isolation Strategy in Health

Separate Yourself from the Pack

Maintaining good health requires discipline and motivation, both of which are attitudes of mind.

To achieve good health can be made easier by joining with a group that helps to motivate each member. This could be a slimming club, an online group of like-minded people, a martial arts school or sports centre... Belonging to such a group makes us more accountable for our actions while providing us with guidance and emotional support. However, it is also true that groups can shrink as members drop out when their motivation fails them, so it is important to use these for support without having to be completely dependent on them.

If you want to achieve lasting health, then you must be prepared to go it alone at some point and not have to rely on others to push you on all the time. Without good health, life can be a misery. Imagine what it would be like to have a chronic illness and live in pain and discomfort and be constantly at the mercy of emotions such as need, tiredness or depression. Whilst part of our health is attributed to genetic inheritance or accident and may not be changeable, you can still, through good habits and attitude, delay or even put off any ill-health inheritance (although we all have to go eventually!). Regular progressive exercise to build and keep muscles and the heart strong, combined with thoughtful and balanced nutrition to fuel the mind and body, are vital to ensuring you reach your potential. However, it has to be maintained throughout your whole life, so it must become more than just a whim. Taking positive actions to achieve good health must be a life choice and one that you will have to maintain on your own. No matter how much support you have around you, your decisions and your actions dictate the state of health you are in.

The only way to build these habits is to do so on your own; you must drive them, you must maintain them throughout your life. This can also mean being aware of the need to isolate yourself from those who would tease you away from your good habits or those who tell you that you're on the wrong track. Study health, educate yourself and apply what you learn.

'It's beautiful to be alone. To be alone does not mean to be lonely. It means the mind is not influenced and contaminated by society.'

Jidhu Krishnamurti

The Isolation Strategy in Wealth

Separating the Wheat from the Chaff

There are those who believe that wealth will change you, but it won't; it's the journey to wealth that will change you. Wealth is not just for the elite, it's for everyone. It's simply the case that some people know how to achieve wealth and most don't.

Achieving wealth needs good planning and using Isolation tactics is equally as necessary to that purpose as are the other four leverage strategies (Energy, Recruitment, Alignment and Pressure). Isolation is the ability to work alone, make your own decisions and have the strength to stick to them. You need to have the independence and self-belief to be able to go your own way in the face of adversity and those who don't believe in you. You must be able to set yourself apart from those who don't want what you want, or who won't pay the price that you are prepared to pay. This can mean leaving behind friends and family who won't join you on your journey, and may begrudge your success and even become your detractors.

Whatever they may say or think and however it hurts, don't let it hold you back from achieving your destiny.

'Isolation is the sum total of wretchedness to a man.'
Thomas Carlyle

The Isolation Strategy in Growth

Success is a Lonely Road

Personal growth is a personal journey made through personal choice. Whilst you will no doubt recruit and align with others, combining your leverage to achieve results together, you will need your personal passion for whatever it is that drives you forward.

Don't expect that others will share this, or that those who do will share it forever. Consider your journey to be like catching a bus to somewhere you want to go to; people will get on with you and some will get on along the way. But not everyone will stay on until the bus reaches its final destination and, although you might not want them to, some important and valuable people will get off long before you, and some will overstay their welcome and you'll wish they got off much earlier. But your journey is your journey and your direction is your direction; if you need anyone to assist you or to combine your efforts with, then you'll need to share the same goals, but even so, your exit strategy (see Proximity) will likely not be at the same point. That's OK, because that's life! But you must accustom yourself to going your own way and to know that, although you will likely have others with you on your way, they will not always be the same people at the beginning and at the end. Don't get too emotional about whether you need or want others with you and don't become too ruthless either.

Do what you need to do; accept help when you can and offer help when you can. You don't have to create isolation to achieve; you just need to understand how it works and how to use it to your benefit.

'Discipline and unconditional support is earned by understanding and trust and inclusion. Not by isolation, not by nasty tricks.'
Colm Keaveney

Summary

You can recognise by now the dual nature of all strategies. In the Isolation strategy, that duality is, on the one hand, to place the enemy in isolation so he feels weak and cut off, but the same strategy may be used to cut yourself off from others at times, in order to make yourself stronger. Isolation works closely with Alignment and Recruitment and it is not necessarily their opposite. It is as distinct as they are and, therefore, works differently when put into action.

Isolation Strategy in Brief

1. Few people want to be alone, isolated or cut off from the group. Without the support of the group, we lack leverage and power and we feel weak and vulnerable.
2. Every warlord or general must lead his army, marshal his resources and supplies, as, without all this, he is alone, removed of his power.
3. Isolation in combat is not always a bad thing and does not always mean we are alone or even at a disadvantage. If we know how to apply the strategy of Isolation we can turn it into an advantage that we can exploit.
4. Everyone is vulnerable to the strategy of Isolation, if not emotionally then practically.
5. We can be in the midst of our closest friends and still feel isolated and alone, but the knowledge that we are loved and valued by our friends and family will bring great solace.
6. At some level we are always isolated. No one can experience what we are experiencing internally in any given moment, no matter how sensitive and empathetic they are.
7. Be aware of the need to isolate yourself from those who tease you away from your good habits or those who tell you that you're on the wrong track when you know you are making a positive change to your life.
8. You must be able to set yourself apart from those who don't want what you want, or who won't pay the price that you are prepared to pay.
9. Consider your journey to be like catching a bus to somewhere you want to go to; people will get on with you and some will get on along the way. But not everyone will stay on until the bus reaches its final destination.
10. Learn to identify when you are going it alone when if fact you should be asking for help, and asking for help when in fact you should be going it alone.

STRATEGY NO. 9

The Leverage Strategy of Alignment

Definition: You Scratch My Back And I'll Scratch Yours

Overview of Alignment

Alignment means to work with, both physically and mentally, to befriend, ally with, and support. In both war and friendship, we create allies to build our strength, giving us the opportunity to achieve more than we can alone. Although the timing of alignment is crucial, the time frame will be flexible. We can align against an enemy temporarily and have duplicitous intent but since that is conflicted, it is therefore fraught with problems. We can gain much more through true alignment, as in friendship and unity. Consider how alignment fits with Expectation, Duplicity and Proximity.

'Successful diplomacy is an alignment of objectives and means.'
Dennis Ross

The Yin & Yang of Alignment

The Yang

alliance
coalition
lining up
joining up
in conjunction
in unison
co-dependent

The Yin

non-alignment
misalignment
going it alone
going against the grain
independence

The Alignment Strategy in Tradition

As Thick as Thieves

Historically, fairgrounds were places where thieves could thrive, with lots of people packed together, being jostled and pushed with the throng of the crowd. Artists and traders would dazzle the crowd with their sales pitches and acrobatics, drawing the full attention of the crowd (see Attraction) who would be so focused on the show that they could be easy pickings for the cut purses and pick pockets moving between the spectators.

Originally an ancient French phrase referring to the number and proximity of thieves working their trade at public fairs – 'like thieves at a fair' – this expression came to England with the Norman Conquest and remained in use, gradually modifying to its current form 'as thick as thieves' by the early 19th Century. Today the phrase is a metaphor describing the extreme closeness of friends and allies.

'When you at last give your life – bringing into alignment your beliefs and the way you live then, and only then, can you begin to find inner peace.'

Peace Pilgrim

The Alignment Strategy in Warfare

If You Can't Beat Them, Join Them

War is only about conflict when peaceful means fail to get what the warlord desires, but war is costly in terms of resources, soldiers, and the destruction caused. Forming alliances is one way to achieve a goal at a lower cost.

Chinese Strategy No. 24 – Borrow a Road to Attack Kuo

The ancient Chinese strategy of 'borrow a road' uses false alignment by coming to the aid of someone in need as a tactic to get close to them in order to take control or attack them (see Duplicity also). The Russian invasion of Afghanistan was such a tactic: the Russians placed themselves in a position to be invited in by the Afghan government to help put down insurgents. Once they had permission to bring their tanks and troops into the country, they took control of the government and replaced it with their own. In the short term, it worked but, as with so many invaders of Afghanistan, they underestimated the Afghan mind set and gradually the Russian occupation failed.

Chinese Strategy No. 23 – Befriend Those at a Distance. Attack Those Close By.

Familiarity breeds contempt and so it's easy to be friendly with those we seldom see, whereas we are so often at war with our families and neighbours whom we see every day. This Chinese strategy dates back to 269 BC and is used to defeat a close enemy by aligning with a distant one, in effect surrounding our closer enemy, defeating him and taking control of his resources (see Recruitment). As your own army swells in strength, you might one day even take on the distant neighbour who helped you (see Duplicity). Both of these ancient strategies use alignment as their primary strategy and duplicity as their secondary one, reminding us how stratagems fit together like jigsaw pieces to make a bigger picture or plan.

Chinese Strategy No. 30 – Arrive as Guest, Take Over as Host

The cuckoo lays its eggs in the nest of another bird who then nurtures the egg along with its own until they hatch. The cuckoo hatches quickly, before the other bird's own eggs, and the chick grows faster. Once the chick hatches, it pushes the other eggs out of the nest so that it can thrive alone. The parents of the cuckoo even choose the nests of birds whose eggs have similar markings so that the egg is not rejected. In some species, the male cuckoo distracts (see Direction) the host parent away from the nest while the female cuckoo lays her eggs.

This is an example of duplicitous alignment (see Duplicity) and is one of the subtlest ways to attack an enemy. In warfare, the cuckoo is the agent who is trained to look and act like the enemy and placed within the enemies ranks (see Isolation), sometimes for years as sleeper agents who work within an organisation, working their way up through the ranks, achieving more and more power and influence, whilst all the time working for the enemy. This is a tactic often used by undercover counter-terrorist agents which allows them to associate with dissident groups in order to collect information.

'Successful diplomacy is an alignment of objectives and means.'
Dennis Ross

The Alignment Strategy in Combat

Pull Yourself Together

Although our enemies become such because we cannot align with them, we can, however, align against them. As an army, we align our forces together, both physically and mentally, and then together against our enemy – just as we have all seen in countless films where two armies line up in opposition on the battlefield of war. Strategy, however, exists to reduce the need to face an enemy full on. We want to utilise battlefield strategies to gain the upper hand without too many losses or injuries.

Even when it comes to body mechanics, we align ourselves physically when we use our punches, kicks, locks and holds. For instance, the right cross can increase the power it generates by aligning the right side joints of elbow, shoulder, hip, knee and ankle and foot to deliver more body weight. Just as angling the punch in a downward tilt can align us with the effects of gravity to increase the power further. Another tactic is to align our body so that we offer fewer targets – which is why boxers lead with the left hand (except southpaws who lead with the right) which protects the vulnerable parts of the body (see Target) from right-handed attacks. This use of the alignment strategy dates back thousands of years to the times of Alexander the Great and beyond. Soldiers in trained armies, such as the Macedonians, were trained to lead with their left, covering themselves with their shields and keeping their stronger right side at the rear holding a weapon. When they faced less disciplined armies, who attacked more as individual warriors than aligned soldiers, this tactic became a formidable shield wall which acted as an almost invincible defence.

Alignment in combat is about the angle of attack, whether it is a straight line toward the opponent's centre line or from the left, right, rising or dropping. The ability to attack from many angles makes us unpredictable (see Expectation) and provides more opportunities to strike (see Opportunity). Whether we attack with punches, kicks, throws etc., the ability to approach a target indirectly makes us less obvious and also gives us the ability to maximise our power. Our bodies are designed to create force in many different directions. The angle we are at, together with the distance we are at (see Proximity), affects the amount of energy (see Energy) we generate against an opponent. As martial artists, we must learn how to align with the biomechanics of our own bodies so that we can attack and defend from the most diverse angles and distances.

The martial arts are a search for truth. It is a search for efficiency, to achieve a result in the best and easiest way possible. In order to do this, we must align with our own resources, which is our mind and body. Alignment in combat means using our skills and abilities in unison to form ourselves into a weapon that is greater than the sum of its parts. As Miyamoto Musashi would say: 'Study this well'.

> **'When envoys are sent with compliments in their mouths, it is a sign that the enemy wishes for a truce.'**
> Sun Tzu

The Alignment Strategy in Relationships

Walk the Line

All relationships, by definition, rely on alignment. But the question is: 'How long can we align for?' In marriage, business or friendship, we align, often intensely and closely, and the strength of the relationship can often be measured in its degree of alignment.

But what happens when that alignment begins to separate, when our ideas or goals change and our partner's may not, or theirs might change and ours remain the same? This creates a divergence where we begin to separate from each other and, unless we can re-align ourselves, the relationship will separate too. Sometimes these divergences can be corrected easily, just as an argument can clear the air and bring us closer together. Sometimes, they can do the opposite and push us further apart. The key is to keep one's emotions in check and avoid saying anything so hurtful that it cannot be taken back. This is difficult to do when you feel upset, hurt, angry and emotional, but self-control and self-discipline are invaluable when dealing with people, and the wise strategist develops these skills in abundance.

Marriages are intended to last forever yet, two thirds of them these days don't make it that far. So, if you're in it for the long term, management of your own alignment with your loved one and your emotions is essential. We all have our own interests and our partners may not share them, or we theirs, but it's important to try to show an interest, preferably sincere, in your partner's interests. Tolerance, patience (see Patience) and understanding are your watchwords and these are needed on both sides of the relationship – in addition to spending time together, sharing stories, hopes and dreams.

The same is true of partnerships and friendships: some can last forever but most won't. It's important to be realistic and not too sentimental about past friendships and partnerships; when they are over, they're over. Remember that many relationships are circumstantial. That is, they exist whilst the circumstances that created that friendship exist: school friends are friends at school, work friends are friends at work and business partners are partners while ever the business continues. Every business partnership and friendship is finite, so once it's over, move on. Take the experience with you but don't hang on to the past.

> **'An alliance with a powerful person is never safe.'**
> Phaedrus

The Alignment Strategy in Friendship

Give and Take

We can achieve so much when we align with ourselves and others which is why friendship, unity and shared goals are the keys of the alignment strategy. To be a good friend is to be truthful, trusting, trustworthy, reliable and predictable.

To be a good friend, we must be a good listener, without judgement or duplicity. We must also expect the same in return, even if it does not come to us immediately – but if we are to be friends, it must come eventually. Friendship is a two-way street and, whilst there will always be times when we give and times when we take, overall the relationship strength comes from a balance of giving and taking.

Alignment is to stand for similar (if not necessarily exactly the same) ideals which is why it is such a powerful force that needs to be harnessed. In friendship, we should be there to stand by our friends, family and colleagues; to support and guide those we care for. But, as stated before, this alignment is a two-way street and true alignment can be demanding and challenging at times. We must trust our friends if we are to stand with them and be able to honour what they are standing for.

Sometimes we may be pulled in more than one direction when our friends have issues with each other, and any action we take for either side can be interpreted as favouritism. We must be able to help but at the same time remain balanced in these situations, and not be drawn emotionally too much to either side without proof. Remember the saying: 'Six of one and half a dozen of the other' which means that what is often purported to be all one-sided is not often truly so. Our emotions make us 'right' but this rightness is the rightness of anger which is rarely, if ever, in balance. In fact, the whole nature of anger relies on being out of balance. So, when helping our friends by aligning with them, your best weapon is to use intellect over emotion.

'Don't walk behind me; I may not lead. Don't walk in front of me; I may not follow. Just walk beside me and be my friend.'

Albert Camus

The Alignment Strategy Personally

In Two Minds

It might seem strange to discuss aligning with yourself but this is an area that is often overlooked. Many people are not aware that they can be anything but themselves, when it is actually often the case. One example of this is defined by the concept of 'cognitive dissonance' – which is when our intentions conflict with our beliefs. It is summed up neatly in the saying: 'Be careful what you really want, as that is what you'll surely get'.

We have to understand that we are several personalities going on inside one body: our emotional personality, our intellectual personality, our physical personality and our spiritual personality. At the best of times, we are balanced between these personalities, but in the average day we can pass through them all. Consider those times when we are conflicted over a decision or situation, when we feel we are 'in two minds' about something or we have a guilty conscience about a past event. These mind sets come from being conflicted with our several personalities; one part of us being out of alignment with another part. Add to this the simplistic conditioning that we carry with us from childhood – part of our needs as a child is to have certainty, fixed answers to problems and our parents give us these in the form of absolutes: good and bad, big and small, child and grown up etc. These absolutes stay with us for many years or until they are re-written in our internal software. Sometimes they are never re-written and remain unquestioned or unchallenged, and become our core beliefs. However, to get what we want from life, we must align our values and beliefs, challenge what we think we already know and decide where we want to go and what we want to achieve. Only then can we be truly aligned with ourselves. And the more aligned we are, the more accessible our aims become and the more quickly we are able to achieve them.

Focus on examining your core beliefs as they occur; challenge what you believe to achieve clarity of your vision. Treat your brain like your body; it cannot walk in two directions at once and if it tries, if will fail and probably fall.

> **'What most people do is try to find a comfortable persona that they're in alignment with and the public likes and appreciates them for.'**
>
> Billy Corgan

The Alignment Strategy in Health

Doing it the Hard Way

We discussed earlier about aligning our different intelligences or personalities so that our goals are not conflicted between what we say we want and what we really want. The saying 'beware of what you really want, because that is surely what you'll get' is equally applicable to our health, as it is to any other part of our lives.

For instance, many people who smoke say openly that they wish they didn't. Yet, soon after saying that, they light up a cigarette! What is the truth? What do they really want? On the one hand, they want to stop smoking but on the other hand, they *really* want a smoke. Others say they want to get fit or lose weight but what they really want is **not** to undergo the pain of exercise and the discipline of dietary control.

Align your goals with your true desire: change your desires to make them match your goals and strengthen your discipline. How? By deciding what will help you best in the short and long-term, and by using that knowledge to build new habits that support your overall goal. The way to build habits is in creating alignment with your true desires. No one wants the pain of exercise; but we all enjoy the buzz that comes from exercise, plus the healthy appearance that it brings. So how do you overcome your initial reluctance to start a new exercise routine? You need to start easy, for example; instead of going for a run when you haven't run for months and feeling afterwards like you are about to die, go for an energetic walk. Find the right level of exercise that is both challenging and enjoyable. Overdoing it only makes us avoid exercise because we don't want to go through this painful process. Finding the right level means the pain level should be quite low during and after exercising. As you get fitter, your comfort area increases and you will start enjoying more challenges. Instead of going for a long run when you can barely walk to the end of the street, try going for a brisk walk every day, gradually increasing the distance and pace. Then, when your body has built a higher level of fitness, step up the intensity. Try walking again, but this time, walk and run from lamp post to lamp post; walk to one, then run to the next, followed by a walk then a run until you can run without stopping. This is a painless way to begin running, but most people don't try it because they want immediate fitness, not gradual fitness. Just like people who want to be slim now but do not want to go through the process of actually losing the weight.

The problem is that lifetime fitness, as well as lifetime health, is a gradual process not a clash of wills, and most people who fail to achieve lifetime good health fail because they are unable to align with their own human nature. Instead, they use force of will which cannot be maintained for more than a few weeks.

Every health habit can be built in the same way as learning how to run, gradually, by aligning with yourself. Take the easy way to get started and build challenges gradually until what was hardship at first becomes easy and the norm.

'Alliance does not mean love, any more than war means hate.'
Francis Parker Yockey

The Alignment Strategy in Wealth

Pull Together

Align yourself with people who can help you build wealth. Emulate them, model their behaviour, educate yourself: there are many books, CD's, videos and seminars that will teach you how to acquire wealth.

Some people have misaligned views on wealth, and perhaps you do too. Do you feel wealth is wrong? That money is the root of all evil or something similar? That the rich get richer as the poor get poorer? If you do, then you can never achieve wealth, as your conditioning and beliefs are misaligned with your desire to provide for yourself and your family, they are conflicted. Examine your beliefs on wealth and rationalise what wealth is. Money is simply a unit of exchange, a value exchange of goods or services. It makes sense to have more money than you need to live on, so you can continue to live in comfort when you are no longer able to work.

To achieve many of your aims in life, you will need money to fund them. So, if you have any doubts about the rightness of achieving wealth, you must deal with them early on or they will sabotage your efforts forever until they are resolved.

'True freedom is where an individual's thoughts and actions are in alignment with that which is true, correct, and of honour – no matter the personal price.'
Bryant H. McGill

The Alignment Strategy in Growth

Don't Re-invent the Wheel

'What has been will be again, what has been done will be done again; there is nothing new under the sun.' Ecclesiastes 1:9. What has this to do with the strategy of Alignment in Growth? It means that everything has been done before; everything you are trying to achieve has already been visualised, attempted and created by others before you. That's not to say that you shouldn't still try, because we all need to find our own way for our own reasons, but there is no point starting completely from scratch if we don't have to. There is no need to re-invent the wheel, so consider what you are trying to achieve and how you can do so more efficiently by aligning with existing knowledge and the thoughts and actions of others that have gone before.

Often our search for personal growth can make us feel like we should do it all on our own (see Isolation), but that's the fool's way to achieve. The wise man is prepared to 'stand on the shoulders of giants'. The knowledge, science, technology and philosophy that makes our world turn today was not invented or thought of today, it has come from no one person. On the contrary, it has come from many millions of other individuals over thousands of years. The point is that you cannot reach for the moon in a single jump; you have to align with previous knowledge and learning by using their experience as a stepping stone.

The AEGIS Law of Judgment says: 'Good judgement comes from experience, experience comes from bad judgement' and personal growth can be achieved much more quickly by learning from other people's mistakes. Once you have decided that you can't do it all on your own you should then set goals that align with each other. Consider how alliances with others can speed your progress and how the knowledge and experience you need can lie in their existing knowledge and experience. Unite with individuals and groups who share your ideals and goals; share resources so you can create more leverage than you ever could alone. Discover your personal gifts and how they will help you and others, but also discover your weaknesses and fix them through study and practice.

Think of yourself as a circle: a wheel will only work when it is fully rounded and fully aligned. When you achieve alignment in all areas of your life, nothing can stop your forward progress.

'Happiness is when what you think, what you say, and what you do are in harmony.'

Mahatma Gandhi

Summary

Alignment is one of the most powerful of strategies if it's used well. It works in friendships extremely well but it can also be a cunning strategy in war. It occurs in three of the 36 ancient Chinese strategies. A key point of the alignment strategy is to find ways to circumvent conflict and to look to the greater power that comes with aligning instead of fighting with others.

Alignment Strategy in Brief

1. In both war and friendship, we create allies to build our strength, giving us the opportunity to achieve more than we can alone.
2. War is only about conflict when peaceful means fail to get what the warlord desires, but war is costly in terms of resources, soldiers, and the destruction caused.
3. Familiarity breeds contempt and so it's easy to be friendly with those we seldom see, whereas we are so often at war with our families and neighbours whom we see every day.
4. The martial arts are a search for truth and efficiency, to achieve a result in the best and easiest way possible. In order to do this, we must align with our own resources: our mind and body.
5. Some partnerships and friendships can last forever but most won't. It's important to be realistic and not too sentimental about past friendships and partnerships: when they are over, they're over. Move on.
6. Friendship is a two-way street and, whilst there will always be times when we give and times when we take, overall the relationship strength comes from a balance of giving and taking.
7. Focus on examining your core beliefs: challenge what you believe in order to achieve clarity of your vision. Treat your brain like your body: it cannot walk in two directions at once and if it tries, if will fail and probably fall.
8. We must align our different intelligences or personalities so that our goals are not conflicted between what we say we want and what we really want. 'Beware of what you really want, because that is surely what you'll get.'

9. Align yourself with people who can help you to build wealth; emulate them, model their behaviour, educate yourself. There are many books, CD's, videos and seminars that will teach you how to acquire wealth.
10. Think of yourself as a circle: a wheel will only work when it is fully rounded and fully aligned. When you achieve alignment in all areas of your life, nothing can stop your forward progress.

STRATEGY NO. 10

The Leverage Strategy of Pressure

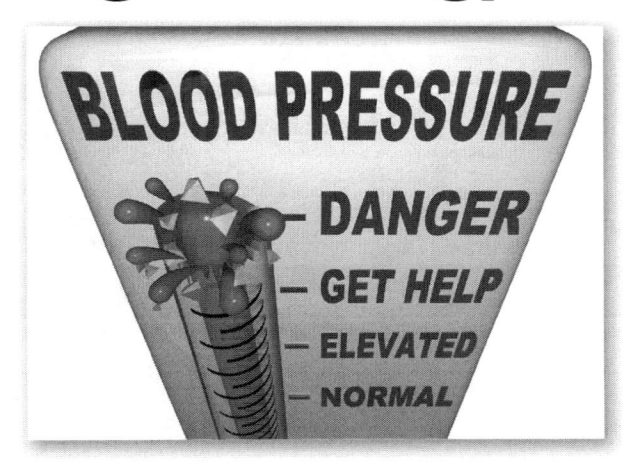

Definition: If You Can't Stand the Heat, Stay Out of the Kitchen

Overview of Pressure

Life carries degrees of stress, from good stress to bad stress. Bad stress wears us down, depressing us physically and mentally, whilst good stress builds and rejuvenates us. The ability to apply pressure on our opponent in combat can overwhelm an adversary, and removing pressure at the right time can turn him into an ally. Our general aim should be to apply pressure to our enemies, remove it from our friends and maintain the right level for ourselves.

'I say there're no depressed words just depressed minds.'

Bob Dylan

The Yin and Yang of Pressure

The Yang
force
push
coerce
steamroll
stress
threat
squeeze
influence
depress
crush
lean on
distress

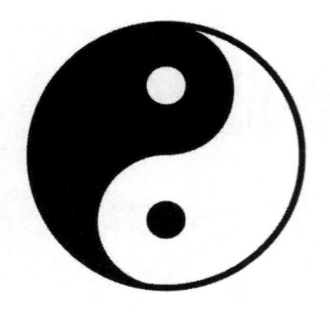

The Yin
relief
de-stress
lift
elate
uplift
pick up
hearten
raise
eustress
impress

The Pressure Strategy in Tradition

Bite off More than You Can Chew

The phrase 'to bite off more than you can chew' means to take on more than you can manage, such as work or effort or other stresses. It dates back to the USA in the 19th Century when people chewed tobacco like people today chew gum. Chewing tobacco came in long strips and one might offer a bite to someone, just as nowadays someone might offer a cigarette. Sometimes greedy people would take a much bigger bite than they could manage in the hope of keeping some for later, causing them to gag on the chunks of tobacco and to risk choking on their big bite. The generous people who were prepared to share their tobacco got wise to this greedy breed and whilst still prepared to make the offer, it came with a warning: 'Don't bite off more than you can chew'.

'God will never give you anything you can't handle, so don't stress.'

Kelly Clarkson

The Pressure Strategy in Warfare

The Heat is On

Pressure in war comes from a position of strength such as taking the higher ground so height and gravity is in our favour. Being larger and heavier works the same way, as does being stronger, better armed, having more soldiers and more skill. Pressure like this applied against an enemy is a powerful weapon, when it is ours to use.

From the German Blitzkreig of World War II, to Rourkes Drift in 1879, to the 300 Spartans at the battle of Thermopylae in 480BC, the Pressure strategy has been an effective strategy, if you have the means to apply it. It is not always necessary to actually have the ability to apply physical pressure, as long as our opponent believes that we do (see Appearance, Toughness and Duplicity).

Chinese Strategy No. 16 – In order to Capture, One Must Let Loose

Sun Tzu observed, in **The Art of War**, that there are circumstances where it is unwise to press an enemy too far, because, if he has nothing to lose, he will fight even more ferociously and the costs to you could be greater than they need be. However, if you relieve the pressure on such an opponent and allow him to escape, you can avoid the costly losses of fighting a desperate opponent. In allowing him to escape (see Proximity) you can conspire to catch him again later when circumstances allow you to take him with less risk (see Risk) or even to recruit him to your side if circumstances prefer it. Showing an opponent respect by letting him go can also be a good way to bring him to your own side. Just as a friend can become your worst enemy, so too can an enemy become your best friend.

> *'A prisoner of war is a man who tries to kill you and fails, and then asks you not to kill him.'*
> Winston Churchill

The Pressure Strategy in Combat

The Killer Instinct

Two powerful weapons in combat are surprise (see Expectation) and speed (see Pace) because they can both create pressure if applied correctly. There is a third element, which increases the effectiveness of any attack, which is to sustain the attack until victory is complete, without giving your opponent time to think or breathe. We call this 'overwhelm' and it can amplify the effects of the smallest advantage (see Exploitation).

Once you have the advantage, you put yourself at great risk if you don't pursue it to its very end. Many fighters have failed because they didn't have that killer instinct to finish the job. We can call it aggression or competitiveness or killer instinct but, whatever name it takes, it is the ability to build and maintain pressure on an opponent often past the point where your emotion says 'stop' or 'take it easy'. This ability can be the difference between win and lose, success and failure, and even life and death.

Pressure is also a physical skill which we must learn to use and also know when to ease off equally in training, competition and self-defence. Applying pressure is one thing, but not enough or too much can cause issues in your launch point (which is preparation and readiness for example). There is a fine line between the concepts of 'enough' and 'too much'. In street survival, 'too much' can lead to serious injuries and even death for your opponent and 'not enough' could have the same outcome for you. So, how do you manage this balance? There is only one way and that is through trial and error, which we know as the Law of Judgement which states: 'Good judgement comes through experience. Experience comes through bad judgement'. This means that when you have experience, you can apply accurate judgement to your decisions but, until you have acquired that experience, you just have to call it as you see it and hope for the best.

'Courage is grace under pressure.'
Ernest Hemingway

The Pressure Strategy in Relationships

'Illegitimi Non Carborundum'

Relationships are all about stress. Think about it: Is there any relationship you have which doesn't cause you stress in one form or another? This doesn't mean that they are always distressing but relationships are always changing and rely on constant management. Relationships are in a constant state of movement and change and it can never be taken for granted that they are settled and stable.

Pressure is stress and relationships are stressful therefore, they are also pressured. Managing that stress, that Pressure, is an everlasting balancing act and, as the saying goes: 'You can please some of the people all of the time and all of the people some of the time, but you can't please all of the people all of the time'. Bearing this in mind, it's important that we apply careful pressure to our relationships. Parents pressure children to achieve results at school, to act or dress in certain acceptable ways or to achieve in sport. Some apply too much pressure on them and some not enough. Some apply the right level of pressure but to the wrong person, and some not enough to the right one. We never really know the level of pressure we should apply, as what works with one doesn't always work with another.

Everyone is different and, even though we all have our predictabilities, we may not always have the same predictabilities at the same time or with the same people. So what is the answer? How do we achieve a balance of pressure within our relationships? The truth is that we cannot always achieve balance and the best thing we can do is to balance what we can. We must be aware that people around us need care and attention, which is a pressure on us and a pressure off them.

This is the nature of pressure in all relationships and it comes from both sides, so it's important to choose which of your relationships you want to be a part of and which you do not. Some need to be developed and some discarded; this way we can manage our relationship stress so that it remains more as eustress (or positive stress) rather than distress.

'Once you agree upon the price you and your family must pay for success, it enables you to ignore the minor hurts, the opponent's pressure, and the temporary failures.'

Vince Lombardi

The Pressure Strategy in Friendship

Take the Pressure Off

Friendship brings the pressure of responsibility, trust and care and this pressure increases when friends are in need.

Our duty as a friend is to relieve that pressure through help and support, but we must also balance this support so that our friend does not fail to stand on his own two feet. Remember the adage: 'Give a man a fish and you feed him for a day. Teach him how to fish and you'll feed him for a lifetime.' One of the best things you can do for a friend is to help him manage the pressure he is under and teach him how to become self-reliant.

Pressure on a friendship can stress it to the point of breaking, especially when it comes from a duplicitous source. There are those who appear friendly but who cannot help but divide and separate (see Isolation and Duplicity) even the truest of friends by spreading gossip and rumour. Watch out for those people who are themselves a stress, who come between other friends to break up their relationship.

Beware also those friends who are always under pressure through only being able to see their own point of view, those who are always at war, in debt or making promises they don't keep. These people create their own stress and often expect you to come to their aid time and time again. But, in so doing so, they are not being friends, they are being users and you should remove the stress they cause in your life by removing them. Until they realise what a destructive and negative force they are, they are no use to anyone and incapable of being a true friend.

'He who is of calm and happy nature will hardly feel the pressure of age, but to him who is of an opposite disposition youth and age are equally a burden.'

Plato

The Pressure Strategy Personally

Don't Stress

We can pressure ourselves just as we can also be the subject of external pressure. Often what we forget is that, in both cases, we can be the author of both types of pressure.

Let us consider how pressure is applied and received on a personal level. We all know people who put themselves under pressure, working long and hard to create success, sometimes to great effect and achievement and sometimes, unfortunately, without getting anywhere. As long as these people can use the other strategies as well, they can certainly do well, but sometimes they just seem to be running faster without achieving anything. This is a dangerous way to use your energy (see Energy) as it drains your physical and mental resources. Many people in this situation can end up bitter and cynical by working harder and harder, applying more and more effort with less and less result.

There is a definition of insanity which says 'Insanity is doing the same thing over and over again and expecting a different result'. Many of us fail to recognise that some of our efforts work just like this: using the same strategy to get different results. Like people who end up in abusive relationships: abusers and abused tend to get the same end result because they keep engaging in the same behaviours. They are attracted to the same types of people and retain the same emotional triggers. They want things to change but they don't examine what it is that actually needs to change. Without a change in behaviour, we won't get a change in results, and without a change in results, the pressure in our life remains and continues to build. The effect of too much pressure can lead to personal overwhelm, where everything gets too much for us and we can suffer breakdown or collapse. Our emotional management systems can no longer cope and eventually we can end up in a state of collapse.

Pressure alone as a strategy is not always enough. No strategy alone will be enough unless we are very lucky, so we have to use the laws of Recognition and Study in order to make the most of it. The former to be conscious of where and how to apply our pressure and the latter to study our results to ensure we are not doing the same thing over and over again and expecting a different result.

'Everything negative – pressure, challenges – is all an opportunity for me to rise.'
Kobe Bryant

The Pressure Strategy in Health

Keep Your Foot on the Gas

The key to the strategy of Pressure is to apply the right kind of stress in the right balance. In our health strategy, this balance is particularly finely tuned. Our health is one of our most valuable assets and any intelligence we have is wasted if we do not have the health to enjoy it. After all, there's no point being the brightest person in the graveyard is there?

With all the things we want to achieve in life, our health can readily be the easiest thing to let slip. The wrong food is much easier to find than the right food and it's easier to be inactive than to exercise. This is how the pressure of life builds up, and our health can be the first thing to go to the wall. We must work hard to keep our health in balance. We need the positive stress it brings in order to keep our bodies working efficiently and, on the extra plus side, good health keeps our emotions and thinking healthy too.

The secret weapon of good health is getting the stress right. Too much training for instance will take too much time and can wear us down, having the opposite effect to what we want. Too little won't keep us fit enough. Achieving this balance will always be an issue and at times we do not get it right and do either too little or too much. This is a balancing act and it has to be managed continually. Fortunately, it gets easier if we build our health habits around things we like to do, and if we remove bad habits, gradually replacing them with better ones.

Don't try to do everything at once, as that pressure will cause pain which results in avoiding (see Proximity) the very thing you need. Make health a priority; apply enough pressure to maintain your health and not too much that it becomes a stress to maintain.

> *'To be a champion, you have to learn to handle stress and pressure. But if you've prepared mentally and physically, you don't have to worry.'*
>
> Harvey Mackay

The Pressure Strategy in Wealth

High Pressure System

There is a sort of in-built mythology in people who are poor which causes them to believe that wealth is somehow magical and that only a lottery win will ever bring it to them.

The good news is that this is nonsense. Wealth is within everyone's reach and its achievement is everyone's responsibility. To look after ourselves in old age without putting stress on the state or our family is our own responsibility. As humans, we are gifted with the biggest brains in the animal kingdom. Doesn't it make sense to use that brain to make our lives easier?

To gain wealth takes three key things: a goal, a system and the motivation to maintain pressure until that goal is achieved. The goal is up to you and such systems can be found in the books of Robert T. Kiyosaki or T. Harv Eker but the pressure to do this is all yours. Achieving wealth is much more straightforward than most people believe, but it won't come to you by sitting back and waiting for it to happen – you must apply constant pressure, at least until you get your money-making machine up and running.

As mentioned before with Pressure, getting the balance right is key and in the early days it can be very difficult. It's easy to get discouraged as initial progress can be slow. But with constant steady pressure it will come, and when it does, it builds up momentum (which is another form of pressure) so that it soon takes less pressure to make bigger gains.

'A man will fight harder for his interests than for his rights.'
Napoleon Bonaparte

The Pressure Strategy in Growth

Turn the Screw

To achieve our goals in life takes passion and effort. Effort is energy (see Energy) but the force it creates is pressure. When the pressure becomes self-sustaining, we have momentum which is where a greater part of our success comes from.

Momentum in personal growth could be described as conditioned pressure, that is, achieving results then raising the bar to the next level. Achieve the results again and raise the bar again. The Law of Conditioning states that 'Repetition is the mother of all skill' and this applies to your success, in creating habits that support your goals. But those habits must be continually refined as you grow, and this takes the application of pressure, both in effort and motivation.

How much pressure and for how long? The answer is: enough and for as long as it takes. It's a moving feast that relies entirely upon you and the goals you are trying to achieve. You can get off whenever you want or you can pursue your growth indefinitely. The amount of pressure you can apply and the amount you can withstand will be key to your success as will the amount of stress you want. Some people thrive on it and others die from it.

Some people thrive so much on stress that they become stress junkies. Think about the rise of extreme sports: hang gliding, base jumping, parcours and the like, all designed for people who need the high stress that danger brings. Salespeople and entrepreneurs too often thrive on the buzz of the big deal or the last minute turnaround. In films or TV, we all love watching programmes that leave us breathless, like the James Bond opening sequences or the thrillers: the lights go out and there's a killer in the house...

Why do we seek this pressure? It would be easy to answer simply by saying that 'it's simply fun'. This is OK, because for most of us it is just that, but for others, that pressure, that 'living on the edge' becomes an addiction. In personal growth, we should seek to balance our stress, remembering that there is an optimum level which is enough to challenge and motivate us but not so much that it becomes a drain on our health (see Energy).

Study and strive to achieve the right level of pressure in your journey of personal growth even though it is almost impossible to constantly maintain an even level of pressure. It is also important to recognise that lack of stress doesn't make us stronger, nor does exposure to extremely high stress. Stress, if it is to help us grow personally, must be the same as stress which makes us physically fitter; it must gradually increase in intensity in order to kick start the bodies to grow.

'When we long for life without difficulties, remind us that oaks grow strong in contrary winds and diamonds are made under pressure.'
Peter Marshall

Summary

Pressure is an important part of leverage strategies and we must understand how it works in order to get what we want. We apply it and we are also subject to it. It is necessary to keep us alive yet too much can kill us. We can use it to do good and also to do evil, to help or to hinder. As ever and as with all strategies, it is double-edged and rarely used in isolation.

Pressure Strategy in Brief

1. Life carries degrees of stress, of good stress and bad stress. The secret is: 'don't bite off more than you can chew'.
2. Pressure in war comes from a position of strength, taking the higher ground so height and gravity is in our favour.
3. There are circumstances where it is unwise to press an enemy too far, because, if he has nothing to lose, he will fight even more ferociously.
4. Paradoxically, once you have the advantage, you put yourself at great risk if you don't pursue it to its very end.
5. Relationships are in a constant state of movement and it can never be taken for granted that they are settled and stable.
6. Friendship brings the pressure of responsibility, trust and care and this pressure increases when friends are in need.
7. The effect of too much pressure can lead to personal overwhelm, where everything gets too much for us and we can suffer from breakdown or collapse.
8. To gain wealth takes three key things: a goal, a system and the motivation to maintain pressure until that goal is achieved.
9. Momentum in personal growth could be described as conditioned pressure, that is, achieving results then raising the bar to the next level.
10. The amount of pressure you can apply and the amount you can withstand will be key to your success as will the amount of stress you want. Some people thrive on it and others die from it.

INVULNERABILITY STRATEGIES

'To Know Your Enemies' Weakness is Strength, To Know Your Own is Wisdom' The AEGIS Law of Vulnerability

Vulnerability strategies seek to reveal, protect and strike at the weakest parts of our objectives, ourselves and our resources. Every goal, no matter how powerful, has its Achilles' Heel, and Vulnerability strategies will uncover and target those vulnerabilities to create weakness or strength wherever it is needed to achieve our expectations.

The 5 strategies of Invulnerability are:

1. *Manoeuvrability* – deals with movement, both physically and mentally
2. *Exploitation* – the manipulation of advantage and disadvantage
3. *Target* – guarding, striking, removal and acquisition
4. *Risk* – managing, removal and creation of danger
5. *Example* – leveraging warnings, deterrents and models

Vulnerability strategies deal with finding and managing weakness as well as its opposite: strength. Protecting, attacking and understanding Vulnerability is of paramount importance in the achievement of our goals.

STRATEGY NO. 11

The Vulnerability Strategy of Manoeuvre

Definition: Float like a Butterfly, Sting like a Bee

Overview of Manoeuvre

When the small is faced with the large, it is outweighed and placed at a disadvantage. A weak opponent cannot stand against a stronger, larger and heavier opponent head on and must, therefore, use his smaller size and greater mobility and flexibility to manoeuvre more quickly in and out of range. When the larger opponent is out-manoeuvred, he becomes vulnerable. When the smaller opponent can manoeuvre, he becomes less vulnerable and more dangerous.

'The difficulty of tactical manoeuvring consists in turning the devious into the direct, and misfortune into gain.'

Sun Tzu

The Yin and Yang of Manoeuvre

The Yang		**The Yin**
act		stand
move		stop
navigate		stay
go		immobility
locomotion		fixed
movability		unmoved
motility		immobile

The Manoeuvre Strategy in Tradition

No Flies on You

This phrase originates from the farmers of horses and cattle in Australia and refers to the fact that cattle that moved around a lot weren't bothered by the ever present flies, whereas those animals that were sedentary and immobile were easy targets – as can so often be seen where cattle standing around in fields are usually covered with flies around their mouths and eyes. In the mid-19th Century the phrase became popular, and remains so today, when describing someone who is quick witted and gets things done.

> *'Battles are won by slaughter and manoeuvre. The greater the general, the more he contributes in manoeuvre, the less he demands in slaughter.'*
>
> Winston Churchill

The Manoeuvre Strategy in Warfare

Keep Them on Their Toes

The ability to move gives us many options in battle: to move forwards, backwards, laterally, up and down; allowing us to attack, defend and counter attack from any angle. If our opponent cannot match our manoeuvres, then we have a major advantage which should never be underestimated.

Chinese Strategy No. 25 – Replace the Beams, Steal the Pillars

Chinese Strategy number 25 deals with weakening the enemy's position by not allowing him to settle. When he is unable to settle, his ability to think, plan and act is compromised and therein lays your chance to move in on him.

During the late 18th and early 19th Century, Napoleon's forces were spreading across Europe. His armies were massive, well trained and devoted to their Emperor. However, his Spanish campaign was dogged by two major problems: one was the tenacity of Wellington's forces and the other, which he never learned how to deal with, was the Spanish Guerrillas. Though ill-equipped and few in number compared to Napoleon's *Grande Armée*, the Guerrilla fighters knew the territory and were committed to beating the French at every turn. They constantly harassed the French troops by sniping at their officers and men, intercepting their couriers and cutting off their supply lines. The guerrillas were vicious and often ruthless – there are stories of individuals setting targets to kill at least 40 French troops per month for example. This constant baiting (see Attraction and Reaction) served to demoralise the French and is considered to be a major cause of their eventual defeat. The guerrillas were swift and mobile, showing that a small opponent can defeat a much larger one with the correct use of the manoeuvre strategy, being the epitome of the phrase 'hit and run'.

'The art of war is simple enough. Find out where your enemy is. Get at him as soon as you can. Strike him as hard as you can, and keep moving on.'

Ulysses S. Grant

The Manoeuvre Strategy in Combat

Hit and Run

Muhammad Ali named himself 'The Greatest' and history has borne him out. He broke all the established rules of boxing; he wouldn't just stand there and fight. He could attack moving backwards, danced around his opponents wearing them down to the point where he could knock them out and seemed to see their punches coming at him in slow motion.

Ali is a study in combat strategy, but his outstanding ability was his mobility, which he used to outpace (see Pace), side step and back step (see Proximity) his opponents, wearing them down with his fast left jabs. So fast was his attack and defence that it was suggested that he saw his opponents move in slow motion. No other boxer has ever captured the public's attention like Ali, who was not just fast with his hands and feet, but also fast with his thinking. Always ready to talk and predict his wins, he was known as the 'Louisville Lip' because of his fast talking style. Ali even invented his own fancy footwork step named the 'Ali Shuffle' and his now famous rhyme:

'Float like a butterfly,
sting like a bee,
your hands can't hit
what your eyes can't see.'

There are few weapons in combat more useful than the ability to out-manoeuvre your opponent. Of course, like any stratagem, manoeuvre cannot work alone and we should always consider how it interacts and supports the other FLITE stratagems, particularly Alignment, Proximity, Pace and Interruption.

Consider Manoeuvre in terms of the biological response of 'fight or flight', that is either advance or retreat in the presence of danger (see Proximity). These are the natural responses that we are born with, but in terms of strategy they are a little too predictable against an intelligent opponent. This is where the strategy of Alignment comes in; the ability to change our position laterally and vertically takes manoeuvre into 3 dimensions, making us more unpredictable and difficult to hit. This difficulty increases even further when one adds pace to unpredictability of movement, revealing the truth of Mohammad Ali's observation: 'Your hands can't hit what your eyes can't see'.

Manoeuvrability relates closely to the law of Balance which states: 'With balance, one can achieve almost anything, but without it we can achieve nothing that lasts.' To manoeuvre requires excellent balance, since every side step, back step, dip, slip and weave compromises this balance. To stand up straight and rigid in combat is a common mistake of the beginner who makes himself an easy target, whereas the master moves smoothly in all directions hence evading attack and still being able to land his attacks effectively.

There are three keys to movement in combat which affect your ability to hit without being hit which are:

1. *Reach* – the distance you can reach with hand or foot without having to step
2. *Step* – the distance you can reach assisted by single or multiple footsteps
3. *Reach and Step* – the distance you can reach by using both your reach plus footsteps

Reach goes forwards, backwards, laterally and vertically, as do steps. For this reason, you must work hard to develop your skill in both areas as they affect power and speed in attack and defence. The ability to manoeuvre is one of the greatest skills of the master martial artist and it requires deep study and practice. An important concept to understand as part of the manoeuvre strategy along with bull's eye distancing (see Proximity) and the 5 standing levels (see Function) are the 5 Levels of Defence (see also Interruption). In unarmed combat, there are 5 levels of defence which are important in manoeuvring:

Level 5 – Avoidance: moving away from the attack (See Proximity)
Level 4 – Block: stopping attacks with parts of your own body such as a hand, elbow, etc. (see Interruption)
Level 3 – Re-direct: deflecting an attack without stopping it (see Interruption and Direction)
Level 2 – Evade: lateral and vertical evasion in defence and attack without meeting any of the opponent's strikes (see Alignment)
Level 1 – Attack: intercepting an attack with an attack (see Interruption)

To understand the implications of the 5 levels of defence is to understand a great deal about how to manoeuvre and its intricate relationship with the strategies of Alignment, Proximity, Energy, Target, Pace and Risk. Using your 5 levels of defence will help you develop your manoeuvre skills. Master the strategy of Manoeuvre and you will be hard to beat.

**'The conventional army loses if it does not win.
The guerrilla wins if he does not lose.'**
Henry A. Kissinger

The Manoeuvre Strategy in Relationships

Jockey for Position

Few relationships are entirely equal; each person brings to it something different to give it balance like the principle of Yin and Yang representing the two necessary opposites which balance all life.

Opposites can work together well and create a good partnership, just like in those performance acts that have the straight man and the comic, or the singer and the accompanist. Each plays their part and complements one another in order to create a balanced whole. In a new relationship too, we can go through a period of adjustment as each member finds their position. This can be an important sorting process: Who will be the leader and who will be the follower? This is not to say that one is necessarily better than the other as, depending on the circumstances, one or other will take the lead when his or her expertise comes to the fore. If the partners are mismatched to their roles, then the relationship will falter before long and can even come to a complete halt. This is where it is necessary to put emotion and friendship to one side to get the best result for the team: you might need to take the role of the leader or your place might be one of being the administrative function or sales person. Whatever your function, you must find your place and give the best you can to that role if you want the whole team to thrive. As the relationship develops, positions might need to change, at which time the manoeuvring begins again to find the right job for each person. Sometimes, there might even be no job for you, and you might have to leave your team and find a new one where your skills will be needed. When this is the case, remember to be flexible and open-minded. Always be aware that every relationship is finite and, therefore, always expect changes to occur and have an exit plan ready (see Proximity).

'Never confuse movement with action.'
Ernest Hemingway

The Manoeuvre Strategy in Friendship

The Social Butterfly

Friends come in all shapes, sizes and types: the lifelong friend, the new friend, the friend of a friend, the loyal friend, the acquaintance, the work friend, the family friend, to name but a few.

One type is the social butterfly: the one who flits from place to place and from friend to friend, never settling for long. This is not to say they are not good friends, they just struggle to settle with one or two key friends in the way that most people do. The social butterfly can be at once charming and fun and then distant and away with another friend. It is just their way, but their constant manoeuvring can be stressful to those they befriend. Ask yourself: Are they there when you need them? Do they give as well as take? If the answer to either of those questions is 'yes', then they are a true friend. But if they only take and are absent when you need them, then they deserve to be relegated to the role of 'fun acquaintance'.

Perhaps you are the social butterfly, unable to settle, always on the move? If you are, ask yourself: 'Is it working for me?' Some people can't settle because they're afraid of being too close for fear of getting hurt. Or perhaps they fear who they are and keep others at arm's length (see Proximity). We do nothing without motive, even if that motive is below the surface and hasn't been verbalised or recognised by us consciously. The key to being a good friend is loyalty and, as long as you fulfil this criterion, you can qualify as a good friend. But if you are too mobile, moving from friend to friend, you may never achieve the real closeness that true friendship brings, forever kept at arm's length.

> **'All change is not growth, as all movement is not forward.'**
> Ellen Glasgow

The Manoeuvre Strategy Personally

Swimming Up Stream

The strategy of Manoeuvre is concerned with either out-manoeuvring the opposition or preventing them from moving (see Function). Sometimes we inadvertently try to out-manoeuvre life, making it the opposition. We try to shortcut things that cannot be cut short or avoid things that cannot be avoided which leads us to becoming stuck and unable to move forward.

Life is governed by several elemental laws (see **Warrior Wisdom** by the author). We can work in unison with the laws, either intuitively or because we know they exist, or we can work against them because we are ignorant of their existence or think they can be by-passed. If you don't understand the laws and strategies that make life function, you will be the victim of your life rather than the victor of it.

How does this relate to the strategy of Manoeuvre? It applies by understanding that manoeuvring has its limitations. For one, you can't manoeuvre backwards in time, nor can you stand still in time; you can only go forwards with time and at its pace. However, if you use strategy well and understand the laws of life (see **Warrior Wisdom** by the author), you can move with life – go with the flow when it's the right thing to do and, when it's not, you can look for new ways to move forward which are still consistent with the laws of life. The key is to recognise when you are moving with your life or when you are trying to move against it, possibly without realising it. It's not always obvious when you're stuck, but gradually you might start to feel a sense of continuing discomfort and frustration. When this happens, it is time to review how you are trying to move: Are you moving with life or against it? The Law of Predictability states: 'If you keep on doing what you do, you'll keep on getting what you're getting' so if you feel like you're stuck in a rut, then the chances are, you're repeating the same behaviour over and over expecting to get a different result. If that is the case, examine your behaviour, actions and efforts to find what is stopping you.

You might have to let go of old behaviours or habits and adopt new ones. Either way, if you step back a little and review your life, you will gain the insights you need to get you moving again.

'I can enjoy anywhere, and I can leave it. Life is about moving on.'
Waris Dirie

The Manoeuvre Strategy in Health

A Rolling Stone Gathers No Moss

There are five key intelligences in life: heart (emotional), mind (intellectual), body (physical), spirit (spiritual) and balance (harmony). Harmony balances out the other emotions and reminds us to attend to each part of our lives.

Balance is never still, just as we are never still – our heart and blood continues to pump even when we are asleep, our lungs are in constant motion. This explains why remaining balanced requires constant monitoring. If we recognise these five intelligences and seek to harmonise them, we will assure ourselves of continued happiness throughout our lives. But if we ignore even one of these intelligences, then we are out of balance and heading for a fall. Maintaining balance is the ability to move and manoeuvre to ensure that we are never too far out of harmony. Of course, every step we take compromises our balance but, unlike walking or running where a single mis-step can cause us to fall immediately, our lives can be out of balance for years and we may not notice it until we are on the edge of a precipice and have run out of options.

The key to lifelong health is balance: balance in nutrition, exercise, learning, relationships, work and study. However, as time passes, we often over-focus on one part of our lives to the detriment of the others. This is bound to happen – you can't avoid it – the skill lies in recognising it when it does and correct this as soon as you can. If you spend too much time working on your relationships, your health will suffer. If you focus too much on your appearance, your work might suffer. It's always a balancing act between the intelligences and as long as you understand that concept, you have half the problem solved.

Consider each one of the intelligences as part of your overall health and manoeuvre between them thoughtfully to maintain a good life balance which will assure you of a long and fruitful life.

'You can only respond to a challenge or opportunity when you recognise that there is one.'
The AEGIS Law of Recognition

The Manoeuvre Strategy in Wealth

Don't Rest on Your Laurels

The attainment of wealth is never over, it never stops. Why? Because prices are always increasing and investments will fall and rise. Why is that important? It's important because, on your journey to wealth and financial freedom, there is no point at which you can suddenly say: 'I've got enough now, so I'll stop'.

The reason for this is that the majority of wealth building comes through using other people's efforts and people always need to be looked after and managed. For instance if you invest in property, your tenants will pay you rent, which is your income, but tenants come and go and when they leave your investment, income stops until you find another tenant. If you have enough properties, you can employ an agent, but still that agent must be managed to ensure that they are getting the best returns for you at the best price. This might sound like being wealthy is hard work. Well, it's much easier than working for a living, where you are only paid for the time you are working. When you are employed or self-employed, your income comes directly from your own efforts; basically, you are paid by the hour, and you are constantly moving and manoeuvring to earn your crust. When you learn how to use your leverage properly, you will have to work less and less for each pound that you earn, but there is never a point when you never have to do something to manage your money. That's not to say it becomes a full-time job, but you do have to manoeuvre your way through managing people, assets and resources, keeping on top of your admin and accounts, or looking for new opportunities and getting rid of investments that are no longer paying their way.

As mentioned earlier, it's all about achieving and maintaining balance: there is never a time when you are static and completely balanced, at least not for very long. There is always something to do, and in time you can use this constant movement and manoeuvre to aid you, so that you grow as your wealth does, allowing you to achieve a position where you can do more of what you enjoy doing, and less of what you must.

'Man maintains his balance, poise, and sense of security only as he is moving forward.'
Maxwell Maltz

The Manoeuvre Strategy in Growth

Run the Gauntlet

The ability to manoeuvre in our quest for personal growth is a key strategy since to circumvent obstacles and learn how to solve problems is important in our success.

'Running the gauntlet' was an old military punishment and the word 'gauntlet' comes from the Scandinavian word 'gantlope' which means 'passageway'. Offenders were forced to run through a passageway of their peers, who would beat them as they passed. Personal growth can sometimes seem like running the gauntlet because growth is about facing new challenges all the time and, at first, we can hit so many problems that we might think our journey is impossible. If we have the right attitude – and understand the concept that if we are constantly facing the same problems, then we must be making the same mistakes – we must therefore search for new mistakes to make. To meet new problems is a sign of growth and, gradually, we meet so many problems that we cease to see them as problems; instead we start to see that every problem is an opportunity (see Opportunity) to learn and grow.

I mentioned earlier the Law of Predictability which says: 'If you keep on doing what you're doing, then you'll keep on getting what you're getting'. It's an important law applied to growth because its shows us that, if we are facing the same problems, then we are not growing. With experience, we can manoeuvre around problems because we see them coming, or we can deal with them quickly because we've faced similar ones before. There's an adage in martial arts which says: 'The fighter who has never been hit is the fighter who has never fought'. You cannot avoid every hit, obstacle or problem but, in time, you will learn the invaluable skill of manoeuvre so that when you are hit, it's only a glancing blow and most of the time you're too fast on your feet to be hit frequently.

'Talent without discipline is like an octopus on roller skates. There's plenty of movement, but you never know if it's going to be forward, backwards, or sideways.'

H. Jackson Brown, Jr.

Summary

Manoeuvre is a useful strategy that forms part of every other grand strategy. We move or stay when we have to or want to but, by being a master of the manoeuvre, we stay light on our toes, alert to danger and opportunity. To manoeuvre takes fast feet and an agile body and mind. When we manage to achieve success through clever movement, it usually brings us a very satisfying result.

Manoeuvre Strategy in Brief

1. A weaker, smaller man cannot stand against a stronger and heavier one head on, and must use his smaller size and greater mobility as his weapon instead.
2. Cattle that move around a lot aren't bothered by flies, whereas animals that are sedentary and immobile are easy targets.
3. If our opponent cannot match our manoeuvres, then we have a major advantage which cannot be underestimated.
4. When he is unable to settle, your opponent's ability to think, plan and act is compromised and therein lays your chance to move on him.
5. In a new relationship, we can go through a period of adjustment as each member finds their position and seeks to find their place in the team.
6. If you are too mobile, moving from friend to friend or relationship to relationship, you may never achieve the real closeness that true friendship or love brings, and be forever kept at arm's length.
7. Every step compromises our balance but, unlike walking or running where a single mis-step can cause an immediate fall, our lives can be out of balance for years before we notice it.
8. On your journey to wealth and financial freedom, there is no point at which you can suddenly say: 'I've got enough now, so I'll stop'.
9. You cannot avoid every hit, obstacle or problem but, in time, you will learn the invaluable skill of manoeuvre so that when you are hit, it's only a glancing blow.
10. To manoeuvre takes fast feet and an agile body and mind so when we achieve success through clever movement, it brings us a very satisfying result.

STRATEGY NO. 12

The Vulnerability Strategy of Exploitation

Definition: Take Advantage of the Fire to Plunder the Goods

Overview of Exploitation

Advantage is what opportunity provides us with, but exploitation is what we do with that advantage. When you have the upper hand, the higher ground, the main chance: this is your advantage. When your position is stronger than that of your target, you have the opportunity to exploit the situation, that is, to make the most of that opportunity or lose it. To do otherwise is not just passive but sometimes can mean complete loss of what you've gained. Sometimes you have to be ruthless with yourself and your target to get the result that you want.

> *'There is no avoiding war; it can only be postponed to the advantage of others.'*
>
> Niccolo Machiavelli

The Yin & Yang of Exploitation

The Yang

use
victimise
mistreat
misuse
manipulate
extort
milk

The Yin

assist
help
support
aid
being charitable
lifting up

The Exploitation Strategy in Tradition

Ride Roughshod

Roughshod refers to horses whose hooves have protruding nails that give greater grip for the horse on slippery or icy ground. During the 18th Century, cavalry soldiers began the habit of leaving their horses roughshod with the intention of causing damage to enemy horses during charges. It wasn't very successful as often it did as much damage to the roughshod horse as it did to the enemy horse, and so the practice dropped out of favour. Today 'to ride roughshod' means to treat people badly, or to exploit one's position of power or influence to another's disadvantage.

'Innocence is thought charming because it offers delightful possibilities for exploitation.'

Mason Cooley

The Exploitation Strategy in Warfare

Don't Look a Gift Horse in the Mouth

When you have the upper hand and the situation has moved in your favour, you must not hesitate to take action. To do otherwise is to risk losing your advantage and that advantage may not come again.

Chinese Strategy No. 5 – Take Advantage of the Fire to Plunder the Goods

When your enemy's house is on fire he's less likely to notice as you steal his car. This is the basis of the strategy 'take advantage of the fire to plunder the goods', meaning to exploit the problems of your enemy.

The ancient Chinese strategy number 5 is 'Take Advantage of the Fire to Plunder the Goods'. One example of this in war relates to a story dating back to China's Spring and Autumn Period and the conflict between Haui Kung and the army of Ch'u. The two armies met on the banks of the river Hung. Kung's forces were already in position before the Ch'u army crossed the river. The Ch'u soldiers were vulnerable during the crossing, but Kung, against the advice of his generals, felt it unfair to attack before the Ch'u army had finished crossing. The Ch'u army was larger and well equipped but Kung still waited until they were fully prepared. When the Ch'u soldiers finished crossing the river, the two armies clashed. Kung was soon defeated and his kingdom was lost. Whereas, if he had exploited his advantage and attacked while the Ch'u were at a disadvantage, he could have won the day but, by failing to exploit his position, he paid a heavy price for failing to use the strategy of Exploitation.

> *'...and being as wicked as any man who ever lived, he exploited his advantage to the full.'*
> Winston Churchill

The Exploitation Strategy in Combat

Kick a Man While He's Down

It sounds pretty harsh to kick someone when they're on the ground or at a serious disadvantage, and in a situation of physical self-defence, it could get you into serious trouble with the law if you can't justify your action.

This strategy is based on the principle of never having to fight the same enemy twice. In a life or death situation, you might consider ensuring that a downed opponent, who might attack again if he can, is too dangerous to be taken lightly. In that situation, you might take serious action to ensure he cannot rise quickly to attack you again. There are some people out there who cannot be given the chance to attack again. That's not to say you should kill or maim – that would be serious indeed and bring you more trouble than you are in already – but when your life is on the line, you must exploit what advantage you have which could require you taking the most aggressive action.

Most situations are rarely so serious, but the principle remains that, in certain situations, you must take the right action. To exploit someone in combat requires that you have what is termed the 'killer instinct', which means the ruthlessness to take appropriate action. On the other side of the coin, we must remember or remind ourselves that, when we are in the grip of fear, anger or high emotion, it might be too easy to take the wrong action. It's sometimes easier to go too far than to control yourself and this is the difference between an intelligent decision and an emotional reaction (see Reaction) – between the good citizen and the thug.

Exploit your combative advantage where necessary, but know where to draw the line between what is necessary and what is too easy.

> *'Who is the most sensible person? The one who finds what is to their own advantage in all that happens to them.'*
> Johann Wolfgang von Goethe

The Exploitation Strategy in Relationships

Two Heads are Better than One

The strength of a good relationship relies on the fact that the sum of the two is greater than its constituent parts. 'Two heads are better than one' is an example of the Exploitation strategy and its purpose.

To have someone who supports you is great and often very comforting, but it's also a lesser recognised advantage to have someone who will also disagree with you when necessary. I'm sure we have seen examples of 'yes men' who toady around the rich and powerful, agreeing with everything they say, afraid to express their true opinion for fear of losing their favoured position. This type of individual is useless to the person they fake (see Direction) their support for.

We all have the capacity to be right and also to be wrong. It's advisable that, when we are right but afraid to act, we have someone we trust to put us or push in the right direction and also to disagree with us when, in our stubbornness, we can't recognise when we are wrong. It is easy to be angry and hurt when those close to us stand up and disagree, but we should make the most of their strength and see it as an advantage to exploit, rather than fear being opposed or being wrong. It takes a certain strength to be opposed without getting upset about it. Even if in the heat of the moment we are angry at being challenged, afterwards when we are calmer and more detached from the event, we should begin to see the truth of their opposition. Never fear being opposed by those close to you who care about you. Instead, listen think and examine what they say to find the truth. Reject their concern if you are certain that is the right thing to do, but do take your time and be strong enough to admit when you are wrong or if something feels like it needs greater consideration. A friend who cares enough to disagree is an advantage, not a disadvantage.

'Almost all of our relationships begin and most of them continue as forms of mutual exploitation, a mental or physical barter, to be terminated when one or both parties run out of goods.'

W. H. Auden

The Exploitation Strategy in Friendship

Not What You Know, But Who You Know

Friendship is based on emotion and the Law of Emotion states: 'Emotion is the fuel that drives motion'. Emotion drives our actions and our friendships. So how does Exploitation work in friendship? Well, the answer is found in the saying above: 'It's not what you know, it's who you know', meaning that the influence you have over someone is often more important than your personal ability or knowledge.

In politics and business, this is known as 'the old boys' network' where previous contacts and associations take precedence over lesser known or less well placed, and even better-qualified, individuals. Although this might seem entirely unfair (unless, of course, it falls in your favour!), it is a fact of life that we can leverage our friendships to our own ends. Good friendships are based on reciprocity, that is, give and take, and whilst we can leverage this, we should always avoid leaning too hard on our friends. This is exploitation of another sort and, while you can get away with it sometimes and still retain the friendship, if you abuse the relationship, you might find yourself friendless.

Exploit in favour of the friendship but never abuse the friendship, if you want it to last, in order to enjoy the happiness and power (see Energy) it brings, as the saying goes: 'Be careful who you step on as you climb your way up, you might just meet them on the way down'.

> *'Friendship is also about liking a person for their failings, their weakness. It's also about mutual help, not about exploitation.'*
>
> Paul Theroux

The Exploitation Strategy Personally

Strike While the Iron is Hot

The moment we live now is a great opportunity for us. Whilst it would be impossible to make the most of every present moment, we should strive to make the most of more of our moments, which is to exploit the opportunities that are all around us.

How do we achieve this? By setting goals, making plans and taking action, we can exploit as many of these opportune moments as possible and, if those plans are worthy, they will bring us more similar moments that we can in turn exploit in the same way. It often feels that all those opportunities are in the future, built on the expectation that the future will be better than the present. But is it? Really? How do you know? The truth is, nothing exterior to yourself can bring you real joy, as all joy comes from within. Many have tried and many still do, and many more in the future will do so again, but all are chasing a fool's dream. You can never be happier than you decide to be in this present moment. The decision to make the most of the moment in order to create joy has nothing to do with positive thinking in the form of a decision which says 'I am happy right now' (like some kind of chant similar to Emile Coue's 'everyday, in every way, I'm getting better and better'). This is a great way to create mental confusion, something also known as 'cognitive dissonance' (Cognitive dissonance occurs when what you say conflicts with what you believe deep inside). It will keep you from achieving what you say you want, because your unvoiced REAL intentions are in conflict with your spoken intentions. Remember the saying 'be careful of what you really want, for that is surely what you'll get' which means that often what we say we want, or think we should want is overridden by what we really want deep down. That want comes from a deeply conditioned part of our minds that we are not always consciously aware of. It might seem a strange thing to say that we don't consciously know what we really (i.e. unconsciously) want but if you take time to consider it, you will see the truth of it.

Real joy comes not from a decision to be happy but from the acceptance that you can be happy, it's a decision that you are anything else. Joy is our natural state, but we choose to be affected by things such as the demands and expectations of others, the news of terrible events around the world that we can do nothing about and the negative feelings of others. Think about the times when you watched either a happy or sad film and you left the cinema feeling either happy after a happy film or sad after a sad film. You need to realise it's not actually the film that has changed your emotions; it's your response to it. It's you have chosen to be affected by the film through suspending your disbelief that it is just a fantasy of which you are the spectator. Once you are prepared to accept that how you feel can only affect you if you let it, and then you can begin to enjoy each moment for what it is. Unless you are unfortunate enough to be living in physical pain, then how you feel emotionally is just a choice you have made in this moment. If you worry over money, relationships, health, success or failure then that worry is your choice, whether you realise it or not. If you had a relationship problem but you didn't know about it, then you wouldn't worry about it. It is only when you learn about it that you start to worry. Since you only worry when you know about the event unfolding (it was unfolding before when you had no knowledge of it and that did not worry you), therefore the feeling of worry is a choice you have made based on a set of rules or values that are conditioned into you. Worry is a fear of something in the future, or a remembrance about something that happened in the past. One way to stop worrying about the past or the future is to live in the now.

Eckart Tolle's wonderful book **The Power of Now** deals almost exclusively with living in the moment and exploiting the only thing in our lives that is real – this present moment. Tomorrow hasn't happened yet and yesterday has gone, so the only real time is this time we are living in now and most of us are in danger of wasting it on things that bring us nothing of benefit, except in the short term.

Time can be spent and it can be wasted, but no time can ever be had again; it is precious and when it's gone it's gone. Make the most of it, exploit it.

'When knowledge is limited – it leads to folly... When knowledge exceeds a certain limit, it leads to exploitation.'
Abu Bakr

The Exploitation Strategy in Health

Don't Push Your Luck

When we are young, we feel we are invincible. We're active, tend to have low body fat, get fit easily, can run for ever, get drunk, be ill and get back out there again. We can smoke, drink, take drugs and eat what we like with no ill-effects on our health whatsoever. But can we? No we can't. Although the ill effects of our self-abuse don't make their presence felt immediately, it's pretty certain that, if we continue with them, they will get us eventually. Nutrition, exercise, drugs and alcohol, if not managed sensibly, can not only spoil our present life, but also shorten our future life.

The advantages we possess when we are healthy can simply slip by us, draining away our vitality. It's not like making a death bed confession when you are faced with a serious illness, only to have your sins forgiven and becoming well again. In real life, you can think 'it will never happen to me' or 'I'll change my ways before it happens'. When serious ill health catches up with us, it is often too late to change our ways. We might get lucky and get only a warning, which frightens us into mending our ways, but conditions like strokes, cancers and heart conditions are pretty much here to stay. They can be managed with drugs, but is that what you want for your life: to be managing your health through drugs just because you couldn't manage it with discipline?

Your health is your biggest asset; exploit it for your own good, which means exploiting it while you have it. Create a discipline that is not a prison or a cage, (see Function) but a support that can evolve over time. Remove unhealthy habits gradually, replacing them one by one – avoiding going cold turkey in a fashion that cannot be maintained – and build new health-supporting habits that will last you a lifetime and can be maintained in the long-term.

'It is the greatest of all advantages to enjoy no advantage at all.'
Henry David Thoreau

The Exploitation Strategy in Wealth

Seize the Day

To seize the day is to exploit the immediate time you have, in other words 'don't put off until tomorrow what you can do today'. Exploitation is often seen as a strategy against others but, like many other strategies, it can also be used for your own good or the good of others.

We discussed in Health above about being careful of thinking that treating your body badly today won't have detrimental effects tomorrow, and we know that if we smoked a cigarette and immediately felt ill we would recognise cigarettes for the poison that they are. In wealth, people often imagine the opposite of this mind set. In health we imagine bad things will never happen and in wealth we imagine that good things will never happen. Human beings are often perverse in this way.

Wealth won't happen by itself, that much is true; we must study and plan for it and then put our plans into motion. In the early days, it can be as simple as saving regularly, building the habit and not dipping into the account before the appointed time. Wealth is not magical, it's methodical and that method is not a secret. It's a matter of exploiting the 'now', doing what needs to be done when you have the best opportunity to do it (see Opportunity).

Today is the best day to get started on building wealth. Start by looking at your income and expenses to eliminate any unnecessary expenditure and re-direct (see Direction) it to your savings. Even to the point of setting up a change jar and every day putting some money in it, no matter how small, and then adding it to your savings every month. Put all your bills on automatic payment and from an account used only for that purpose that has enough paid into it every month to cover them. Keep your living money separate so you never spend your bills money. Next, look for ways to increase your income: What can you do to build some passive income, or at least some extra income? A job in a bar, teaching a class in something you're good at, car boot sales, anything that will bring in extra cash that you can add to your savings. It is vital to build a savings habit and eliminate bad spending habits. If you are a regular spender, then that's going to get in your way of getting wealthy because saving is the first part of building wealth.

Here's a great way to exploit your income to the fullest in order to build savings. It's based on how differently poor people and rich people save money:

- ***Poor People*** – spend their money first and save what is left over at the end of the month. However, just as work expands to fill the time available, so does spending expand to take the cash available. Most of the time, there is just no cash left to save at the end of the month. Don't kid yourself that you'll be disciplined enough to put some money aside this way, it's the poor man's way of (not) saving money.

- ***Rich People*** – save first and live on what is left till the end of the month. They calculate how much they can save each month and set up an automatic regular payment into a savings account. You'd be surprised how much you can save this way, even ending up putting an amount away that stings a little so your savings grow faster. It requires less discipline than the poor man's method; it's the rich man's way of (actually) saving money.

To use the strategy of Exploitation in building wealth you must take advantage of every chance you have to start the discipline of saving and in the meantime build upon your financial education so that when it's time to invest you have the right vehicles to make your savings grow even faster. Don't wait for wealth to happen on its own, instead exploit the opportunities you have now to build it for your future. Too many people expect to be wealthy someday in the future, that tomorrow will be better than today, but as we all know 'tomorrow never comes'.

> *'Instead of loving people and using money, people often love money and use people.'*
> Wayne Gerard Trotman

The Exploitation Strategy in Growth

Don't Push People Around

As we have seen, exploitation can be used in both a positive and negative manner but it's not always clear to us when we are exploiting or being exploited.

Your personal growth is driven by ambition which, like exploitation, has its soft and hard edges. Sometimes we can get so involved with our journey and our forward motion that we forget to thank those that have been helpful or even instrumental in our journey. We have to stop sometimes and consider where our gratitude should be aimed. At other times, we might exploit others, to the point of ruthlessness, if they stand in our way. This approach might be necessary if they deliberately try to block us – and some will! However, we may inadvertently trample on some people because we are too focused on ourselves and fail to consider any feelings but our own.

The strategies of Alignment and Recruitment are key strategies that we should keep in mind in order to balance our exploitation tactics, as they remind us that it is better to work with others than to be in conflict with them. So, whenever possible, share what you have, through exploiting kindness and help, this way you need never worry about who you might have wronged on your way to success.

One area to exploit mercilessly though, is yourself, by making the most of your own gifts, moving away from your weaknesses and toward your strengths. It is not for nothing that the strategy of Exploitation is one of the Vulnerability strategies, as the AEGIS Law of Vulnerability says 'to know your enemy's weakness is strength, to know your own is wisdom'. It's therefore important to identify where you are personally strong or weak so that you can work to your strengths and away from your weaknesses. Personal growth is about making the most of your life. In order to do that, you must also make the most of what life has granted you with. One of the greatest gifts to exploit is the attitude that supports you, to see the best in every situation, to want to change and grow and the passion to see it through to the end. Conversely, you should examine your weaknesses and work to eliminate them so that they don't hold you back. At the start of your journey for example, your desire likely outstrips your education and certainly outstrips your experience. The key part of personal growth is education (including experience) which brings knowledge and then wisdom. In fact, wisdom is really the application of experience, and so all personal growth is really a pursuit of wisdom.

Once you find your strengths and weaknesses, you must set a plan to fix them and that fixing will never really end; things change over time and you have to change yourself in order to keep up with them.

> **'A person who won't read has no advantage over one who can't read.'**
> Mark Twain

Summary

As the Law of Judgement says: 'Good judgement comes from experience and experience comes from bad judgement'. When you are given an advantage, you must judge whether to take it or not, to consider how it can serve you and whether it fits with your core principles. There are opportunities all around us and Exploitation is about how we use them; there are times when it is appropriate to use them and others when it is wiser to hold back.

Exploitation Strategy in Brief

1. Advantage is what opportunity provides us with, but exploitation is what we do with that advantage.
2. 'To ride roughshod' means to treat people badly, or to exploit one's position of power or influence to another's disadvantage.
3. When you have the upper hand and the situation has moved in your favour, you must not hesitate to take action.
4. Exploit your combative advantage where necessary, but know where to draw the line between what is necessary and what is too easy.
5. A friend who cares enough to disagree is an advantage, not a disadvantage.
6. Exploit in favour of the friendship and never against it.
7. Time can be spent and it can be wasted, but no time can ever be had again; it is precious and when it's gone it's gone. Make the most of it, exploit it.
8. Your health is your biggest asset; exploit it for your own good: create a discipline that is not a prison or a cage, but a support that strengthens over time.
9. Don't wait for wealth to happen on its own; instead exploit the opportunities you have now to build it for your future.
10. Share what you have, through exploiting kindness and help, and then you need never worry about who you might have wronged on your way to success.

STRATEGY NO. 13

The Vulnerability Strategy of Target

Definition: The Achilles' Heel

Overview of Target

Everyone and everything is vulnerable in some way, no matter how big or strong or tough and whether animal, human, building or organisation... The strategy of Target is focused on finding that vulnerability and use it either against an enemy or to promote a life goal. Every step forward in any field of endeavour has been achieved because someone believed it was vulnerable to their efforts and identified where that vulnerability lay. If you ever feel a goal is invulnerable, it only means you just haven't found its vulnerability yet. In that case, you need to either use the targets you know or find the targets you need. As the law of vulnerability states: 'To know your enemies' weakness is strength, to know your own is wisdom'.

'Success is steady progress toward one's personal goals.'

Jim Rohn

The Yin & Yang of Target

The Yang	The Yin
mark	off-target
bull's eye	misplaced
victim	off the mark
objective	inaccurate
aim	blind
place	aimlessness
goal	divergence
prey	

The Target Strategy in Tradition

The Achilles' Heel

In Greek mythology, Thetis was a nymph who wanted to make her child immortal and sought to do so by dipping him in the river Styx. The Styx was the gateway between the living world and the underworld and the river possessed of magical powers which made anything immersed in it invulnerable.

Although she immersed him almost completely, the part of his body by which she held him – his heel – was not touched by the water and thus became a vulnerable target. Achilles was thought invincible and became one of the greatest of the Greek heroes, but he was eventually killed by Paris who fired an arrow which struck Achilles in his vulnerable heel. Ever since that time, the term 'Achilles' Heel' has been used to describe a person's most vulnerable point.

'Whoever is winning at the moment will always seem to be invincible.'

George Orwell

The Target Strategy in Warfare

A Chink in Their Armour

We are all vulnerable to something; this is the key to the Target strategy and an empowering concept against even the most powerful of enemies. Find the chink in their armour and you find the seeds of their defeat.

Chinese Strategy No. 2 – Besieging Wei to Save Chao

When faced with a foe that is large and powerful, you cannot face him directly unless you have equal or better strength. The way to fight such an enemy is by using the Target strategy. Find where he is weak and attack him there.

For example in the Spring and Autumn period of ancient China, the state of Chao was attacked by the powerful army of Wei who besieged its capital Han Tan. Chao requested help from the state of Ch'i who provided an army led by general Tien Chi and tactician Sun Pin. General Tien ordered his troops to attack the besieging Wei troops, but Sun Pin suggested another plan. He said the army of Wei was too strong to face, but their own capital was only manned by a small force of veterans and was therefore vulnerable. To attack the Wei troops head on would have been too risky (see Risk) as their whole force was too strong but to attack Wei's capital while its army was attacking Chao's capital, meant Wei's forces would be divided on two fronts and therefore weakened. This strategy of finding a weak spot in Wei's army gave Chao victory.

Chinese Strategy No. 18 – To Catch a Thief, Catch his King

This strategy is also known as 'kill the head and the body will fall' and is a specific Target strategy designed to find the enemy's weakest point. Nothing can survive without its head and mind. So, if you can identify that point in battle, victory is assured. Against an army, the head is the leader or leaders who lead through inspiration and purpose. The leader is the one whom the army follows, whose purpose they support, and without whom they have no purpose or direction.

In the British army today, the Rifles Regiment still exists, consisting of 'chosen men' who were hand-picked for their independent self-reliant natures and their skill in marksmanship. During the battles of the Napoleonic wars, they made themselves a particular nuisance by skirmishing among the enemy lines; in small groups, they hit vulnerable targets – including the officers themselves – so that their men had no one to lead them and they fell into confusion and disarray.

In ancient days, the leader of the army was such because he led his army into battle and his soldiers were spurred on by the image of him charging into the fray, risking everything for his cause. Because he risked his life in that cause, he was the inspiration for his troops. If he was struck down in their sight, it could mean the end of their ambitions and their direction, often leading to their defeat. In warfare today, junior officers still lead their men into battle, and so become ideal targets for enemy snipers.

The key to using a specific target to defeat your enemy is simple: once you can find an enemy's weakest point and strike it, then victory is yours.

> **'He who is not courageous enough to take risks will accomplish nothing in life.'**
> Muhammad Ali

The Target Strategy in Combat

Know Your Enemy

In self defence against an unknown opponent, which is what the study of physical martial arts intends to prepare us for, we learn how to deliver attacks to the body's most vulnerable and most available targets. For instance, on the head we target the eyes, ears, temples, nose, jaw and chin, and each martial artist has a weapon designed to attack these targets at all ranges of personal combat. On the body there are even more equally valid targets: throat, solar plexus, heart, kidneys, groin etc., and a good martial artist can attack these from many distances and angles (see Alignment and Proximity). Over years of practice, the martial artist drills his technique until it becomes second nature and rehearses strategies to meet many situations, so that if he has to defend himself for real, his trained instincts will 'kick in' and he will automatically hone in on his opponent's most vulnerable areas.

In mutual combat such as a sporting competition, we can research our potential opponent and study his style, methods, strengths and weaknesses and then gear our practice toward the ideal game plan to beat him specifically. When you know your opponent's weakness and strength, and you also know your own, then the targets become obvious; you can gear your practice, your techniques and strategies toward getting the easiest victory, to the point where you no longer have to think about them consciously and your body simply responds to the situation in the most efficient way.

> *'Either I will find a way or make a way.'*
> Hannibal of Carthage

The Target Strategy in Relationships

Beauty is Only Skin Deep

In the strategy of Attraction, we discussed making ourselves an attractive target to draw in our enemies. It is also a Focus strategy, intended to lure an enemy toward a false target.

In relationships, we are biologically drawn to the most physically attractive partner: strong, muscular, fit and healthy, all in order to better propagate our species. Intelligence and compatibility are not needed biologically, only physical strength, fertility and reproduction are. It is only in more recent history that humans have chosen mates based on a potentially lifelong relationship. Choosing a lifetime partner is rarely based on looks, although that may be what draws two people together at first, but after that there must be an emotional, intellectual and spiritual connection, as well as the initial physical attraction that gets things started.

In targeting a partner, whether it is in love, friendship or business, we should look for people that we can enjoy spending time with and share a common purpose. If we don't have this, then the relationship lacks the foundation it needs for the long term. The AEGIS Law of Base says 'A tall building needs a deep foundation' and we must consider our relationships and partnerships as being like tall buildings which, if they are to last, must have a strong base. Target people to enter relationships with on more than just the way they look and take time to get to know your future partners before you commit too deeply. Initially, we know our partner as both young and strong, but eventually, all that will fade away with age and we will be left with old bodies. However, the person that we are inside will remain after our looks have faded, so if we only target partners based on their looks, we will soon be disappointed and want to move out as age catches up with them. But if we target our partners based on their personal qualities which will not fade with age, then we can target true happiness.

'Discipline is the bridge between goals and accomplishment.'
Jim Rohn

The Target Strategy in Friendship

Choose Your Friends but Not Your Family

The common phrase 'you can choose your friends but you can't choose your family' is usually used when we feel frustrated with a family member. Yet, we can look at it from a different angle: Whilst it is true that we can't choose the personalities of the people in our families, we can, however, choose the personalities of our friends. That is, we can target who we are friends with.

Does this seem a little mercenary? If so, then perhaps you have the wrong view of how friendship works. Friendships can often happen by chance, but they continue to exist through many other factors, such as experience, attitudes and expectations, amongst others. This creates rapport which creates affection which sustains friendship. It has been calculated that we earn a salary within plus or minus 20% of what our friends earn. This demonstrates one way in which we connect. Therefore, if we want to improve our personal life as in Growth, Health and Wealth (see below), that process should put us in touch with others who are doing the same as us. We discussed, in the strategy of Exploitation, the concept of 'It's not what you know but who you know' and friendship is a great way to get ahead in life.

Just because you decide to target the kinds of friends you make, does not in any way detract from the quality of the friendship. The quality of a friendship comes from the interaction of the friends, but you should always choose friends who complement your own personality and aspirations, and avoid those who either don't complement what you are or do, and/or try to hold you back. In short, you should target good friends who will help you grow, and remove those who do not support you. It is possible to remain friends through pure affection and respect, as long as both your attitudes are supportive, but do be prepared to shed those friends that will not share in your journey, and try to hold you back.

'Learn from the past, set vivid, detailed goals for the future, and live in the only moment of time over which you have any control: now.'

Denis Waitley

GAME PLAN

The Target Strategy Personally

Be a Hard Target

In combat, we have to target the most vulnerable parts on an opponent so that he can be neutralised effectively, but we should also look at why the conflict occurs in the first place.

Perhaps it's because you look like a target. Much of what people put up with at home, school and work years ago is now classified as bullying and intimidation (see also Pressure, Exploitation and Isolation), and is much less acceptable, but any bullying that you face today probably means you've been a target before. How do bullies choose their victims? To answer that question, let us look at the face of the bully. Often bullies have been or are being targeted themselves, and might be conditioned to think that pushing another individual around is acceptable behaviour. Another type of bully is the person who is easily threatened by people who are different or hold different views to themselves, (which is basically fascism – a person who is reactionary (see Reaction) and dictatorial). Fascism is based on fear, fear of others who are different and what their views and actions might lead to. This fear threatens the fascist/bully, and they react by attacking the threat, which in this case might be you.

Does this mean you should change your views, your looks or your actions? Of course not – you are not the problem, the bully is the one with the problem. However, there are things that you can do to prevent you from being an easy target. Part of the bullying problem comes from:

You are different and, therefore, threaten the bully

You are probably the weakest-looking target available.

Now you can't do much about your size, but you can change your passive behaviour and body language (which invites the bully, see Attraction) to a more positive and assertive behaviour. This doesn't mean swaggering about like a local thug, but it does mean picking up some habits that show others that you are not a target.

Many top martial artists took up the study of martial arts because they were being bullied or feeling threatened, and often martial arts have helped. There are a number of ways to turn yourself from being an easy target to being a hard target. The key is that you must take action if you are being targeted through someone else's problem. Often the cure for bullying is not the dramatic

180

film style option that sees the bully beaten by his victim. Instead it is simpler, such as changing your body language, making stronger eye contact, being more assertive and speaking one's mind. Standing up to a bully is to remove yourself as a target, to cease to be a target by removing the vulnerability that placed your there in the first place.

> **'Vulnerability is not weakness.
> And that myth is profoundly dangerous.'**
> Brene Brown

The Target Strategy in Health

Feet of Clay

The term 'feet of clay' comes from a Bible story and refers to a statue of bronze and brass whose feet were made from a mixture of clay and iron. Clay and iron don't mix well, so the statue, no matter how grand it might have appeared, would always be flawed by the fact that its foundation was weak.

This story is suggestive of the legend of Achilles, but how does this apply to the Target strategy of health? Good health is a holistic process covering nutrition, heart conditioning, muscle strengthening, flexibility, emotional, mental and spiritual conditioning. If we fail to cover all these areas of health, we create a target for ill-health to creep up. In much the same way as a chain is only as strong as its weakest link, our bodies are only as strong as their constituent parts.

It's not uncommon to see fit looking people light up a cigarette after training. For instance, that was even a common habit amongst professional ballet dancers who smoked cigarettes as a means of keeping their weight down. But what is the point of looking fit and training hard regularly to keep fit, if after the session we light up? Another example of this sort of imbalance is someone who lifts weights and is very strong but doesn't have the lung power to run for a bus. Any neglected area of our health becomes the target for potential ill-health. Our health is a delicate mechanism; it works like an eco-system that must be kept in balance if we want to have a long lasting and pain free life.

It is important that if we find an area of our life that is weak, we can target it to bring it back into balance. Never take your health for granted, it is a gift which should be treasured.

> **'People with goals succeed because they know where they're going.'**
> Earl Nightingale

The Target Strategy in Wealth

Keep Your Eyes on the Prize

It may not seem obvious but in order to become wealthy – that is to become financially free – we should set a goal for how much we need to accumulate to achieve that freedom.

Once we apply the strategy of Target to our wealth building, we give our brains something concrete to achieve since any goal that we achieve tends to be visual, specific and measurable. After that, we should consider two key things:

a) Find the most vulnerable part of your target
b) Understand where you are most vulnerable to not achieving it.

Vulnerability has two parts to it: its weakness and its strength. Keep these in mind in your goal to achieve wealth and you will help yourself enormously. To find where your wealth goal is vulnerable, you must consider your own strengths. What are your skills (see Exploitation)? What abilities do you bring to the equation? Perhaps you have a fairly secure job which is not too demanding on your time and would allow you to start a small business that brings in a second income? Or you have a really good credit rating which allows you to access a line of credit which could be used toward your investment? Maybe you are a good money manager who is already sitting on solid savings which could be invested?

Alternatively, look at your weaknesses. Are you a spender? Do you live on credit or are you a sucker for being sold things you don't need? Or do you like to treat yourself to things you don't really need but make you feel good? All this must be considered as part of your wealth building strategy. Target your weaknesses and learn to manage or remove them. Target your strengths and build on them.

> **'Setting goals is the first step in turning the invisible into the visible.'**
> Tony Robbins

The Target Strategy in Growth

Can't Hit a Target You Can't See

In order to develop yourself through the pursuit of personal growth, you must set clear targets for what you want to achieve, and the more precise those targets are, the more achievable they will become.

Initially, you may not have a clear idea of what it is you want but, as you try and as you achieve, you will become clearer in what it is you want (and often this comes through experiencing what you don't want). In time, you will gain clarity and, as each of your goals is achieved, you will learn and shape what you really want from life so that your initial goals will seem to be tiny in comparison to all you have achieved since you started on your journey. There are two key types of goals that you should be aware of, especially in your early days:

   a) **VVG** or Very Vague Goals – those are goals that are not specific or measurable. Any goal that is not specifically defined and exact will cause our brain to struggle to visual the outcome. Our brains are very visual instruments in nature, and as the saying goes: 'A picture is worth a thousand words'. So, if we can vividly detail and describe what we want then the better our brain can set about achieving what we want.
   b) **VPG** or Very Precise Goals – these are the goals that are definitely specific, easy to visualise, with the addition that they have a specific date for their completion.

It can be difficult at first to set truly precise goals, or even very achievable or challenging goals, but with time and experience you will get better. A great way to manage the goals that you target is to first consider what you want before you set out, and then to write down in detail what you want to change. Also, you can model yourself on those who have achieved what you desire. Or you can set up vision boards. A vision board is a visual image of what you want, using pictures which you can draw or taken from photographs, the internet and magazines, which you can use to colour in the exact detail of what you want from your life. The more precise your images, the more likely you are to achieve your goal. Place your vision boards where you can consult them and view them often to constantly reinforce your goals. They will not only bring definition to your desires, but also help to keep you motivated. Motivation will waiver from time to time, especially when times are hard, so make the most of any tools that will help to keep you on track. Remind yourself of your targets at every opportunity and take pride in your achievements, no matter how small. Refer back to your boards to remind you of what you have visualised and achieved and you will see how your journey is progressing, which will help to keep you going.

'*Goals allow you to control the direction of change in your favour.*'
Brian Tracy

Summary

The strategy of Target is essential to all achievement and should be considered in relation to its counterparts in the Invulnerability section: Manoeuvre, Exploitation, Risk and Example. The Target strategy seeks to find the strength and weakness of every desired goal and to recognise that some targets are always more vulnerable than others.

Target Strategy in Brief

1. Everyone and everything is vulnerable somehow, no matter how big or strong or tough and whether it is animal, human, building or organisation.
2. When faced with a foe that is large and powerful, you cannot face him directly unless you have equal or better strength. The way to fight such an enemy is by using the Target strategy: Find where he is weak and attack him there.
3. Gear your practice, your techniques and strategies toward getting the easiest victory, to the point where you no longer have to think about them consciously and your body simply responds to the situation in the most efficient way.
4. The person that we are inside will remain after our looks have faded, so if we only target partners based on their looks, we will soon be disappointed and want to move out as age catches up with them.
5. It is possible to remain friends through pure affection and respect as long as both your attitudes are supportive, but do be prepared to shed those friends that will not share in your journey and try to hold you back.
6. Standing up to a bully is to cease to be a target by removing the vulnerability that placed your there in the first place.
7. If we find an area of our life that is weak, we can target it to bring it back into balance. Never take your health for granted, it is a gift which should be treasured.
8. To become wealthy – that is to become financially free – we should set a precise goal for how much we need to accumulate to achieve that freedom.
9. In order to develop yourself through the pursuit of personal growth, you must set clear targets for what you want to achieve, and the more precise those targets are, the more achievable your goals will become.
10. The Target strategy seeks to find the strength and weakness of every desired goal and to recognise that some targets are always more vulnerable than others.

STRATEGY NO. 14

The Vulnerability Strategy of Risk

Definition: Nothing Ventured, Nothing Gained

Overview of Risk

Every action comes with risk; some with little risk and some with much risk. Often, the greater the potential reward and the greater the risk, and the lower the risk, the lower the reward. Risks can be lessened through study and experience and increased through ignorance and egotism. If you want to make great gains, then you cannot avoid risk. Learn to manage it and reap its rewards: you should not fear all risk and nor should you embrace all risk; as the Law of Assessment says: 'Getting the best out of any outcome is the balance of risk against reward'.

'Of course risk-taking does not always pay off, but it's a lot of fun!'

Mary Wesley

The Yin & Yang of Risk

The Yang

hazard
peril
chance
gamble
venture

The Yin

secure
safe
certainty
risk-free
sureness

The Risk Strategy in Tradition

Chance Your Arm

'To chance one's arm' is to take an uncalculated risk where the outcome is far from certain. It's not known for sure where the phrase comes from, but one suggestion dates back to the late 1500s in Ireland, where a feud between the Ormonds and the Kildares resulted in the Ormonds taking refuge in a cathedral for safety. The Kildares could not enter the premises and the Ormonds could not leave, so the conflict was at a stalemate. Eventually, the head of the Kildare family offered a truce, which the Ormonds would not believe in. He had a hole cut in the cathedral door and put through his arm through the door as a gesture of his sincerity, risking the chance that it might be cut off by the Ormonds inside. Though the risk was great for Kildare, it paid off as the Ormonds clasped it in friendship – and peace was restored.

*'The enlightened ruler is heedful,
and the good general full of caution.'*

Sun Tzu

The Risk Strategy in Warfare

Don't Count Your Chickens

The development of the Risk strategy is the development of the oblique attack. In all warfare there are two types of attack:

a) **Direct Attack** – which is to meet the enemy head on, strength for strength and, 'may the best man win', no matter what the cost.

b) **Indirect Attack** – which is to achieve our aims without meeting the enemy head on, to use deception and subterfuge, so as to minimise the risks to ourselves, and our soldiers.

Direct attacks are costly, wasteful and only the most foolish generals engage the enemy head on, if there is any alternative. Indirect strategies are more subtle; they use guile and deception to achieve their aims. The difference between the two is for reasons of risk. The wise warlord always looks for the way of least risk.

Chinese Strategy No. 17 – Cast a Brick to Pull in Jade

All battle strategies involve risk and, whilst this ancient Chinese strategy is mainly a draw strategy (see Attraction), a key part to it is the bait that it risks to achieve its ends. Bait is essentially a small risk to grab a larger gain and the strategy of 'cast a brick to pull in jade' is at the core of many battle plans which involve risking a smaller force to tease the enemy out of its stronghold. To risk a large force into unknown territory is risky to the point of foolhardiness, but let us look at an example where this actually happened.

The battle of Isandlwana in 1879 pitted the most powerful Empire in the world against (what they thought was) a bunch of primitive natives in South Africa. A slow-moving, red-coated British force entered Zulu country completely unprepared for a highly trained and well-led Zulu army who, though they were largely equipped with only spears and shields, knew the country and could move very fast (see Pace). The British force, however, was slow, cumbersome and wearing red – which meant they stood out like a sore thumb. Instead of sending out scouting parties, the British waded into Zulu country unaware that the Zulus had amassed a huge force of 24,000 just waiting for the British. The result was a massacre of the British forces, which lost over 1400 soldiers to the Zulus.

The British made a number of mistakes at Isandlwana, but one of the most disastrous one was to underestimate the Zulus and fail to manage their risk by sending out a smaller force to scout out the territory ahead of the their main army.

'Prophesy is a good line of business, but it is full of risks.'
Mark Twain

The Risk Strategy in Combat

Leap in the Dark

All combat carries a risk of injury or even death, which is one of the reasons we avoid it. Violence is nasty, aggressive and egotistical. It panders to our most primordial instincts and is rarely a cure for any problem.

However, those of us who practise martial arts have a fascination for it, because it can teach us so much about ourselves and our lives if we study and observe it closely. Those on the outside of the martial arts sphere often comment on martial artists being humble and mild mannered, and there are several reasons for this:

1. Martial artists know enough about violence to have the sense to avoid it; one way to avoid it is to be humble, modest and non-threatening.
2. The practice of martial arts confers a quiet confidence which fosters the belief that others are less threatening and, therefore, there is little need for macho posturing.
3. Every good martial artist knows that no fight is ever certain, even for the very skilled. Win or loss can turn in a moment, so martial artists rarely seek trouble unless they are certain that it is completely necessary and that they can secure an edge that will turn things in their favour.

If we focus on the latter reason, we come back to the management of risk. The Law of Assessment states: 'Getting the best out of any outcome is in the balance of risk against reward' and combat increases the potential of that risk to the very highest level. The outcome of any combat is always uncertain to a large degree and, therefore, the risk is always high. Any outcome that cannot be well predicted and carries high risk is a leap in the dark, a gamble which should be avoided whenever possible.

Martial artists, including soldiers and generals, also know that fighting is the last resort, only entered into after all other avenues have been explored. They know that few problems can be solved with violence, and they save theirs for those situations where it cannot be avoided. This brings us to a boxing adage relating to risk: 'Sometimes you have to take one to give a better one'. This presumes that we know the amount of risk we are going to take – which we rarely do in reality – but there are times when we have no choice, and it may be the only option we have.

Conversely, to do nothing in the face of violence is also a risk. Your religious beliefs may preclude it, but that goes against the biological 'fight or flight' instinct which is programmed into all of us to help us survive as a species. To fail to fight is to risk death, and death, taken to its final conclusion brings extinction, which defies the laws of nature.

At some point we must draw the line at how much we are prepared to take in the face of violence, and we have two choices – fight or flight. The third option (which is to do nothing) is sometimes simply too risky and fails to be an acceptable choice.

> **'Risk comes from not knowing what you're doing.'**
> Warren Buffett

The Risk Strategy in Relationships

Out of the Frying Pan, into the Fire

There is an old adage which goes: 'The grass is always greener on the other side of the fence'. All relationships, be they emotional or practical, can be split by one of the partners thinking that the grass is greener elsewhere.

Any relationship that works well does so because each partner works at the relationship. Relationships will break down if any partner stops playing their part, or if they feel they have a better opportunity elsewhere.

Sometimes a working relationship is a case of 'better the devil you know than the devil you don't'. But this is often true only as long as it fulfils the aims of the partnership and brings satisfaction to all sides. When a partner leaves the relationship, they risk what they already have against what they feel they will gain elsewhere. Will the risk be worth it? Or will they leave only to find they have made a mistake and possibly burned their bridges behind them?

This is always the danger of moving relationships, so how can we reduce the risk and be surer of whether to stay or go? The only way to answer this question is to reduce the risk by removing your emotions from the equation and looking at the problem with cold logic. Add up the pros and cons, put your thoughts on paper and balance out what you have, what you might gain and what you stand to lose.

Will this bring a certain answer to your problem? Of course not, only experience will tell whether you jumped from the frying pan into the fire. But this method will at least help you make a choice based on a methodical way of assessing your risks rather than merely being guided by your often unreliable emotions.

> **'Most people would rather be certain they're miserable, than risk being happy.'**
> Robert Anthony

The Risk Strategy in Friendship

It Ain't Over Till It's Over

Friendships are emotional and, when it comes to strategy, emotion is often a killer. Good strategists do their best work under the influence of logic and logic is never emotional.

In fact, emotion is the frequently used tool of a good strategist. In friendship, we are almost always in the presence of emotion, which is difficult to deal with logically; however, there are times when only logical reasoning is needed.

Imagine a situation where a friend breaks up with a partner, perhaps one that you didn't approve of. You are called in as the compassionate friend to listen to their outpouring of grief over the broken relationship. Now you are in a situation where you can give your honest opinion of the ex-partner. Dangerous ground to be in, but it is only human to give your opinion. But then, they get back together again and this puts you in a difficult position because your friend now knows that you don't actually like his partner. And it's pretty likely that your friend has told their partner everything you said about them. Now you're in a bad place because there is a rift between you, your friend and their partner. The key in this situation is to minimise the risk of alienating friend and partner by not expressing your opinion in the first place, staying calm and helping your friend without taking sides.

You're still in a position of some risk if you do so because, when your friend pours their heart out to you, they will often expect you to fully take their side and, as they say possibly horrible things about their ex, they can fully expect you to do the same. In this scenario, you have to tread carefully and hold your tongue as much as possible. Remember with relationships that 'it ain't over till it's over'.

'The policy of being too cautious is the greatest risk of all.'
Jawaharlal Nehru

The Risk Strategy Personally

Better the Devil You Know

Our personal attitudes to risk must be examined and understood if we are to live a life free from negative conditioned habits. From our very earliest childhood, we are constantly watching and learning and, with everything new that we experience, we make a decision and judge what we have learned.

The judgements we make as young children are made from the standpoint and mental capacity of a child but, as we grow older, they become deeply ingrained in us, even when the original reasons are long forgotten. So, as adults, we carry rules that govern our lives and decisions, although we don't remember how or when we decided to adopt those rules, or even notice that they are guiding our lives.

Some of these rules may be still valid, but others might no longer be applicable. That's why we can often feel conflicted over important decisions where our logic says one thing yet our inner voice says another. Can you imagine having an important choice to make and turning to ask the advice of a 5 year old? It would be ridiculous of course: a 5 year old has no experience, or full understanding of the situation. Yet, the emotional part of our decision-making process, that part that we often trust so much, which we might refer to as our gut feeling, could be based on a judgement of certainty that we adopted when we were a child.

How do we avoid putting our decisions at risk like this? The only way to make an informed decision is by thoroughly observing, examining and analysing our beliefs, questioning everything we know, keeping what is valid and eradicating what is not.

'A life unexamined is not worth living.'

Socrates

GAME PLAN

The Risk Strategy in Health

Playing with Fire

Health, both mental and physical, is our most treasured possession, yet we often take it for granted and we often abuse it.

We tend to think that whatever health we have now is what we'll always have, or that ill-health or accidents will never happen to us. Only when it does actually occur, do we start to make the changes we should have made many years earlier. If you smoke all your life, then the chance is high that smoking will be the cause of your death, usually after many months or years of worry and pain for yourself and your family. At that point, all those years of 'just having a cigarette' and planning to give up tomorrow, may be brought into sharp focus as a highly irresponsible way to play with fire.

There are two sides of risk:

a) Risking too much
b) Risking too little

To risk too much is to take high risks that bring sometimes big and sometimes small gains if we succeed, but they always carry a high potential to stumble and fall. Low risk is to risk little to seek security, to stay safe, and this also usually brings only little reward. How does this work in health?

To smoke, to drink too much, to eat junk food, to work too long and too hard without proper rest is to take a high risk view of your health. People who do this feel that 'it will never happen to them' or 'what's the point?' They often have a fatalistic view of life that whatever will happen will happen, and there's nothing they can do about it. People like this will often quote stories about someone they know who was as 'fit as a fiddle' but died suddenly of a heart attack. Sadly, some healthy people do die young, but most don't. Why take the risk of damaging your health just for a bit of immediate pleasure now that has no benefit in the long-term?

The low risk people don't take risks, they fear injury, or they fear pushing too hard that they might hurt themselves. They fear making mistakes and overestimate how costly and how painful any loss might be. As the saying goes: 'Success is not forever and failure is rarely fatal.' This means that when we win, it won't last forever and when we lose, we won't lose everything; instead we'll often only lose a little if we lose at all. Few decisions, if they go wrong, will leave us homeless, completely destitute or even dead, but low risk people avoid risks as if they will. Their perception of risk is skewed by their attitude to it.

Both sides of the risk spectrum must be managed to find the right level of risk for each situation. Sometimes, we must take a risk to get a result, such as taking regular exercise and eating well, where the risk is the pain of keeping it going in the long term. At other times we must hold back, like when we want to train at too high an intensity for too long, thereby risking injury or making ourselves susceptible to illness or exhaustion.

Our health is always going to be a challenge, a risk we juggle. Yet, we simply don't know what our genetics have in store for us or what accidents might lay ahead, we might be destined to live long and with all our faculties intact, so it's important to plan ahead so we keep our bodies in as good a shape as possible for as long as possible.

Good mental health combined with good physical health is surely something we all desire and it can be ours if we manage our health risks the right way.

'The risk of a wrong decision is preferable to the terror of indecision.'

Maimonides

The Risk Strategy in Wealth

Speculate to Accumulate

It's commonly said that we must 'speculate to accumulate'. Yet, it is so often uttered by people who don't do either, that this phrase seems to have little meaning any more.

Most people don't manage to build wealth because they think it's impossible or they believe it's as risky as betting on a horse race. To build wealth does involve taking risks – although rarely to the extent that people imagine. There are several ways to build wealth which are:

1. Spend less than you earn
2. Save the excess
3. Invest the savings into a higher investment area
4. Re-invest the gains
5. Study carefully where you invest

At which of the above points is there a high risk? It can only exist in point 5, and only if you fail to make adequate study of your investment area, be it property, shares, building a business or whatever. The final thing necessary to acquire wealth, and a key to managing risk, is discipline (see Patience). Wealthy people have this in abundance and they need it too, because there will be times when an attractive investment offers itself but might not fit their investment criteria. At times like these, the wise investor sticks to his plan; every now and then he will take a risk and speculate, but always with amounts he can afford to lose. The key to building wealth is to manage investment risk. If you err on the side of caution you stand to make too little and if you err on the more reckless side then you stand to lose too much. The mid-ground of securing your gains and only risking what you can afford to lose is the way of the wise investor.

Building wealth is simple, but we must understand the risks and lessen them through study. We must understand ourselves and our susceptibility to taking either too much risk or not enough. Consider why you are reckless or cautious: is it because you have lost too much or never lost? Or is it not related to investment at all? Are you reckless because you love the high risk like a 'base jumper' loves high emotions (in which case you may get rich but lose it all through too much risk.) If you are too cautious, then why is that? Is it because you fear failure in the eyes of others perhaps?

In both of these cases, the risk taken by both types of investors is not linked to money but to some other emotional issue. In either case, you must attend to these issues or they will hold back your wealth building. Wealth building is not an emotional business, it is instead a logical and cool headed process based on knowledge and method.

'The man who knows it can't be done counts the risk, not the reward.'
Elbert Hubbard

The Risk Strategy in Growth

Can't Make an Omelette Without Breaking a Few Eggs

On our journey of self-discovery, which is our personal growth, we sometimes have to make tough decisions, and they are usually tough because they involve taking risks. Risk is a strategy and also the consequence of a strategy, so how can we use the strategy of Risk in our personal growth?

Risk is something to be managed, if it is to be used well, and to manage it well, you must understand it well. The motivation to take risk lies in the potential reward it will bring if we succeed. We must understand the difference between high risk and low risk and how some decisions may be high risk but give higher rewards, and some decisions may be low risk and give low or no rewards. It is often incorrect to think that the opposite of high risk means safety and security. On the face of it, deciding to stay safe through a low risk decision looks like it should bring safety, but, for someone who wants more from life, staying safe won't move you forward very far, if at all – which is how that safe decision has a high risk consequence! Therefore, if you want to get a good job with lots of security, your decision is based on low risk, but the high risk consequence is that no job is ever truly secure, and those that seem secure usually don't pay well – so you have a high risk of being poor in retirement!

This means that, if you want to move forward with your life, you have to consider all sides of the risks you want to take and don't take. You cannot live your life without some amount of risk taking; it is something that is always with us, which is why it's worth giving it some serious study.

> **'Only those who will risk going too far can possibly find out how far one can go.'**
> T. S. Eliot

Summary

Risk is there to be used, and, to be used well, it must be managed. No one is all high risk and no one is all low risk; everyone is comprised of a mixture of both. The secret is to know when to risk and when to hold fast, keeping in mind that we will only really know for certain what is the right thing to do after the event. Study the risk in every situation and make the best decision you can make with the time you have available to decide.

Risk Strategy in Brief

1. The greater the potential reward, the greater the risk, and the lower the risk, the lower the reward.
2. 'Getting the best out of any outcome is the balance of risk against reward'.
3. 'To chance one's arm' is to take an uncalculated risk where the outcome is far from certain.
4. To risk a large force into unknown territory is risky to the point of foolhardiness.
5. All combat carries risk of injury or even death, which is one of the reasons we avoid it.
6. Good relationships, be they emotional or practical, can be risked by one of the partners thinking that the grass is greener elsewhere.
7. The secret is to know when to risk and when to hold fast, and in remembering that we will only really know for certain what the right decision is after the event.
8. Our personal attitudes to risk must be understood if we are to live a life free from negative conditioned habits.
9. Health, both mental and physical, is our most treasured possession; don't risk today's pleasure against tomorrow's health.
10. On our journey of self-discovery, which is our personal growth, we have to make tough decisions, and these are tough because they involve taking risks.

STRATEGY NO. 15

The Vulnerability Strategy of Example

Definition: Make Sacrifices

Overview of Example

We can make an example of another person or we can be the example to other people. In conflict, we use the strategy of Example to frighten others through threat, either direct or indirect, or to inspire our own soldiers through our model behaviour. The fear of the threat can do our work for us, like when it involves making a threat to one individual, whilst implying a threat to another. In friendships and relationships, we can gain trust and respect by making ourselves the example for others to emulate.

'Society is always taken by surprise at any new example of common sense.'

Ralph Waldo Emerson

The Yin & Yang of Example

The Yang

instance
illustration
exception
model
representation
lesson
warning
sacrifice

The Yin

common
normal
unrepresentative
average
usual

The Example Strategy in Tradition

The Whipping Boy

In the Middle Ages, princes and the very wealthy had their sons educated with a special proviso. While most scholars who misbehaved would be beaten by the master for their misdemeanours, it was unthinkable for a prince or the son of a duke or an earl to be beaten by a lowly school master. So instead, the master would focus his beating on a specially provided 'whipping boy' who took the punishment for a high-born student. The whipping boy would be a child from a poorer family, who offered him for the task in exchange for payment and privileges, which could be substantial. The downside was that of course, if the aristocratic youth misbehaved, then the whipping boy would be thrashed as an example to the real transgressor.

'If you must hold yourself up to your children as an object lesson, hold yourself up as a warning and not as an example.'

George Bernard Shaw

The Example Strategy in Warfare

Fear is the Key

To make an example in war is to make a threat to one person or group (see Pressure) to demonstrate the vulnerability (see Target) of this group by sacrificing another (see Risk). Its successful use can create leverage over others, often without having to go through with the threat.

Chinese Strategy No. 11 – The Plum Dies in the Place of the Peach

In around 480 BC, the Persian army, under the command of Xerxes, attacked Greece with a view to taking over the entire country and adding it to the massive Persian Empire. The invasion was blocked on land and sea, but it is the land battle of Thermopylae that has found its way into popular history as 'The Last Stand of the 300 Spartans'.

The mountain pass at Thermoplylae was one of two easily defended approaches into the Greek mainland and, although there were narrower passes through the mountains, the Persians didn't know where these were until the Greek Ephialtes betrayed their position. The battle ran over 3 days and saw the 300 Spartans plus Thespians, Thebans and Phocians, with a total force of around 1600 soldiers, holding the opening of the pass which spanned around 100 metres. The Greeks were very well trained, especially the Spartans led by King Leonides. They used large shields and long hoplite spears to form a phalanx across the pass and stopped attack after attack by thousands of Persian soldiers, including the fearsome Immortals, but every assault was thwarted. The Persian army is thought to have been as many as 150,000 but thanks to the narrow pass, a good knowledge of military strategy and a high level of training, the Greeks held them off for 3 days, until they were betrayed by Ephialtes, who showed the Persians secret mountain passes which led them to the rear of the Greek forces. The Greeks, therefore, had to fight with their meagre forces, on two fronts, and lost the advantage that the narrow pass had provided (see Exploitation). Almost the entire Greek force was killed but, despite their small number, they took with them around 20,000 Persian troops.

The battle stands out as not only a sacrifice of the few to save the many, but also an example of superior training and equipment. The example set by the brave Greeks at Thermopylae has served as an inspiration which has lasted over 2000 years because a tiny force of men sacrificed their lives in order to save their country from an invading enemy.

Chinese Strategy No. 26 – Point to the Mulberry, Berate the Pagoda

Little is known of the famous Chinese strategist, Sun Tzu, or even whether he was a real person. However, his legacy on strategy, compiled in his book **The Art of War**, written over 2,000 years ago, has been hugely significant. Legend says that Sun Tzu was proposed as a general to serve the emperor. Although he came highly recommended, little was known about him. The emperor agreed to employ him if he could first demonstrate his leadership by training his 1,000 concubines how to march like an army.

Sun Tzu stood in front of the concubines and gave his instructions, but the concubines paid no attention and simply stood around chatting. Faced with this insubordination, Sun Tzu took radical action and ordered that a group of the concubines were executed in full view of the rest. This certainly caught their full attention and, by the end of the day, the concubines could indeed march like an army. Whilst the emperor was sad to have lost his concubines, he had to agree that Sun Tzu could get the job done, and employed him on the spot. By making an example of a few unruly people, Sun Tzu brought 1,000 under his control.

Chinese Strategy No. 34 – Self Injury Scheme

We discussed the Focus strategy of Function when we looked at the Battle of the Red Cliffs and how Cao Cao's fleet was defeated by being tricked into tying his ships together, and so was unable to manoeuvre against his enemy's fire ships. The fire ships were initially allowed near Cao Cao's fleet under the guise of surrender. There was another part to the strategy which was used to convince Cao Cao that the surrender was real. Strategist Huang Kai, who devised the plan, had his own part to play personally. He arranged to be seen while he vehemently disagreed with the surrender plan in open meeting with his commander, for which he was taken out and given 100 lashes. The punishment was very real and it was weeks before he was well again. Meanwhile, the spies who witnessed the very public punishment of Huang Kai's apparent insubordination used this as evidence to convince Cao Cao that the surrender was indeed real. Hence, the battle was won through Huang Kai's personal sacrifice in making an example of himself.

> *'Go before the people with your example,
> and be laborious in their affairs.'*
>
> Confucius

The Example Strategy in Combat

Make an Example, or Go Down Fighting

In combat, it can be frightening enough to face one opponent, but to face two or more is far worse. One use of the Example strategy in self-defence when faced with multiple opponents, if one has the opportunity (see Opportunity), is to choose the biggest enemy (see Target) and challenge him (see Isolation and Delay), or simply attack him with speed and overwhelm (see Pace and Pressure). Your attack must be ferocious and ruthless (see Toughness) with the intent of beating him quickly so that his partners become unsure of using you as their target. Once they see the toughest of them beaten, it should take the heart out of them. Do they want to risk the same treatment (see Risk)? Is what they will get worth the hassle? Either way, if you can beat any one of them convincingly, you'll have to face one less opponent and, if you lose, at least you'll have the satisfaction of having been able to fight back to some extent. If you can avoid fighting, and talk your way out of the situation, all the better, but sometimes violent action cannot be avoided, and when that is the case, you must know how to take violent and aggressive action.

If you cannot win, at least you can go down fighting and take some of your enemies with you on the way, in the hope that your example could dissuade these same attackers from picking on someone else in future.

> **'Example is the school of mankind,
> and they will learn at no other.'**
> Edmund Burke

The Example Strategy in Relationships

Lead From the Front

In partnerships and teams, it's often thought that leadership is simply a command from the rear, sending others forward to do the work. Of course, in some cases, that's the way it is. But true leadership involves more than just telling others what to do, it means doing it first as the example to those you are leading.

In order to create a partnership or team that is bonded together, that will work together and makes sacrifices for each other, we must follow an example. A leader is so designated because he or she has certain specific qualities or skills, and has gained the trust of the group through experience and training. As Tony Robbins says: 'A leader must know the way, show the way and go the way' if he is to be a true leader. A leader only appears to lead from the rear because, in order to get to where he is, he has led from the front, proving through experience to be worthy of the position of leader.

A leader must be prepared to make the final decision on any action, but also be able to listen to his team. A leader must be tough (see Toughness) and set the standard for all the behaviour of the group, which is why some leaders, especially politicians, fall particularly hard when their behaviour falls short of that expected from someone in their leadership position.

If a leader is seen to have lower standards than he demands, he will not last long in his position.

> **'Parents must lead by example. Don't use the cliché: do as I say and not as I do. We are our children's first and most important role models.'**
>
> Lee Haney

The Example Strategy in Friendship

Give Trust to Gain Trust

There is an old story of a man found shivering in front of a fireplace where wood is stacked ready to be lit. His guest says: 'Why don't you light the fire and get some heat?' to which the old man replies: 'I'll give the wood flame when it gives me heat.' The morale is that, sometimes, we have to make the first move to get the things we want, even if we feel it is unfair or inappropriate at the time.

Friendship is based on trust and trust has first to be given before we can expect to receive it. To do so can place us in an emotionally vulnerable position; we must take the lead and set the example by being fully prepared to give before we can receive. Once we do, the example we set can be the solid base upon which the friendship stands.

In disagreements with friends, we might not wish to make the first move, because we feel that to do so might be an acceptance of guilt in the dispute. Or we might feel that our ego may be bruised, and our friend's stroked, by giving them a result which they might claim says, 'he needs me more than I need him'. Or 'he knew he was in the wrong, that's why he came crawling back'. A good question to ask oneself in this situation is: 'Would I rather be right, or would I rather be effective?' This helps to focus us past our egotism and instead, seek the best result for both sides.

Sometimes we have to focus on the bigger picture to get the right result, which means looking to the future of the friendship instead and putting aside any petty hurts.

'Let not him who is houseless pull down the house of another, but let him work diligently and build one for himself, thus by example assuring that his own shall be safe from violence when built.'

Abraham Lincoln

The Example Strategy Personally

Do As I Say, Not As I Do

So often in life, we come across people with double standards and, whilst this can be simple duplicity (see Duplicity) which aims to deliberately deceive, often our double standards come from the conflicting beliefs that are conditioned into us from childhood.

As children, we pick up and learn from many different people in our lives, each with differing views and attitudes. When we're young we need certainty, so we accept these views at face value, and usually without question, not realising that they are often in conflict with each other. The problem is that, these conflicting views stay with us and can cause us real hardship as we get older. They become the rules, principles and ideologies that govern our adult lives. However, unless we examine and either dispel or confirm these rules through rational observation, especially on important issues, such as race, religion, honesty, truth, sex, trust, money, etc., we will be responding automatically, and often wrongly, on issues that matter. I knew someone once, who thought all black people should be sent back to their own countries. When he was challenged about his friend next door, who was black, he said 'oh no, he's alright, he's a nice guy'. This person had conflicting views that made no sense. He was prepared to make an example of an entire group of people through deporting them, but ready to make an exception of one because 'he was OK'. We must, therefore, at some time in our lives, question the examples and lessons that make up our belief system, those tenets that we follow and live by. They may not be as right as we think and they may not be serving us anymore.

We need to observe ourselves and our behaviours to find our true beliefs, to question our conditioned beliefs and the examples we have been set, to see whether they are consistent with whom we really are. To do otherwise is to set poor examples to our juniors and at best, we will end up looking foolish, or at worst we can become a potential danger to society.

'A person always doing his or her best becomes a natural leader, just by example.'
Joe DiMaggio

The Example Strategy in Health

Practise What You Preach

We have discussed before how the body we inhabit is like the car we drive or the house we live in; it is a vehicle that keeps us safe and warm. But often we treat our home and car better than we do our own bodies. How often do we see people with power and intelligence who spare no time for their own health? They have so much intelligence in some areas, but they lack the intelligence to look after their most important possession: their own health.

As we grow older and our lives often become easier and more settled, we tend to become more sedentary, yet our eating and drinking habits remain the same as when we were young and active, and may even increase. The result is that, in middle age, we get fat and unfit, which we blame on old age; we become the example of a middle aged person accepting that role as if it were inevitable, which it isn't.

At what age do we become middle aged? The answer is that there is no such thing. Society considers a person to be middle aged based probably on the Bible's '3 score years and 10', so that at 35 we are suddenly half way through our lives. The typical example of the middle aged man or woman is not a very attractive one. Fortunately, more and more we see people who set new examples of what 'middle age' might mean; one that is not characterised by falling into poor health habits, but which demonstrates that, by keeping fit and eating well, we can live our life to its fullest, despite the years passing by. Of course we all age, gradually and gently, but our habits and choices don't have to be those typical of a stereotype of old age, since we have the power to keep our standards high, set our own example and live that way.

We need not follow the example of others either, taking life easier and easier, for no other reason than that it is easy. Being overweight and out of condition, taking little exercise, and eating food low in nutritional value are choices that we make every day. This has nothing to do with the aging process. Instead, we can set our own example of middle age, one that includes fitness in all areas of our lives.

> *'Few things are harder to put up with than the annoyance of a good example.'*
> Mark Twain

The Example Strategy in Wealth

Success Leaves Clues

All around us, there are people who are rich and famous, and many people feel that the rich are somehow gifted, special or different, or that their wealth comes from exploiting others (see Exploitation).

This might be true in some cases, but it is not true in most cases. One person having wealth doesn't mean that someone else has to lack it. There is enough wealth for all of us; it is not a finite thing. In truth, wealth is infinite and present all around us. Just because you know of someone who has set a bad example of a wealthy person, doesn't mean that it is typical of all wealthy people, or even that you would have to become that way yourself if you achieved wealth. It's up to you to become wealthy and to set your own example of what a wealthy person can do with their money. Consider this too: Who are the biggest givers to the needy through charity? Who are the employers who share their wealth through payment of wages and salaries? The answer is, of course, the wealthy. Consider this also: you are currently paid what you are worth. That might seem harsh if you feel you are not being paid well, but it is true that you are currently paid to the maximum of the value you provide to the organisation you work for. How can you earn more? By providing greater value. There is no secret as to why some people achieve wealth and others don't; if you were worth more, you would be paid more.

It may sound cruel, but it is true. In order to earn more, you must find a way to be worth more and therefore create more for yourself and your business, whether you are an employee or the CEO. This could mean: acquiring more skills, applying your knowledge more effectively, using your time and resources more efficiently...

The good news though, is that anyone can become wealthy by learning the techniques and systems of the wealthy. How can we discover the secrets of creating wealth? It's simple: by learning from the examples of those who have already achieved wealth. There are hundreds of books and courses available to teach you the simple secrets of building wealth, and platforms such as Amazon, YouTube or eBay where products can be turned into cash.

Books and courses on wealth building can now be downloaded to your electronic device and be in your hands within minutes. Whilst not all these products are exactly what you need and you might need to read and study several to learn what you need to know, everything you read will be of use in some way. At the very least, they will provide experience, and a tightening up of your goals on your journey to personal riches. Sometimes, to find what is useful you must experience what is not useful.

Wealth, therefore, is not magical. It is methodical and, thankfully, you need not experience the pain that many have on their journey to riches. All you need do is to read, study, follow the instructions, and put into practice what you learn from those who have set the example by going before you, and writing down how they did it so you too can benefit from their system.

'Imagine for yourself a character, a model personality, whose example you determine to follow, in private as well as in public.'

Epictetus

The Example Strategy in Growth

Be the Example

Your journey of growing as an individual is one that will take you away from the place of discomfort where you first started – with that feeling that life must hold more, that you deserved and expected more than your current life seemed to offer.

Your journey, therefore, began because you wanted more from life and, in order to get more, you have to be more. That is part of the growth process and it cannot be shortcut. Each step on your journey requires that you take a step in the direction you intend to go despite any fears or worries that might hold you back (see Risk). This often takes courage (see Faith and Toughness) because growth means moving into the unknown – a leap of faith – and each leap brings growth, experience and knowledge, which can change you as a person.

You must set for yourself an example which is a created image, an image that is entirely in your head to which you must try to adhere. It is possible that only those who witness your journey will see the change, but this doesn't matter. Create the image of who you want to be and the life you want to lead, and try your best to make your experiences reflect that example. You can't cut corners in your personal growth, or life will just make you repeat the experiences again and again until you do it the right way in order to help you move forward.

The Example in personal growth really is the example you set for yourself. You cannot fake it, you can only live it and be it; that is the only way to grow.

'I'm a survivor – a living example of what people can go through and survive.'

Elizabeth Taylor

Summary

It is interesting to note that, of the 36 Chinese strategies of the martial arts, the strategy of Example is the one that appears most often. Example is something you set and something you follow, it is both a threat and something to aspire to. Consider how it fits with the other strategies to become part of your overall plans for success and, most of all, set an example for yourself to follow.

The Example Strategy in Brief

1. We can make an example of another person or we can be the example for other people to follow.
2. To make an example in war is to take action against one person or group in order to demonstrate the vulnerability of another.
3. By making an example of a few unruly people, Sun Tzu brought 1,000 under his control.
4. When faced with multiple opponents, choose the biggest one and challenge him, make an example of him, so that others fear to challenge you.
5. A leader must know the way, show the way and go the way.
6. If a leader is seen to have lower standards than he demands, he will not last long in his position.
7. Friendship is based on trust and trust has first to be given before we can expect to receive it.
8. Learn from those who have set the example by going before you and writing down how they did it for you to benefit from.
9. The example in personal growth comes from the example you set for yourself. You cannot fake it, you can only live it and be it; that is the only way to grow.
10. Example is something you set and something you follow, it is both a threat and an inspiration. The secret of example is knowing when to be either.

TIMING STRATEGIES

'The Greater Part of Success is in the Timing' The AEGIS Law of Timing

Timing Strategies deal with the control and timing of events and situations. As the AEGIS law of Timing states, the major part of success is in the timing of events. Time at its core is simply the interval between two or more events and we can change the timing of events by changing the frequency or pace of those that are within our control. This takes a certain skill as we can be early, late or on time for any event and the skill in Timing is to be able to judge the right time to act to your own best advantage.

The 5 strategies of Timing are:

1. *Patience* – the ability to wait for the right time
2. *Interruption* – the ability to block, deflect, evade and create events
3. *Pace* – the management of speed in events
4. *Opportunity* – the ability to respond to events
5. *Delay* – the ability to manage the timing of events

Timing is a major controller in strategy. Without proper timing in attacks and defences, one will lack speed, power and overall efficiency. If the right thing happens at the wrong time, then impact is lost and so timing in physical events is of paramount importance. Timing comes through judgement, assessment, predictability and repetition and requires constant attention to get the desired results.

STRATEGY NO. 16

The Timing Strategy of Patience

Definition: Good Things Come to He Who Waits

Overview of Patience

Patience is the waiting game, biding your time until the right moment comes. There is a right time for everything and it takes control to wait, especially whilst those around you demand action and accuse you of procrastination. But if you have the courage to wait until your target is most vulnerable, then victory can be made easy. All patience needs is discipline, which is the management of your emotions, the ability to prevent yourself from rushing in by imposing your intellect over your feelings for the sake of your plan and the result that you desire to achieve.

> *'We could never learn to be brave and patient, if there were only joy in the world.'*
> Helen Keller

The Yin & Yang of Patience

The Yang

forbearance
tolerance
restraint
sufferance
imperturbability

The Yin

impatience
passion
excitement
irritation

The Patience Strategy in Tradition

At the Eleventh Hour

This common phrase dates back to the Bible, from Matthew 20:9, and relates to the Parable of the Labourers. Twelve-hour days in the vineyards were the norm, and employers would only employ the minimum number of labourers needed, in order to save money on wages. But, as the day progressed, if they found out the workers could not complete the workload before it became too dark to see, more labourers would be hired at around 5pm ('the eleventh hour') in order to finish the day's workload. So the less fortunate labourers had to wait patiently all day for their chance to work and to earn some money; hence the modern meaning of the phrase which means to wait for something until the very last moment – 'the eleventh hour'.

> **'He who is prudent and lies in wait for an enemy who is not, will be victorious.'**
>
> Sun Tzu

The Patience Strategy in Warfare

Patience is a Virtue

Patience is the mastery of emotion, which cries out for immediate results, and in war a commander must master his emotions, or be drawn into battle before the time is right.

The heat of battle is a frightening and unpredictable situation filled with chaos, noise and death and it is easy to make your move before you are fully ready. 'If you can keep your head when all about you are losing theirs and blaming it on you' is a quote from Rudyard Kipling's **'If'** and pretty much sums up a commander's position in war. The ability to stick to your guns and be patient, especially under pressure, is a skill indeed. The opposite of patience is to rush, to charge in, to be unable to wait. The wise strategist must have patience in abundance. The Law of Launch Point, the Law of Emotion, the Law of Judgement and the strategy of Faith are all key elements to the execution of the Patience strategy.

Chinese Strategy No. 9 – On Distant Shore Watch for Fire

This is the 9th of the ancient Chinese strategies of war. It recommends waiting until the opponent is in disarray, not yet ready or having internal turmoil to deal with, and then attacking him while he is disadvantaged. If you can wait until your opponent is at his weakest point before you make your move, you can gain an easy victory.

After the fall of the Han dynasty, China fell into many years of civil war, known as The War of the Three Kingdoms. One of the outstanding warlords and strategists of this time was Cao Cao (also known as Ts'ao Ts'ao) who used many different strategies to achieve his aims, one of which was 'on distant shores watch for fire'. In 207 AD, two brothers – Yuan Shang and Yuan His – who were his enemies, escaped after the battle of Kuan Tu, and sought refuge with another of his enemies, Liao Tung, who had successfully resisted Cao Cao before. The brothers felt safe aligning (see Alignment) with another of Cao Cao's enemies and, in any case, they also felt that they could subdue Liao Tung if things turned badly. Cao Cao's generals recommended attacking the kingdom of Liao Tung to destroy the brothers before they could regain their power base, but Cao Cao refused as he believed it was unnecessary since he predicted there would be internal conflict between the brothers and Liao Tung before long. He ordered his generals to wait for the conflict which he knew would grow between the brothers and their new ally. Soon after, envoys came to Cao Cao from Liao Tung with the decapitated heads of the two brothers. The internal conflict he had expected had come to pass.

By waiting patiently, Cao Cao had gained what he wanted without the loss of a single soldier. In allowing internal strife and patience to work for him, Cao Cao got what he wanted.

> **'How poor are they that have not patience!
> What wound did ever heal but by degrees?'**
> William Shakespeare

The Patience Strategy in Combat

Ready, Steady…

The pre-emptive strike takes the initiative to start the fight before our opponent is ready, as it gives him no time to prepare and respond. The opposite strategy would be to wait for him to attack, so that you can defend against his attack and counter with your own.

In the heat of a fight, strikes are being thrown back and forth in rapid succession, but some fighters prefer to wait patiently for their opponent to attack first. They are ready with their counter, waiting for their opponent to commit himself with either hand or foot, knowing that, once he is committed to a course of action, he will struggle to change plans and can be lured onto a powerful riposte (see Attraction). Being able to wait like this requires patience and courage. This can also be misinterpreted as fear of engaging your adversary and can be used to throw them off your scent.

In self-defence, you may be faced with a potential threat and decide to wait for the right moment to attack so that you get the best result possible. In this situation, you can combine the pre-emptive strike with a patient demeanour, waiting for that moment when your attacker is in the best position for your onslaught.

Wait for the time that is best for you and worst for him. Take away his initiative and you can reduce the threat considerably. If your strategy works, you might even be able to remove his threat completely.

> *'Patience, persistence and perspiration make an unbeatable combination for success.'*
> Napoleon Hill

The Patience Strategy in Relationships

Stick to Your Guns

It's difficult enough to make a decision and see it through to the bitter end when there is only you involved, but in a partnership, whether it is a marriage or a business, it can be even worse.

When you make a personal decision to do something that will take time and patience to see it through to the end, you can use two strategies to help you reach your goal. First, you might decide to keep your decision to yourself and not tell anyone about it. If you then change your mind or lapse on your commitment, no-one will be any the wiser about your failure and it will be easier to get back on with your plan. However, if you are really serious about sticking to your plan, or you know that you have only one chance to get it right, a good idea is to tell your friends or colleagues what you are intending to do. This way you can use your motivation not to lose face in front of others to help keep you on track, even to the extent of asking your friends to remind you of your commitment if they see you waiver in your intent.

In a group decision, the power of social proof can come into play in the same way; each member of the team can remind the others of their decision, to help the team work together so that they all stick to their guns. The expression 'stick to your guns' is fairly self-explanatory. It came about in times of war, when officers would charge their men to stay with their weapons under the heaviest of fire, to prevent them from up and running away in the heat of the battle, or firing before the time was right. The strength of the adage applies to all important decisions requiring patience, but also reminds us that patience also can often require us to have the courage of our convictions and act in spite of our fear.

It can happen that one of the partners in the group won't stick to the plan. This can be a bad thing if he goes against the group decision, but it can also sometimes be a good thing, if the original plan is proving not to be as good as initially thought. If the decision not to stick with the plan is motivated by a genuine reason, rather than lack of courage or strength of character for example, then do not let yourself be pressured by the group to act against your principles. If you cannot adapt to fit in with the plan, it is better to quit and break away, at least for a while.

'I'm extraordinarily patient provided I get my own way in the end.'
Margaret Thatcher

The Patience Strategy in Friendship

Bite Your Tongue

There are times when friendships can sorely test us, such as when we go to help someone in need and they are in such a bad place that they lash out at us, as if we were the problem.

Perhaps they see us as part of that problem, or maybe they don't see that they have a problem at all and end up rejecting our help. It puts us, as friends, in a difficult position: do we persist against their wishes or back off until they are in a better frame of mind? Sometimes, they may never regain their senses alone and, when that happens, we have to be patient with them, listen to them, sympathise with them and be the shoulder and support they need in their time of need. It's not easy though, to keep your cool when a friend is blaming you for their troubles. It's easier to retaliate in the same way because hurtful comments, blame and rejection are painful to us all, no matter how much control we exert over our own emotions. But the best response we can offer is really our patience, by ignoring our friend's response and recognising that their attacks on us are simply a response to the pain they feel. We can often say things that we don't mean when we're emotional, things that aren't true or fair, but when emotion takes over, we often lose our ability to be rational. Remember that anything said in the heat of the moment, no matter how hurtful, is their pain speaking and not their true feelings, so bite your tongue and wait for the crisis to pass.

If you can do this, you will have proven the strength of your friendship, your patience and, eventually, you should receive some kind of apology after the crisis is over. In circumstances like these, we find that patience is truly a virtue.

'Be patient and understanding.
Life is too short to be vengeful or malicious.'
Phillips Brooks

The Patience Strategy Personally

Control Yourself

In the series 'Star Trek', Mr Spock was a Vulcan who relied solely on logic to make his decisions. His whole race had worked to employ intellectual decisions over emotional ones. The reason for this was that his race was extremely emotional which had almost cost them their entire civilisation, so they had decided to work together to banish emotion and focus only on logic.

The relevance of this example, in applying the strategy of Patience to our personal life, is to warn us against the over-reliance on emotion. Our emotions have no thought, only feeling; they cannot reason and drive our response to 'fight or fly', to move toward or away from a situation. To fight or to fly are important reactions (see Reaction) in life or death situations which demand an immediate action one way or the other, but they are not part of any Patience strategy.

This important force of will – this discipline over emotion – is relevant because you only have to look around you to see that people who live on their emotions tend to be unhappy, not achieving much with their lives, and are often out of control. This is because their emotions are making more of their decisions than is their reasoned logic. Emotional people often over-eat, under-exercise, smoke, drink and have volatile relationships; all because they let emotion, rather than their intellect, run their lives. Emotional people are at the mercy of anger, hate, upset, depression and, equally, happiness and pleasure. But what stimulus is deciding which emotion is at the fore? Is it one they can trust, or one that will lead them into danger?

Just because we feel a certain way, whether it be happy or sad, does not mean that that emotion is a true evaluation of the present situation. Let's face it, any emotion we have could be chemical, brought on by too much coffee or other stimulant for instance, or even a biological response that has been brought on by an involuntary imbalance. Emotions can be brought on by unconscious habits and circumstances, by outdated experiences; becoming a simple stimulus and response mechanism, just like Pavlov's dogs, who were trained to salivate at the sound of a bell.

Emotion, therefore, is not the truth; neither is it necessarily a lie, so we must apply our logical intelligence to decide what to do next. Patience does not come from emotion, it comes from logic. So if you make decisions and you later feel like changing your mind, you should carefully examine your motives logically before you make any change.

Patience takes self-control and self-control comes from our intellectual intelligence, not our emotional intelligence, so never change a good decision for purely emotional reasons. Always apply logic first, so that you can make patience work in your favour.

'Have patience with all things. But, first of all with yourself.'
Saint Francis de Sales

The Patience Strategy in Health

Softly, Softly, Catchee Monkey

We have discussed elsewhere the reason why so many people focus past their health and once again it comes to emotion over logic. Emotion wants what it wants right now, no waiting, just action and immediate results.

In the right place this is the right thing to do, but we must never just act for action's sake, without thought, if we want to benefit from a long and healthy life. We must apply ourselves thoughtfully if we want to be healthy, harnessing our emotions rather than being harnessed by them.

To see and feel the changes in ourselves that result from our healthy living discipline takes time, self-control and patience. If you want to see a change in your physique, it will take weeks, months and years maybe, and the same applies to your overall health or mental well-being. Of course, we often feel better by just having made the decision to adopt new habits but this will wear off quickly and after that we must have patience, courage and faith (see Faith) that our strategy will pay dividends in the long run.

The Law of Conditioning controls habits and it states: 'Repetition is the mother of all skill'. Repetition takes a lot of self-control including the patience to stick with your chosen health regime. Results take time and time means patience, but we can make our patience work for us by harnessing our emotions in support of the task ahead. If we want to start exercising, for instance, we can plan it out beforehand, and part of that plan should include factoring in that time when we won't feel like exercising. This is guided by our emotions that want us to stay in our comfy bed, or sofa; to stay in front of a warm fire instead of jogging along a cold street. It's natural for us to want comfort over hardship, but comfort won't keep us healthy. This is why we have to plan those times and devise strategies that will help us overcome the emotions that desire immediate comfort over gradual fitness.

To harness your emotions, you need to focus on linking positive emotions with your exercise schedule. For example, don't make your programme a shock to your system, but start slowly and even con yourself by saying to yourself 'I'll just do a short workout today' and then, once you're started and your 'happy hormones' have kicked in, you'll most certainly find that you'll want to continue, instead of quitting early. Using some psychology on yourself in this way really does work – despite the fact that you know you're using the strategy against yourself, interestingly.

Another Patience strategy is to start slowly and gently, gradually increasing the intensity and allowing your body and mind to enjoy the process before you up the intensity level. Warming up before a workout is designed exactly for this purpose, but often in our (emotional) hurry to get the workout over with we dispense with the warm up, and thereby lose its beneficial effect. Think of it like this: you're not just warming up for this workout, but for the next one too. Once you're in the flow of the session, any thoughts of stopping are banished as your enjoyment and enthusiasm increases. It's a simple strategy, but an effective one.

Avoid always working out to the state of complete exhaustion because, although you will be on a high at the end of the session, your emotions will remember the hardship of the workout and unconsciously you'll start building a barrier in your head to put off that pain from happening again. This often happens with people new to exercise; they do too much too soon and fall off the wagon before they've even got started. They push themselves too hard and only remember the pain and not the gain.

So be patient with yourself, start slowly, enjoy the process as much as you possibly can, and this way it will be easier to keep going with your routine. Then your patience and persistence will be borne of desire, rather than self-control, which is the easiest way to apply the strategy of patience.

'Patience is bitter, but its fruit is sweet.'
Jean-Jacques Rousseau

The Patience Strategy in Wealth

Good Things Come to He Who Waits

The building of wealth definitely needs patience, which is not to say that becoming rich can't come quickly; it can. In fact, the whole process of building wealth is to grow our investments at a faster rate than the price of inflation through compounding its growth exponentially.

The average earning employee will probably earn a million pounds over his 40 year working life but will spend most of that money on his way to retirement. But imagine if you could make that million in 10 years instead of 40 and then live off the money and its continued growth for the rest of your life, doing exactly what you want instead of working the 9 to 5 drudge every day for 40 years... The idea with wealth is: instead of working comfortably for 40 years and retiring for the last 10 years of your life, you should work hard for 10 years and then live in comfort until you die.

However, no matter how brilliant your plan and how fast your wealth grows, you must still exercise patience and restraint, by carrying out 'due diligence' before investing. Due diligence is the research and care taken before investing your money. If you invest in an area you know nothing about, you could easily lose your money. Good investors thoroughly research their investment area before ever risking (see Risk) a penny. You must first investigate the market, study it, learn about it and, best of all, invest in something you know about through personal experience. Never invest more than you can afford to lose. Know your market, and learn the potential pitfalls of the investment before you make your move. But what happens if you get a time-sensitive 'hot tip' and need to act fast? If you have to act so fast that you cannot perform your due diligence, then forget it. If you do miss out on a genuine opportunity, it's OK. Other opportunities will present themselves and you will get another chance to invest later.

A rash investor is often a poor investor. Be patient, do your research and enter into all your investments thoroughly prepared. Remember: 'Fools rush in where angels fear to tread.'

'Have patience. All things are difficult before they become easy.'
Saadi

The Patience Strategy in Growth

Rome Wasn't Built in a Day

When we make our decision to set goals for our personal development, where we want to be, compared to where we are right now, might seem like a million miles apart.

So much to do and so many goals to hit before we get there; it can seem like a daunting task and many people who begin their journey fall by the wayside after just a short while, disheartened and disappointed. They lose their motivation and many feel like failures, or that the life they imagine can never be theirs. Where they want to be and where they are now is just too great a leap and the task ahead can appear so daunting that they give up before they ever even get started.

Here's the cure: don't worry about how fast you get to where you're going because, if you keep hold of the right attitude, you will soon learn that it's not the destination that counts, but the journey itself that is the most important adventure. Personal growth is not about speed and it's not necessarily about getting to a precise destination either. It's about the gradual process of positive change and the acquisition of new habits, education and experience. Personal growth at its most basic level is about achieving a life of joy, instead of a life of pain. Personal growth is about finding out what is causing you pain and gradually eradicating that pain and replacing it with a state of joy; a state that we are all born in, but that we lose along the way, as we lose sight of what is really important. This is why some of the wealthiest and most successful people in the world live simple lives, because their journey has uncovered the secret that life is not about the acquisition of possessions. In fact, true success often involves the losing of possessions as we realise how unimportant they are to a life filled with joy.

Understand this: If you could achieve your ultimate goal suddenly, tomorrow, then you'll find that you are mentally and emotionally unprepared for it and consequently you are likely to lose that wealth as quickly as you found it. We've all heard of lottery winners winning millions only to be broke again after a couple of years, and the reason for this is that they are not ready for wealth; mentally and emotionally they lack the maturity they need to live the life of a rich person. So they mismanage their money, they spend instead of invest, and they can't cope with the sudden freedom from their work or career. They end up self-sabotaging themselves and soon find their wealth spent, wasted, and they're forced to return to their previous life of 9 to 5 drudgery.

If you want a better, more rewarding life of personal fulfilment and achievement, then you have to enjoy the process as you travel along your way. Take pride in the smallest steps forward and be philosophical about your failures. Remember that you will probably never achieve the growth you initially set out to get because growth is a moving feast. When you achieve one goal, your ideas will have already grown beyond that goal toward another beyond it, as the achievement of each goal shows us the achievability of the next.

As each goal is achieved you will gradually and steadily grow as a person, becoming wiser and more at one with yourself along the way – so be gentle and patient with yourself, and enjoy the journey!

'A man who is a master of patience is master of everything else.'
George Savile

Summary

Patience truly is a virtue; it is self-control, self-denial, discipline, conditioning, will-power and, often, just plain hard work. But what is difficult today often brings greater and longer lasting rewards tomorrow. Those who achieve little are often at the mercy of their emotions, needing to have immediate pleasure to avoid the pain of their lives. They are like children, not able to see the bigger picture or that the greatest successes in our lives have to be worked at.

By applying a little discipline and patience to your thinking, you can have a truly rewarding life and patience will prove to be one of your greatest weapons.

Patience Strategy in Brief

1. Patience is the waiting game, biding your time until the right moment comes.
2. Patience is the mastery of emotion, which cries out for immediate results.
3. If you can wait until your opponent is at his weakest point before you make your move, you can gain an easy victory.
4. Patience may sometimes be seen as fear of engaging our adversary, unless, of course it works, and then it is seen as being part of your plan.
5. If you are serious about sticking to your plan, it is a good idea to tell your friends or colleagues what you are intending to do, so they can remind you when your resolve is failing.
6. Never change a good decision for purely emotional reasons. Always apply logic first, so that you can make patience work in your favour.
7. There are times when friendships can sorely test us; in circumstances like these we find that patience is truly a virtue.
8. Be patient with yourself, start slowly, enjoy the process as much as you can, and this way it will be easier to keep going.
9. Be patient, do your research and enter into all your investments thoroughly prepared. Remember: 'Fools rush in where angels fear to tread'.
10. Don't worry about how fast you get to where you're going, it's not the destination that counts, but the journey itself that is the most important adventure.

STRATEGY NO. 17

The Timing Strategy of Interruption

Definition: Stop Him in His Tracks

Overview of Interruption

There are times when we must stop what is happening, either by prevention or intervention, and sometimes the moment comes when we must take control of the situation and prevent events from moving further, for our own safety or for the safety of others. This is the strategy of Interruption which includes all defence and attack and whose purpose is to stop, block, interrupt, prevent and anticipate perceived and actual threats, both physically and verbally. The opposite of interruption is permission which should also be studied as a different use of the same strategy.

> *'People who say it cannot be done should not interrupt those who are doing it.'*
> George Bernard Shaw

The Yin & Yang of Interruption

The Yang

hinder
stop
break
halt
obstruct
intercept
block
deflect

The Yin

permit
allow
flow
free
avoid
evade
duck
slip
dodge

The Interruption Strategy in Tradition

Saved By the Bell

This phrase is generally associated with the sport of boxing. It was originally thought to be used when a fighter was in trouble and his opponent was about to finish him off. Before he could strike the finishing blow, the bell sounded the end of the round and the other fighter was saved. However, according to Albert Jack's entertaining book **Red Herrings and White Elephants**, the phrase actually comes from an event in the 19th Century when a Horse Guard was accused of falling asleep on guard duty. In his defence, he stated that he had heard Big Ben sound 13 times so he must have been awake. When his story was checked it was found that, owing to a gearing problem, Big Ben actually had sounded 13 times, rather than 12, so the guardsman was indeed 'saved by the bell'.

'A sense of humour is a major defence against minor troubles.'
Mignon McLaughlin

The Interruption Strategy in Warfare

Stop Him in His Tracks

To interrupt is to stop, block, and impede your enemy in his threat toward you. To hit or strike is also an interruption but it is important to understand that part of the Interruption strategy deals also with its opposite. It includes also permitting and allowing, which might be to create flow in order to allow a more powerful interruption as when 'an irresistible force meets an immovable object'.

Beware the Ides of March

In 44 BC Julius Caesar was gaining power in Rome and becoming more and more like a king intent on reducing the power of the Senate. Caesar had immense wealth from his campaigns and the support of the people. If he managed to gain absolute power, the Senate sensed that their days would be numbered. A group of the senators hatched a plan to assassinate Caesar when he was in the senate, where only other senators were permitted. On the 15th of March, despite warnings from his wife Calpurnia's prophetic dreams of disaster, he made his way there. 40 senators attacked and killed Julius Caesar, thus interrupting his rise to further power. The senators were above reproach, since they were too powerful in their own right to pay directly for their crime. However, in the long run, their plan failed as Julius had named his nephew Octavius as his heir; he became the Emperor Augustus, first Emperor of Rome and founder of the Roman Empire, and reigned for over 40 years.

The Phalanx

An ancient battlefield weapon, dating back over 4000 years, the phalanx consisted of soldiers creating a shield wall by holding shields in the left hand and long spears in the right hand. The second line of soldiers thrust their spears over the shoulders of the front rank and behind each rank was another line of armed soldiers, each one ready to step into the breach to support the line. The phalanx created a rectangular formation that could move forward, well protected and with great force, to push back the enemy. By moving together in tight formation and shielded on all sides, the phalanx would block an enemy's advance and cut a swathe through their centre, resembling something like a modern tank against foot soldiers. The phalanx was widely used by ancient armies and was a favourite of Alexander the Great. Against armies who didn't advance in such tight formation, the discipline of its ranks would halt the oncoming tide of the enemy.

Also, in warfare, the Interrupt strategy was used by each individual soldier as he blocked, deflected and intercepted each blow of his opponent with his sword or shield. If his timing was right, he would stop his opponent mid-flow without blocking, and evade his enemy's attack using a 'stop hit' by passing both sword and shield and connecting directly with his target with a direct strike.

'The quality of decision is like the well-timed swoop of a falcon which enables it to strike and destroy its victim.'

Sun Tzu

The Interruption Strategy in Combat

Don't get Me Started!

Surprise in combat is a great weapon (see Expectation) and part of any surprise strategy consists of interrupting whatever your opponent is doing with your attack.

One way to create this interruption is with a pre-emptive attack. A pre-emptive attack is initiated before our opponent can initiate his attack. The Law of Launch Point says 'Ready, steady, go!' and the power of this law is found in taking action before our opponent is ready, forcing him into a period of shock where he will need time to recover his senses and composure. By this time, you should, hopefully, have escaped (see Proximity) or overwhelmed (see Pressure) him completely. The pre-emptive attack intercepts our opponent, blocking him before he can begin. It is an effective Interruption strategy used in self-defence to give us an edge in combat, and provide us with thinking and acting space.

When using the pre-emptive strike in a self-defence situation, it is important to prevent difficulties with prosecution. You need, of course, to be sure that there will be an attack and that you are acting in self-defence. Yet, remember that in Britain at least, the pre-emptive attack is an entirely legal response to an impending threat.

Another important part of the Interruption Strategy in the martial arts, which also connects with the Law and Strategy of Proximity, is the concept of the 5 Levels of Defence. The 5 Levels of Defence describe the 5 types of reaction (see Reaction) to attack as follows:

Level 5 – Avoid: The flight response to avoid or move away from the threat. This is the lowest level of defence because it offers the least options since we cannot run away forever. Nonetheless, it is an effective short-term tactic and may be enough to save ourselves.

Level 4 – Block: Stop the attack, usually with another part of our body, like a hand or elbow. This keeps us closer to the action and allows a faster response and better positioning to counter-attack (rather than avoiding the attack totally). Its drawback is that we put ourselves in the way of injury through blocking.

Level 3 – Re-Direct: To deflect the attack, to interrupt its flow without actually stopping it. This allows for a faster counter-attack because the opponent's momentum continues forwards, thus bringing him into our range (see Proximity) more quickly.

Level 2 – Evade: To evade the attack laterally by side stepping or slipping the blow so that it misses us altogether. The strength of this defence is that we can achieve a simultaneous counter attack or 'stop hit' to an exposed target (see Target) on our opponent's body.

Level 1 – Attack: The highest level of defence. The AEGIS Law of Guard states 'Attack is the best defence' which is to take the initiative in a dangerous situation or in competitive sport combat – in street defence it can mean the pre-emptive strike we discussed earlier.

Consider in the above levels how interruption and flow interact with each other and how both are used in combat. Allowing your opponent's attacks to flow past you is the best way to escape them, whilst at the same time your attacks interrupt his body as they strike.

The better you can reach the higher levels of defence against your opponent, (with 5 being the lowest level and 1 being the highest), the more you will develop your own flow and the more you will interrupt your opponent's flow. To interrupt his flow creates a winning scenario for you and you can then consider combining other strategies into your game, especially isolation, pressure, target, faith (especially yours, but your opponent's as well). To be outmatched by a stronger opponent is one thing, but to be outmatched by a cleverer opponent who out-thinks you and makes you feel like a child in comparison to his mastery is altogether more frustrating (see Function and Faith).

'The great defence against the air menace is to attack the enemy's aircraft as near as possible to their point of departure.'

Winston Churchill

The Interruption Strategy in Relationships

Snap Out of It

We discussed above the frustration and doubt that an interruption can cause. It can be seen as insulting and disrespectful to interrupt someone and this sometimes leads us to the point where we are forced to listen to all sorts of people who get so carried away talking that they don't know when or how to stop. Being polite, we are forced to listen so as not to seem rude by stopping them.

A good habit to get into in a relationship is to make sure you are allowing your partners to say their piece. To block them is to disrespect them, to regard their thoughts and opinions as being of lesser value than yours. This is tantamount to bullying, which is not a good way to build a successful relationship. Blocking what they say, belittling their ideas and interrupting them before they have completed their sentence are a great way to shorten the life of a relationship. If that is not what you want, then you must allow their voice to be heard. Listen, nod, affirm, ask questions about what they say, show interest in their opinions and, where you feel it or where they need it, show your support for what they say. The opposite of interruption is permission; to live in a tolerant world we must permit others to say their piece, just as they must allow us to question what they believe. A successful society is not one that simply acquiesces to everyone's point of view, but instead has the freedom to disagree with impunity, within the bounds of reasonableness.

The key is to judge when to listen and when to interrupt, based on what response you want to gain or what point you wish to make. There is a saying which goes 'we have two eyes, two ears and one mouth, and we should use them in that order.' This should give you a clue as to the priority of listening, observing and speaking up in order to create more flow and fewer blockages in your relationships.

'Circumstances may cause interruptions and delays, but never lose sight of your goal.'
Mario Andretti

The Interruption Strategy in Friendship

Do Interrupt

To interrupt someone while they are speaking is considered rude and can be a major source of offence. Blocking someone's speech and train of thought is both irritating and annoying for the person interrupted and, when used as a weapon, it is a useful tool to get an emotional response (see Reaction) out of our adversary. Toward a friend, it would often be inappropriate to cut them off in such a way, although there are times when it is for the best to interrupt a negative or destructive train of thought.

In moments of high stress, we can suffer an emotional lockout where we only focus on our anger or our fear. We may become depressed or over excited, feeling that there is no way out of a situation. This could be happening for many reasons, such as a divorce, break up, bankruptcy or bereavement. All of these, we will eventually get over, even though at the time they can seem like never-ending problems.

One way to help someone through these times, as a friend, is to change the state of the person suffering. This can be done in several ways, one of which being to get them away from the source of their stress: a day out, a weekend away, a party amongst friends… anything which can interrupt their emotional entrapment. It may take some time to achieve this but sometimes it could also be as instantaneous as a proverbial slap in the face. Often it can be an argument or thought that sums up the situation with a clarity that manages to shock our friend back to reality. It need not be something clever and it could be as simple as: 'Pull yourself together!' The key is to interrupt, block and break the damaging thought process before it gets too severe.

There is a concept in psychology known as 'mnemonic lockout', where a person suffers from an inability to shift their train of thought away from their negative and destructive mind set. It is thought that people who commit suicide are subject to this terrible fixation, unable to see any way out of their current problems and pain. The only way out they see is to take their own lives. Sufferers of depression, too, suffer similar lockouts and part of their treatment is often to build strategies to break their negative thought processes.

In less serious situations, we all at some time suffer from feelings of doubt (see Faith) and pessimism and we develop our own strategies to shake ourselves up and interrupt our negative thinking. In friendships and partnerships, it is useful to have another person or group who can re-direct our thinking (see Direction) back to one of optimism and hopefulness.

'The strong man is the one who is able to intercept at will the communication between the senses and the mind.'
Napoleon Bonaparte

The Interruption Strategy Personally

Stuck in a Rut

There are times in our lives when we feel stuck or stopped; everything seems to be going against us or just going wrong one way or another. Times like these are opportunities for our negative thoughts and emotions to foster and take over; which is when it is necessary for us to take the same action with ourselves as we would with our friends.

In those cases, we have to shake ourselves up, change our routine and break our own rhythm. The Law of Predictability states: 'If you keep on doing what you do, you'll keep on getting what you get', but it's not always easy to recognise that we are doing the same thing over and over. Often it can feel like the right thing because it is what we have always done. So, finding where we are going wrong takes an examination of our life and habits. To live our life without examination of how we act and interact with others and deal with problems, opportunities, motivations and habits is to live without using our full intelligences; like a trained animal who responds to its conditioning instead of using its thinking abilities. This is completely contrary to any plan for personal improvement.

In order to progress in life, we must move forward and away from our current life. We must change some of our habits, as well as our thinking, and here lies the difficulty: some things don't need to change and some things do. It can take a long time to recognise behaviours that are blocking us and some of us never quite manage to do so, which leaves many feeling that 'life is a bitch and then you die'. We must realise that our sense of progress is purely perceptual; it is only one image of where we think we are compared with another of where we think we should be.

To change our behaviour, we must interrupt our behaviour patterns, our habits, and ensure that we do not end up standing in our own way. If we examine our habits and conditioning, we will find those that serve us and also those that hinder and block us. If we don't look for what is blocking us, we can end up complaining, blaming and judging – as so many do daily – trapped in our limited thinking, and believing that it is life that is at fault, rather than ourselves. Life is life –

one cannot fight it – one must seek to understand it and flow with it and, through understanding, find joy in it.

Our true progress in life is, therefore, a self-imposed perception and perceptions can be false. We must recognise that, even when all our dreams come true, our success must not interrupt the basic rules of daily life. We still have to attend to very basic things just like anyone else does. As the saying goes: 'Before enlightenment, fetch water and chop wood. After enlightenment, fetch water and chop wood', the basic essentials of life never change. Even though we manage to interrupt our old habits with new ones that serve us better, both psychologically and practically, we must still retain those fundamental things that will always be present and necessary to ground us in the now.

'Never interrupt your enemy when he is making a mistake.'
Napoleon Bonaparte

The Interruption Strategy in Health

Interrupt, Interruptions

Many of our strategies focus on why health is important and, in the Interruption strategy, we will look at how we can maintain our healthy lifestyle throughout our lives.

We know we should exercise our body and mind and aim to eat well. In order to implement our plans and to build new habits, it is important we find a way to interrupt our old habits. It's a perverse twist of fate that it always seems easier to develop bad habits than to build good ones. It can certainly be difficult to swap things that give us immediate pleasure for things that will give us more eventual benefit, as our rewards are delayed to some future date. This requires a high level of patience (see Patience) and emotional control to help us build a whole set of new habits.

The Law of Conditioning states: 'Repetition is the mother of all skill' and any new habit needs not just be blind repetition, but quality repetition. To get quality repetition requires making your new habit an attractive proposition (see Attraction). One way is to introduce just one new habit at a time, then build it in isolation (see Isolation), condition yourself to it and, when it has become second nature, introduce the next thing you want to change. If you interrupt all your bad habits by changing them all at once, your body and mind will rebel; it will take great resolve to overcome this rebellion and often will-power will not be enough – which makes it so difficult to maintain, much like New Year's Resolutions that fall by the way side soon after they are set.

The other side of the Interruption strategy to consider is when we get interrupted in our progress forward by our conditioned habits. Habits are conditioned, rhythmic patterns just like the Circadian rhythms that our body uses to set internal clocks and reminders for all our involuntary processes (such as our heartbeat or breathing patterns). However, unlike Circadian rhythms which ensure that we unconsciously continue with our most important habits, personal habits can be easily interrupted if they are missed even for just one day. Changes in your schedule, from workload to holidays, will all work to break the rhythm that you are building to improve and maintain your health, and it can take time and motivation to re-start a broken routine. If you begin a new routine of fitness or diet, you can make great progress for a few weeks and months, only to be interrupted for a day or two. It can then take months to re-establish your routine again. As the saying goes 'it takes thirty days to build good habits, and only one day to break them'. The answer, of course, is to build a motivation around the new habit that will support it and to remain conscious and constantly reminded of why the habit is important to maintain.

Use notes and alarms to keep you conscious of the new habit you are trying to build, especially in the early days, and use motivational quotes, vision boards, videos and audio recordings to keep you motivated toward your task.

'The effectiveness of work increases according to geometric progression if there are no interruptions.'
André Maurois

The Interruption Strategy in Wealth

Don't Stand in Your Own Way

To create wealth, you need to develop good habits and maintain their rhythm until, and also long after, you achieve your goals.

Life will try to interrupt your good intentions, systems and routines by throwing disturbances and challenges your way, but your greatest weapons are your attitudes and your ability to recognise when you are being interrupted and the necessity to get back on track. There are important keys to building wealth including: time, systems, persistence and expectations, and you must develop all of these key areas in order to create and hold onto your financial growth. Don't let your old conditioning interrupt your progress. We are all conditioned from childhood on how to feel about certain aspects of life and some of this conditioning will stand in our way, so this must be overcome before it sabotages our growth.

There are so many reasons for us to have greater wealth, but there are also many things that can get in our way to interrupt our progress; from people who will tell us that money is the root of all evil, to those who will try to borrow from us, waste our money, give bad advice, tell us we've changed for the worse and try to bring us back down to their level. Our key to building wealth relies on the consistency of our effort and, whenever our rhythm is interrupted or blocked, getting back on track as soon as possible. Remember that if you are poor now, it is because your conditioned habits and behaviours are keeping you poor.

There is a corollary to the Law of Predictability which says: 'If you want something you've never had before, you have to do something you've never done before' so recognise that you must interrupt your old habits and replace them with new ones that will permit you to build and maintain a wealthy lifestyle.

'The average American worker has fifty interruptions a day, of which seventy percent have nothing to do with work.'

W. Edwards Deming

The Interruption Strategy in Growth

The Glass Ceiling

We have seen both sides of the Interruption strategy: the blocking and deflecting side on the one hand and the permitting and flowing side on the other hand. We also saw briefly, as in Wealth above, how our own conditioning and thinking patterns can block our development.

It's like a glass ceiling that we hit as we rise but, because it is invisible, we tend to believe that life is getting in our way rather than ourselves. This is a crucial point in personal growth – don't stand in your own way. How? By not accepting setbacks as failure, but rather seeing them as experience and growth. We only fail when we don't try and we don't fail every time, so, even if you don't seem to be moving forward at all, you are actually moving. A useful saying here is: 'Frustration comes before a breakthrough, and confusion comes before understanding.' When our minds tell us we are not progressing, we are in danger of stopping ourselves and giving up. In the early days of our goal setting, this can be easy to do as we will often suffer more setbacks and may be more receptive to feelings that 'we'll never do it'. Remember and recognise that you can't control everything, and often, the harder you try, the more frustrated your attempts will be. But, if you study the AEGIS Laws as set out in the book **Warrior Wisdom** by the author, you will soon understand how to use these elemental laws that govern all our behaviours, how to work with them, and how to recognise when you are trying to work against them. Without an understanding of the elemental laws of life, we can easily fall into the trap of trying to go against the flow of nature.

When we try to go against the flow, we can stall our progress to the point of stopping altogether. Just like banging our heads against a brick wall: it's nice when we stop. The key to Interruption is therefore to prevent the interruption of our progress, but certainly to encourage the interruption of our failure and failings.

'When your work speaks for itself, don't interrupt.'
Henry J. Kaiser

Summary

The Interruption strategy is all about flow, one of the most powerful forces in your life. This strategy deals with how to create it and how to block it, how to create progress and also how to prevent it. Look for how things flow in your life and the life of others, and discover how you can combine it with the other strategies for best effect.

Interruption in Brief

1. The strategy of Interruption includes all defence and attack: to stop, block, interrupt, prevent and attack both perceived and actual threats.
2. In warfare, the Interrupt strategy was consistently used by each soldier as he blocked, deflected and intercepted the blows of his opponent with his sword or shield.
3. Blocking someone's speech and train of thought is both irritating and annoying but, when used as a weapon, it is a useful tool to get an emotional response (see Reaction).
4. Judge when to listen and when to interrupt, based on what response you want to gain or what point you wish to make.
5. Allow your partners to say their piece. To block them is to disrespect them, to judge their thoughts and opinions as being of lesser value than yours.
6. To change our behaviour is to interrupt our behaviour patterns and our habits, to ensure that we do not end up standing in our own way.
7. Use notes and alarms to keep you conscious of good habits, use motivational quotes, vision boards, videos and audio recordings so you don't interrupt your progress.
8. You must interrupt your old habits and replace them with new ones that will permit you to build and maintain a wealthy lifestyle.
9. Sometimes there's a glass ceiling that we hit as we rise but, because it is invisible, we think that it's life that is getting in our way rather than ourselves.
10. The Interruption strategy is all about flow: how to create it and how to block it, as well as how to create progress and how to prevent it.

STRATEGY NO. 18

The Timing Strategy of Pace

Definition: More Speed, Less Haste

Overview of Pace

The Law of Acceleration states: 'The control of speed is the ultimate control of any situation'. Speed provides opportunities and can either speed things up or slow them down. Speed can be fast or too fast, or it can be slow or too slow. Getting the right speed is the key; not to rush or to dawdle but to achieve the optimal speed for the situation. Determine the right speed and strive to achieve that speed, and you will become a force to be reckoned with.

> **'My life is like a speeding bullet that just hasn't hit the target yet.'**
>
> Kid Cudi

The Yin & Yang of Pace

The Yang
speed
quick
fast
sharpish
accelerate

The Yin
slow
snail's pace
decelerate
sluggish
lagging behind

The Pace Strategy in Tradition

Going Nineteen to the Dozen

'Going nineteen to the dozen' means 'going fast' and, at first glance, one might surmise, unreasonably fast. How else could you go 19 into 12? But the real meaning comes from the early days of steam power.

One of the earliest uses of steam power was to pump water out of mines, often susceptible to the build-up of water, resulting in serious problems of flooding for the miners. When a pump was working at maximum output it could pump 19,000 gallons for every 12 bushels of fuel burned. Hence the expression 'to go 19 to the dozen', which still today means 'to go at full speed'.

> *'It generally happens that assurance keeps an even pace with ability.'*
>
> Samuel Johnson

The Pace Strategy in Warfare

As Fast as Lightning

The AEGIS Law of Implementation says: 'Nothing happens until something moves' and getting there first and fastest is a key to winning in war.

Acting first, and making that action a fast one, creates a shock in your enemy which gives you the advantage (see Exploitation) that can lead to victory. Great speed is difficult for the brain to assimilate and if that speed is against you it can cause you to mis-function (see Function). Like a rabbit caught in the headlights of a car, everything happens so fast that it just freezes, neither fighting nor taking flight. Not pleasant for the rabbit but against a dangerous enemy, it is an ideal situation.

Blitzkreig – The Lightning War

In the early part of the Second World War, an apparently new strategy was implemented by German troops: the 'Blitzkreig' or lightning war.

German troops overran their enemy with ground troops, supported by tanks and air cover from the Luftwaffe. Their advance was fast and relentless, creating a momentum (see Pressure) that seemed unstoppable. This was the first time in history that such a sustained attack could be applied with such weight from both ground and air, and it packed a determination that was terrifying to witness.

In fact, the German command claimed that they did not deliberately invent the blitzkrieg strategy, but that it was simply the result of technology coming together in the most obvious way at the time. If Hitler had not procrastinated at the crucial moment, there would not have been a way out for the Allied forces on the beaches of Dunkirk. Hitler often gave orders that he would then have second thoughts about, and finally order that action be delayed (see Delay). He did so during the attack that pushed Allied forces back to the beaches of Dunkirk. The German commanding officer realised that if he did not act quickly, the Allied forces would gain a foothold in France which could block the German invasion of France. As Hitler dallied and doubted himself (see Faith), his commanders in the field knew their advantage was slipping away, so the General in charge ordered the attack anyway. However, all this happened too slowly and Hitler's delay saved the Allies, who were still forced to retreat (see Proximity) but did so with the bulk of their soldiers intact. This avoided the massive losses that swift action would have wrought on them.

Pace means speed, which is also acceleration and velocity. The Law of Acceleration says that: 'The control of speed is the ultimate control of any situation'. In war, speed can be the ultimate weapon.

To move faster than our opponent, to attack faster than he can defend, to defend faster than he can attack and to strike before he can recover, gives us an almost unbeatable advantage.

> **'In philosophy, if you aren't moving at a snail's pace, you aren't moving at all.'**
> Iris Murdoch

The Pace Strategy in Combat

Beat Them to the Punch

What makes us faster or slower than our opponent? There are a number of factors which affect speed, the two main ones are:

a) The speed of recognition
b) The speed of reaction

Some of us are born with the ability to recognise and react at a faster pace than others but, with training, we can all learn to react even faster.

Two keys to greater speed are:

a) Repetition of relevant movements
b) Movement hierarchy

Relevant movements are those movements that one feels are most likely to be needed in a given combat situation, whether weapon-based or unarmed. There are 5 types of attacks that someone might prepare for in combat:

1. Awareness that an attack could occur
2. Expected attack
3. Unexpected attack
4. Mutually agreed combat
5. You as the attacker

Once we decide what attack type is most relevant to the type of combat we are training for, we then learn and practise a system of strategies and techniques over and over, based on the assumptions of how attack and defence work in our given situation. We do this in order to build muscle memory, familiarity and reaction times so we are able to quickly recognise and respond to the combat situation that we anticipate might happen.

We practice our techniques and strategies in thin air, against targets, with cooperative opponents and then uncooperative opponents and each rehearsal will serve to build our speed as the movements become more and more familiar and efficient. Our speed will grow alongside our muscles and fitness and our movements become more automatic and second-nature.

The second part of speed is **hierarchy of movement**, which deals with the order of movement and body position. For example, in boxing the lead hand is the major weapon to initiate attacks, as it is in front of the right hand, it is closer to our opponent and, therefore, capable of reaching the target more quickly. The reasoning here is that, because the lead hand is faster than the rear, the lead hand takes priority. Another area of priority could refer to energy: a kick is slower, less agile and takes more energy than a punch, so a punch takes priority over a kick.

These are only brief examples of how to use pace in combat and it is a subject you should apply yourself to. Learn not only to develop greater speed, but also to use slower speeds, which may be equally useful, as the change of gear can be less perceptible in its own way and work in your favour.

As the Law of Acceleration states: 'The control of speed is the major control of any situation.' Especially in combat, speed is one of the major deciding factors you can have in turning the tides in your own favour. No matter how strong and powerful you might be, if you are too slow, then you will always be at a disadvantage.

'Quiet minds cannot be perplexed or frightened but go on in fortune or misfortune at their own private pace, like a clock during a thunderstorm.'
Robert Louis Stevenson

The Pace Strategy in Relationships

The Speed of the Team

Partnerships bring a source of leverage to businesses, that, when working alone, they often cannot achieve (such as in expertise, finance or connections…). Also, as long as everyone fulfils their part and the business thrives, most problems should remain small and easy to be dealt with.

If, however, one of the partners is not moving at the right speed, by failing to convert sales, complete tasks or manage staff, for instance, then the partnership will face problems. A partnership is a team, and a team needs not only to have the same goals but, crucially, move at the same pace.

This is not always easy to do, as it requires balance, and balance always has to be managed since every step we take constantly compromises it. Nevertheless, if we focus on the team itself and match its pace by fulfilling our duties when expected of us, then any temporary imbalance can be corrected quickly.

But, if we cannot match the speed of the team by either going slower or faster, then it might be best to split the relationship. This might be a pity and a costly decision, so, if you are the one going too slow and you want to save yourself and the partnership, you have to be prepared to lift your game. If, on the other hand, you are the one going at the fast speed and leaving the others in your wake, then maybe you just have to accept the disparity and slow down for the benefit of the partnership as a whole.

A team that is strongly bonded, with well-defined roles and goals and which is moving together at the same speed can be unstoppable.

'Adopt the pace of nature: her secret is patience.'
Ralph Waldo Emerson

The Pace Strategy in Friendship

The Pace of Change

Friendships can be long-standing or brand new; the time is hardly relevant as sometimes a friendship can develop very quickly if you discover rapport between yourself and a new person.

It might be that you trust the other person immediately, through being matched in type or interests, fostering a sense of having known that new friend for much longer than you have. Other friends of longer standing might be threatened by it, and this can create friction. Friends are often competitive for your affections and new friends can push older ones out of the picture, which gives you an issue to manage – and can end up with you becoming a peacekeeper. At other times, a friendship might grow gradually and increase in closeness owing to factors which heighten the trust between you both, such as being thrown together in adversity for instance.

It might be sometimes that a new 'friend' suddenly enters your life for the wrong reasons – perhaps taking advantage of your circumstances or good nature to obtain money, a space to live or something similar (see Duplicity), and so it is wise to show restraint at times in new relationships. Emotion doesn't understand pace; it only understands reaction (see Reaction). It is your intellect and logic that come into play to impose a sense of control over the speed of how quickly things happen (see Risk), not how you feel about a specific situation.

However, friendship is a real treasure and the speed that it happens at is not connected to the depth of the relationship, there is no minimum time limit on developing rapport and affection. Whether it happens quickly or slowly, and however it brings you together, it is something to hold onto and to work at keeping together.

> **'The underlying principles of strategy are enduring, regardless of technology or the pace of change.'**
> Michael Porter

The Pace Strategy Personally

The Rat Race

No two people are alike; we all move at our own pace, and sometimes that pace may be at odds with other people's personal comfort zone. At these times, we can either decide to go with the flow or resist the speed, whether it be fast or slow.

Some things, like technology for instance, seem to be moving faster than we can cope with, especially if we're older and less comfortable with it. But the pace of change around us is happening whether we can cope or not. If you live and work in a typical big city and big company, your pace of action will be particularly dictated by others – and you might thrive on that pace or you might feel like you're stuck in the rat race and just want to get out. A fast-paced life, with deadlines and targets in a cut-throat business, suits some but many, after years of merely tolerating it, manage less and less and, in time, just want to escape from it. Most people don't get the chance to slow things down until they either retire or are let go by their employer, but others do make their preparations early on to leave the fast-paced life sooner and swap it for a pace that fits with their idea of a good life.

Working to a pace that is not your own is OK for a while, but it removes your ability to choose, thereby removing your sense of freedom (see Function). However, with the right planning and action, we can change our lifestyle completely. Technology makes it possible for us to leave the office, but still work for the company, remotely, at home. We also have plenty of opportunities nowadays to set up our own businesses through Internet-based companies, franchises, and so on. Information is everywhere and cheaply available to teach us how to save and invest with a view to stepping out of the rat race early.

If you feel your life is running at someone else's pace and you're not happy with it, then know that you can change that. It is in your hands to construct an effective strategy and implement it. You don't have to put up with the pace of life you have for ever, it's up to you to synchronise its pace with yours.

'If a man does not keep pace with his companions, perhaps it is because he hears a different drummer. Let him step to the music which he hears, however measured or far away.'

Henry David Thoreau

The Pace Strategy in Health

Busy Bodies

Our bodies are the vehicles we travel in and, like any vehicle, they need to be well fuelled, carefully driven and regularly serviced. Our bodies are designed to move around and be active, and also to take sufficient adequate rest.

Too much moving around can be as bad as not enough, and it always comes back down to balance. Our hearts, as an example, beat throughout our lives. The heart, being a muscle, becomes stronger with sensible use (not too much for too long, nor too little). The strategy of Pace tells us to get our hearts pumping at a higher pace. If we do this regularly, with sufficient rest in between, gradually increasing the intensity throughout our lives and finally keeping that routine interesting so that we are motivated to keep going year after year, then we will stay as healthy as we can hope to be. This means, barring accidents and unlucky genetics, we should have a long fruitful and healthy life.

The pace of our lives can be the cause of a great deal of bad stress. To combat this, we need to fight back with our own positive stress. It's easy not to exercise or eat well, and yet our heart, organs and muscles are designed to respond to the positive stress (i.e. 'eustress') of planned exercise. By building our capacity to withstand eustress through planned exercise, rest and mediation we can also increase our ability to manage and cope with negative stress.

Use the strategy of Pace in your life by getting your heart to beat faster, stronger and more regularly, at least 3 times every week, and rest well in between. Don't push yourself too hard, nor too little, and work to get the pace of your life just right.

'Extroverts may get places faster, but for introverts it's all about working at the pace you need and, at the end of the day, performing at your best.'

Douglas Conant

The Pace Strategy in Wealth

Interesting Wealth

The secret to creating wealth is to make money faster than you spend it, and to invest the difference in a place where it will continue to grow at a faster rate than inflation: simple when you think about it!

Well, if it were, everybody would be doing it. However, it is basically as simple as that: the key is to get your money working for you, because, if you're living on earned income and just saving what's left over at the end of the month, then you'll never create the wealth you need. How does money work for you? It works by creating something that people want and will pay you for, and that you can deliver and be paid for quickly at a good profit. Once you have created some profit, you need to invest your surplus into an area that will grow your money faster than the rate of inflation. If the inflation rate is 3% and the interest on your money is 3%, then you're obviously not outstripping inflation and, therefore, your money is not working hard enough. However, if you can get 10% return on your money instead, then your money is starting to work for you, as it's growing faster than prices are rising. If you then re-invest your profit it will, through the principle of compound interest, grow even faster.

Compound interest is the secret to wealth building. For example, paper is thin – that's the nature of paper. Yet, if you fold a piece of paper in half and then fold it in half again, it will double each time. If you could fold it in half 50 times, it would be so thick that it would reach the moon!

Most of us in the West will earn over a million pounds in the 40 or so years of our working lives. The problem is that this sum will take 40 years to acquire. If we could use compounding to speed up the pace of our earnings and instead earn a million pounds in 5 or 10 years instead of 40, then our lives would change out of all recognition. No more the drudgery of the 9-5 rat race! Instead, we can have a life that goes at the pace we choose rather than the pace chosen by the company we work for.

'I returned, and saw under the sun, that the race is not to the swift.'
Ecclesiates 9:11

The Pace Strategy in Growth

Ready, Fire, Aim

Growth is about positive change, i.e. changing what you are unhappy with and becoming someone you would be happy to be. How long does it take to change? It takes the time it takes to make the decision to change.

Now your journey of change and personal development may last a lifetime, but who you become is something that grows as you do. Initially, you might just want to be less stressed or more educated for example, so you set your goals for what you want to change and by what date. When you achieve those goals, you realise that your goals have moved to another level, and so you set new goals and by what date, repeating the process over and over. There is always something that we want to change in ourselves if we wish to continue to grow, and there are so many areas of potential growth that the journey can literally take a lifetime. Also, as you progress, you will find not every goal will be about a change in you, but also changes you want to make in others and their lives.

Just because you're not where you want to be yet is irrelevant; the key is that you have begun your journey. Like going on holiday; you might not have arrived at your destination yet, but you have at least made it to the airport. With holidays, our elation begins the moment we leave the house, so why not treat ourselves to the same feeling when we decide on a challenging new goal? Achieving a goal can sometimes take time, because it involves re-conditioning habits that are often deeply ingrained. So that initial decision you make to change will, in itself, have to be made and re-made constantly.

Growth is a moving feast; the decision in itself is quick yet the journey is long. But then growth is not a sprint, it's more of a marathon and every mile achieved gives us a sense of movement forwards.

'Ambition never is in a greater hurry than I; it merely keeps pace with circumstances and with my general way of thinking.'
Napoleon Bonaparte

Summary

Fast or slow, life is about achieving results and some are quick to happen and some are slower. Often, we want things to move faster, to get to where we want to be, and, when we get there, we want things to slow down so we can appreciate them more. It's like booking a holiday; we want the time between now and the holiday to fly by, but we want the holiday to last forever. Much of your speed is out of your hands, but for those areas where you can exercise some sort of control, use that control to give yourself the edge you need to achieve your goals.

Pace Strategy in Brief

1. Getting the right pace is the key; not to rush or to dawdle but to achieve the optimal speed for the situation. Determine the right speed and achieve that speed, and you will become a force to be reckoned with.
2. Acting first, and making that action a fast one, creates a shock in your enemy that gives you the advantage that can lead to victory.
3. Some of us are born with the ability to recognise and react at a faster pace than others but, with training, we can all learn to react even faster.
4. A team that is strongly bonded, with well-defined roles and goals and which is moving together at the same pace can be unstoppable.
5. Friendship is a real treasure and, whether it happens quickly or slowly, and however it brings you together, it is something to hold onto and to work at keeping together.
6. You should never have to put up with the pace of life you have. It's up to you to synchronise its pace with yours.
7. Don't push yourself too hard, nor too little, and work to get the pace of your life just right.
8. The secret to creating wealth is to make money faster than you spend it, and to invest the difference in a place where it will continue to grow at a faster rate than inflation: simple stuff.
9. Growth is a moving feast; the decision is quick yet the journey is long. But then growth is not a sprint, it's more of a marathon and every mile achieved gives us a sense of movement forwards.
10. Much of your speed is out of your hands, but for those areas where you can exercise some sort of control, use that control to give yourself the edge you need to achieve your goals.

STRATEGY NO. 19

The Timing Strategy of Opportunity

Definition: Strike While The Iron Is Hot

Overview of Opportunity

There are times when fate or planning puts an opportunity before us, but we can really only call it an opportunity if we: (a) are in a position to act and (b) act on it. There are always opportunities around us at any given moment, some big and some small; we need to either actively look for them or create them ourselves. If you can't see them, you aren't looking hard enough. An urban myth says that the Chinese for 'challenge' and 'opportunity' is the same and one word. It's an interesting story, though sadly not accurate; because it is true that they are basically the same concept – as summed up neatly in the phrase 'every cloud has a silver lining'. We never know for sure whether a problem will bring good or bad news but we can be assured that failure to act will bring nothing.

> *'When written in Chinese, the word 'crisis' is composed of two characters. One represents danger and the other represents opportunity.'*
>
> John F. Kennedy

The Yin & Yang of Opportunity

The Yang

chance
possibility
opening
shot
crack
break
window
luck

The Yin

challenge
bad luck
hazard
disadvantage
problem
misfortune

The Opportunity Strategy in Tradition

Give Him a Break

In olden days, street performers would take a break during their acts, so they could pass round the hat for their audience to have the opportunity to give money for the performance. This was known as 'taking a break'.

In the 19th Century, the term was adopted by the criminal fraternities to help their fellow criminals recover financially on leaving prison. The friends of ex-convicts would pass round a hat to their group who would drop coins in to help, so that the ex-convict had some funding to live on after being set free.

'Discourage litigation. Persuade your neighbours to compromise whenever you can. As a peacemaker the lawyer has superior opportunity of being a good man. There will still be business enough.'

Abraham Lincoln

The Opportunity Strategy in Warfare

Don't Miss a Trick

Abraham Lincoln once famously said: 'I will prepare myself and one day my chance will come.' In warfare, we are constantly faced with challenges that can become opportunities, so we should ask ourselves: What is the difference between the two?

Put simply, a challenge is what you are unprepared for and an opportunity is what you are prepared for. Either can morph into its opposite depending on what you do when you face them. The AEGIS Law of Launch Point says 'Ready, Steady… Go!' and represents that perfect converging point at which preparation meets readiness. Being in the right launch point can often be the decisive factor in turning a potential challenge into a welcome opportunity. In warfare more than anywhere else, one must be prepared and ready to act, without delay.

Chinese Strategy No. 12 – Lead Away the Sheep When Conditions Are Right

The 12th of the ancient Chinese strategies deals with taking advantage of the smallest opportunity when it is presented. Battle is a situation where many single acts of combat play out concurrently, and the outcome of each individual combat added together often defines the result of the overall battle. The outcome of any battle is, therefore, subject to not just one chance, but hundreds and possibly thousands of chances which come together to create either victory or defeat. It is for this reason that we don't know what result any single opportunity will bring, and that we must, in war at least, take any and every opportunity that is presented to us.

The Battle of Agincourt

The Battle of Agincourt in 1415 was a famous victory for the English, and is often depicted as being won by the might of the English archers, who were accurate, fast and out of reach (see Target, Pace and Proximity). However, the truth is rather different and victory actually came through the French failing to exploit the situation the English Army was in (see Exploitation).

The English soldiers were tired after marching over 260 miles back toward Calais, yet the French failed to turn the English exhaustion to their advantage. The English archers were indeed skilful with the longbow, but the site that the French army chose, to prevent the English withdrawal to Calais, gave the English an opportunity which they exploited to the full. The French blocked the English along a narrow strip of land bordered by trees which created a channel along which the French soldiers could advance and destroy the smaller and fatigued English. However, the land between the two adversaries had recently been ploughed and on top of that, it had rained heavily overnight. The French pressed forward through the muddy fields, hemmed in on either side by trees; the French foot soldiers' every step was heavy in the thick mud and the press of the tight rows of soldiers meant they could not move backwards or manoeuvre very well (see Proximity and Manoeuvre). The English archers rained down their deadly arrows on the French and those who made it through had to navigate the mud and their fallen comrades. So bogged down were the French with heavy armour, their dead and the deep mud, and forced forward by the press of those behind their numbers, that they could barely take full steps in their advance toward the English. The English Men at Arms faced them directly, awaiting their 'tired steps' (see Energy) whilst the English archers placed at each flank made short work of the French forces.

The English won the day and the rest is history. The English were considerably outnumbered (see Recruitment) and had marched 260 miles over the preceding few weeks (see Energy); they were tired and many were ill with dysentery but a fortuitous set of circumstances turned the tide in their favour.

'Ability is nothing without opportunity.'
Napoleon Bonaparte

The Opportunity Strategy in Combat

Rise to the Challenge

Every move in combat creates an opportunity and a challenge for one of the protagonists. An opportunity for one side is very often a challenge for the other.

Martial artists create opportunities through their training and conditioning over many years of study; their constant practice is a rehearsal for when life gives them an opportunity to use those skills for real. If and when that opportunity does come, it will challenge the quality of their practice and what many martial artists forget is that what they have learned may not be what they need.

What does this mean? It means that many martial arts systems do not teach self-defence; they teach a tradition, a history of what they think the ancient masters practised and which, for them, has become the truth. What they fail to understand is the difference between a tradition, i.e. a ritual and a history, and a practical system of self-defence. These two things – tradition and efficiency – are definitely not the same thing, yet most martial arts styles continue to teach ancient techniques against outdated weapons (e.g. the 6ft Bo staff, the sword, halberd, sai, nunchaku etc.), focusing only on repeating what they have been taught instead of what is necessary in the modern world of flick knives, hand guns, tasers and Mace. Instructors create scenarios based on what rarely happens, rather than what often happens. Which is why we often end up seeing defences used against silly wrist grabs, frontal chokes and so on... many practiced at inaccurate ranges. What many martial artists practice to make themselves better combatants is often going to provide an unwelcome challenge to them, if they are ever faced with a life or death situation.

In order to keep growing and bettering your martial arts study, you must constantly challenge what you know, to assess its 'relevance'. Ask yourself: Is what I practise going to be relevant for the combat I might find myself in? What is the type of attack I might face, in what situations, and in which places?

Remember that combat is simple and that your approach should be so too. To be able to defend yourself takes 5 key things, represented by the acronym *F.A.S.T.R* which stands for:

- *Fit* – aerobic fitness to last for as long as necessary to beat the threat
- *Aggressive* – that attitude of 'no quit' and harnessed anger and emotion
- *Strong* – the physical ability to meet strong or stronger opponents
- *Training* – conditioned techniques, reflexes and strategies
- *Relevance* – training which fits the situations you are likely to meet

If you are strong but not fit, you might run out of steam (see Energy). No matter how skilled you are, if you can't go the distance, you are severely disadvantaged. If you are not aggressive (for this read **VERY** motivated to protect yourself), you will lack the necessary will and controlled anger to put fear into your foe (see Toughness and Appearance). If you are strong in body and will, you can also maximise even small opportunities that are available to you. Finally, if your training is not relevant, you might find that you have turned up to a gun fight armed only with a knife. The way most systems teach martial arts would mean the quick demise of most Masters who put tradition before efficiency. Consider how the archers of Agincourt would have fared if the French had been armed with modern day SA80 Assault Rifles... Combat, like life, progresses; technology improves and so combat must adapt to meet ever changing circumstances. Sadly, in the martial arts, the student rarely challenges, questions or tests what he has been taught.

Consider very carefully what it takes to become effective in your martial arts practice; accept nothing at face value, challenge and test everything. This is the only way to create opportunities and defy challenges in combat.

> **'The good fighters of old first put themselves beyond the possibility of defeat, and then waited for an opportunity of defeating the enemy.'**
> Sun Tzu

The Opportunity Strategy in Relationships

Opportunity Knocks

There is a saying which goes: 'If you have two people in your team that agree on everything, fire one of them'. Teams thrive on cooperation, but they must also be able to air their views openly and to conflict with the group.

Relationships thrive on agreement, but they can also grow through disagreement. Conflict breeds growth. Conflict is a challenge and an opportunity; if we avoid challenge we also avoid opportunity, as they are two sides of the same coin – they are yin and yang. Every invention, discovery and innovation has been the result of a challenge which was turned into an opportunity. Every failing in one area has created an improvement in another area and so we must work on our relationships with this in mind.

We cannot get on with our team and partners all the time and it's impractical to think we can. But, just because we cannot always agree, does not mean the relationship cannot work. We have to work at our relationships, face the challenges and work to overcome them; we have to take a mature attitude and commit to making it work rather than just jumping ship at every challenge. A team is based on the Alignment and Recruitment strategies which are based on cooperation, and building that cooperation into opportunities. Strength comes from this unity, but we must expect challenges; the key to managing them is to consider the strength that comes through bringing a variety of opinions and experiences to the team.

Put your ego aside and look to a bigger future through the relationships you belong to and the opportunities you can create together.

'A pessimist sees the difficulty in every opportunity; an optimist sees the opportunity in every difficulty.'
Winston Churchill

The Opportunity Strategy in Friendship

A Window of Opportunity

Friendship is always a responsibility of trust, expectation, reliability and affection; so is it true that it does not also present opportunities, as Gibran suggests below? Friendship is a complicated issue and can be demanding at times, more of a challenge than an opportunity – but why should that be?

To start with, in order to be a good friend, we have to be there when our friends are having challenges in their lives, to support and comfort them. It may also be that we need to help them recognise where opportunities lie too. It can seem like an uphill struggle at times, trying to lift a friend who may not only be down, but resistant to being lifted up again. But it should not all be one way traffic, because being a friend means that we should be able to call on our friends in the same way. Such is the nature of true friendship and this support is one of the greatest opportunities that friendship brings.

It can be invaluable when we are so entangled in our own problems that we are unable to see the wood for the trees, and a good opportunity could be missed. In that case, a friend distanced somewhat from the situation could be just the advisor needed to push us on or steer us away.

Friendship can indeed provide many challenges but true friendship will also bring far more opportunities through the strength of its unity and support.

> *'Friendship is always a sweet responsibility, never an opportunity.'*
> Khalil Gibran

The Opportunity Strategy Personally

Make the Break

Opportunities and challenges are all around us, but so often we hear people declaring how bad their lives are or how bad the government is, or how bad the weather is, or how cruel their spouses are...

If we listen to the naysayers, we'll never get anything done, as they always know the reason why we shouldn't do something and none of the reasons why we should. Oscar Wilde once said 'a cynic knows the price of everything and the value of nothing' and, whilst we can all have times of anger and complaint, in the main, we must hold ourselves and our pessimism in check. Without this, life will only ever bring us challenges that we cannot overcome, and none of the opportunities that we can harness.

People who complain about their lives are not open to the opportunities that exist all around them, and they also won't see or support the opportunities that surround you either. It can be that these people put the dampers on your goals and dreams to the point where you might have to cut their negative influence from your life. Unfortunately, some of these negative people might be close relatives, which is doubly upsetting, but nonetheless, if you have someone close to you who is an emotional vampire and sees a challenge in every opportunity then cutting them from your life can be an absolute necessity. Do it quickly and don't look back. In fact, you'll soon find that you won't miss them; quite the contrary, you'll probably feel like a weight has been lifted from you.

Either way, as you rise to the opportunities that you find and create on your journey, the negative people will naturally be left behind. Remember it is their choice; they could come with you if they changed their mind set. It is their opportunity, if they choose to take it.

*'Don't worry when you are not recognized,
but strive to be worthy of recognition.'*
Abraham Lincoln

The Opportunity Strategy in Health

No Such Thing as Coincidence

What is the challenge with good health? First, the benefits are often not seen for weeks, months and even years. We may get to the end of our lives and realise that we have lived long, healthily and happily, and even then not know for sure if this is because of our healthy lifestyle or just down to good luck.

There are those who say there is no such thing as luck or that we make our own luck through good habits and attitudes. Luck is opportunity, and it is certainly true that we create our own opportunities and challenges, so it seems, by the same token, that we must also create our own luck. If we agree that luck is, to a certain extent, self-created through our actions, it must, therefore, be something that can be manipulated by us. And hard work appears to be the crucial factor; hard work in the form of not only physical, but also mental application. In fact, our mental abilities are likely to be in better shape at the end of our lives than our physical abilities, which tend to deteriorate more quickly. We might be lucky to be blessed with good genes that grant us a long and healthy life no matter our lifestyle, but why take the chance? Why not take the opportunities to learn how to be healthy and how to maintain that health throughout our lives, from the knowledge readily available all around us, in books and videos, and easily accessible from the World Wide Web?

Why miss the opportunities provided by this amazing information age, just to avoid the brief challenge of getting up early to go to the gym or to choose food that takes time to acquire a taste for, in favour of the quick-to-eat salt and sugar-filled packet food that has little nutritional value but is easy to find, cook and eat?

'Opportunity is missed by most people because it is dressed in overalls and looks like work.'

Thomas A. Edison

The Opportunity Strategy in Wealth

Don't Miss the Boat

Louis B. Mayer once said: 'The harder I work the luckier I get', suggesting that luck or opportunity is something we create ourselves, instead of what most people seem to think, which is that opportunities are something which just occur randomly and externally to us. If we can make our own opportunities then it follows that life is full of opportunities as long as we are open to recognising them.

The Law of Study states: 'The more you know, the easier it is to know more.' This links to what Sun Tzu observed, in that the more we educate ourselves and acquire knowledge, methods and systems, and the more able we are to recognise similarities and likenesses in other areas. Because most things, no matter how different they may seem initially, respond to the same laws of life and are based on the same foundation, with experience it becomes easier to see their similarities. How does this relate to wealth? To build wealth, it is necessary to recognise that the opportunity to attain wealth is all around us, and the more we explore and create wealth, the more we will recognise further opportunities that are similar.

The saying goes that 'the rich get richer and the poor get poorer', which is true somehow because the richer you get, the more opportunities you create and the fewer challenges you encounter. 'Every cloud has a silver lining' is the adage of the rich because they always find the seed of something good in even the greatest of challenges. Being poor is an attitude: the poor are poor because they fail to see the opportunities and only see the challenges.

The biggest difference between the rich and the poor is not money, but how they think. The Law of Attitude states: 'it's our attitude, not our aptitude that determines our altitude' and this law is the bedrock of all success, wealth included.

'Opportunities multiply as they are seized.'
Sun Tzu

The Opportunity Strategy in Growth

Carpe Diem

'When life hands you lemons, make lemonade.' This saying was first credited to Elbert Hubbard in 1915 and has been modified since into its current succinct form, telling us to make the most of what we have.

Our growth as individuals is the application of this saying, taking the lemons we are given (the challenges) and turning them into lemonade (opportunities). We have discussed at length the nature of opportunity and its opposite, challenge, but always bear in mind that an opportunity and a challenge are one and the same: 'one man's meat is another man's poison'. How does this work for our growth? It works by recognising that what you have may not be what you want in terms of job, career, home, car and happiness, but within all of that can be found your opportunity, the seeds of your success. You have skills already in your hands, developed through your experiences to date, and those skills are your potential. Education, experience, physical or mental gifts, the knowledge of what you both love and hate and that certain thing that you are passionate about and pursue out of love: these are your opportunities.

Your present challenge is having a life or lifestyle that you don't always enjoy, and your opportunity lies within what you already know. Your opportunity lies within your dissatisfaction because all growth is born of discomfort and pain – and you must feel that already or you wouldn't be reading this book.

Look at your life critically; examine all that you have and all that you want. Regret none of the experiences, take responsibility for all that has happened, both good and bad, and recognise that, if you are responsible for getting to this point so far, then you also have the power to get to the point where you really want to be. All that you have has occurred through choice, some of it good and some of it bad. However, if you learn to identify the bad choices and eradicate them and recognise the good choices and repeat them, then you will have created a new opportunity which is this: you are the writer, designer, producer, director and star of your life. You have all the control over what you do and in that potential lies great power (see Energy).

This recognition and acceptance of responsibility can be the most empowering thing you can learn and, potentially, your greatest opportunity in life.

'*I will prepare and someday my chance will come.*'
Abraham Lincoln

Summary

The Law of Recognition states: 'You can only respond to a challenge or opportunity if you recognise that there is one'. The good news is that there is always a challenge and always an opportunity present somewhere, and sometimes an opportunity can turn out to be a challenge and sometimes a challenge can turn out to be an opportunity in disguise. The only way to find out which is which, is to assess and then act.

Opportunity Strategy in Brief

1. The Law of Recognition states: 'You can only respond to a challenge or opportunity if you recognise that there is one.'
2. In warfare, more than anywhere else, one must be prepared and ready to act without delay.
3. We cannot know in advance what result any single opportunity will bring, which is why we must, in war, take any and every opportunity that is presented to us.
4. Every move in combat creates an opportunity and a challenge for one of the protagonists. An opportunity for one side is a challenge for the other.
5. Accept nothing at face value: challenge and test everything. This is the only way to create opportunities and defy challenges in life and combat.
6. Friendship can provide many challenges, but true friendship will bring far more opportunities through the strength of its unity and support.
7. Rise to the opportunities that you find on your journey; leave negative people behind. They can join you when they change their mind set.
8. If we agree that luck is self-created through our actions, it must then also be something that can be manipulated by us through hard work and good attitude.
9. The Law of Attitude states: 'It's our attitude, not our aptitude that determines our altitude.' This law is the bedrock of all success in health, wealth and growth.
10. The recognition and acceptance of personal responsibility is the most empowering lesson you can learn in life and is also, potentially, your greatest opportunity.

STRATEGY NO. 20

The Timing Strategy of Delay

Definition: Play for Time

Overview of Delay

Time waits for no one and yet no one wants to be rushed, though there are often times where we want to rush others, or they us. There are times when we must slow things down so that they move at our pace rather than the pace of an enemy or other exterior circumstance. The Law of Acceleration states: 'the control of speed is the greatest control of any situation' and in warfare we must move at a speed that is often the opposite of what our opponent needs. Speed is a powerful weapon, it can be constant or variable, fast or slow, predictable or surprising and we can be prepared for it or completely taken aback by it. Delay (and its opposite: Immediacy) deals with the management of speed. Delay can be part of an important tactic to create anticipation, which is a powerful tool in drawing a response (see Attraction) from an opponent as well as a friend. Never underestimate the power of Delay and its ruling Law of Timing: 'The greater part of all success is in its Timing.' The prize does not always go to the fastest, sometimes a slower pace is what is needed in order to win the race.

> *'Truth is confirmed by inspection and delay; falsehood by haste and uncertainty.'*
>
> Tacitus

The Yin & Yang of Delay

The Yang

postpone
put off
defer
retard
wait
hold
pause
dampen
stall

The Yin

hurry
rush
speed up
act
go
just do it
quicken

The Delay Strategy in Tradition

Hang Fire

The musket became popular during the 17th Century as a battle weapon, but it had an issue: there was a delay between pulling the trigger and it actually firing, owing to the time it took for the fuse to ignite the gunpowder. This worrying pause became known as 'hang fire'. When an enemy charged forward toward them, newer recruits would often panic and fire too early, losing their advantage (see Exploitation). Soon, the phrase came into common usage as an instruction from officers to their soldiers, to hold off action and delay a while before the attack. Today the phrase 'hang fire' means to wait before taking action in order to get the timing just right.

'A right delayed is a right denied.'
Martin Luther King, Jr.

The Delay Strategy in Warfare

Penelope and Odysseus

The 36 ancient Chinese strategies of war do not have any specific reference to the strategy of delay, so this illustration of the tactic was drawn from Greek Mythology instead, specifically 'The Odyssey' by Homer. Odysseus, the hero of Troy, was delayed for 10 years after the fall of his city. During the absence of Odysseus, his wife Penelope was besieged by suitors who believed Odysseus to be dead and pressed her for a decision to re-marry. Penelope knew that, in her position, she may be forced to take on a new husband, but held the faith (see Faith) that her husband would return, despite his 20 year absence, and she determined to delay her suitors' advances for as long as she could.

Penelope managed to keep them at bay for many years by claiming that she would make her decision once she had completed weaving a tapestry in honour of Laertes, the father of Odysseus. Each day she would weave the tapestry and each night she would undo her work, so that the tapestry was never finished. She kept this up for 3 years – until her suitors discovered her secret and forced her to make her decision. She agreed to marry the suitor who could string Odysseus's bow and fire an arrow through 12 axe heads. Unbeknown to anyone, by that point, Odysseus had returned, disguised as a beggar. He proved to be the only one who could string and fire the bow, first hitting the target, and then killing all the suitors.

> **'Delay is preferable to error.'**
> Thomas Jefferson

GAME PLAN

The Delay Strategy in Combat

Bide Your Time

We can delay fighting and we can delay in fighting. Both give us time to prepare, to think and to plan, but they can also be tactics used to psych out an opponent.

In competition fighting, such as boxing, an opponent may delay his entry into the arena, leaving his adversary waiting as a way to build tension and demonstrate disrespect, making his opponent emotional. The famous Japanese swordsman Miyamoto Musashi was considered the finest in all Japan in the 16th Century, in a country which adhered to strict codes of behaviour and etiquette. One of Musashi's favourite strategies was to arrange a duel at an appointed time, and then show up very late. This showed great disrespect and, consequently, when Musashi finally arrived, his opponent was angry and stressed. Musashi would take immediate advantage (see Exploitation) of his opponent's emotional upset to gain quick victories, often by arriving late and rushing suddenly straight at his opponent. At other times, Musashi would hide nearby, biding his time for the moment when he calculated his opponent would be at his most vulnerable (see Exploitation). Musashi mixed his delay tactics with its opposite – which is to rush in without formality – and was considered a master of sword strategy in his time.

'You may delay, but time will not.'
Benjamin Franklin

The Delay Strategy in Relationships

Take a Time Out

The strategy of Delay is a useful tactic in relationships and partnerships as a method to get what you want, not only for yourself but also for your partners. Sometimes, it is the ability to walk away when angry or upset and sometimes to leave someone 'hanging', waiting for a decision or result, as in playing the 'waiting game'.

In a marriage, this second kind of tactic should be avoided if you want a good relationship, but in business negotiations, it is a valuable tool providing you can control your emotions well enough and have the leverage necessary to back up your delay.

Using delay to take time to cool off, so you don't do or say something rash in a relationship, is a wise approach to prevent yourself from doing or saying something that you might regret; hence the saying 'bite your tongue', meaning 'prevent yourself from saying something that might end up damaging you'.

Delay is the control of emotion. Emotion has only two choices: move toward or move away. The Law of Emotion says 'Emotion is the fuel that drives motion' and, whilst we often feel that long lasting relationships thrive on emotion, this is not often true. A long and successful relationship doesn't thrive on emotion; it thrives in spite of emotion. Certainly, there are times of great joy and sorrow in all relationships, but the best relationships survive these times of extreme emotions, particularly if one partner is up when the other is down. Relationships are not built on emotion, they are based on passion. Not the passion we associate with new relationships filled with infatuation. True passion is long lasting and much deeper than emotion, and it is built on deeper ties and bonds which sustain a long relationship. A key to a successful relationship, the strategy of Delay is a major tool for success, helping us to overcome the dangerous emotions that could at times destroy it.

Delayed gratification is a tool to excite the emotions and a loving relationship between partners can use this to spice up their romance. In times of stress though, we can also use this as a way to delay (possibly indefinitely) saying anything that might be regretted later – or which might benefit from being phrased differently or more carefully. Delaying our emotional responses can sometimes be just the right thing to do if we want to keep the peace or consider the best response.

'Never let the sun set on an argument.'

Ephesians

The Delay Strategy in Friendship

Bite Your Tongue

We discussed earlier, in the Focus strategies, the tactic of 'Reaction' – which is to rouse an opponent to an emotional and unthinking response which can be used to our advantage.

The opposite of reaction is no reaction, and one way this manifests itself is in delaying action. This is not an easy thing to do when our blood is up after we have been emotionally hurt, insulted or harbouring a feeling of being wronged in some way. But one of our greatest weapons in these situations is to delay our actions. We are sometimes riled to action (and some of us more than others). Some people are emotionally based, that is their major intelligence, their main way of dealing with life is through their emotions. This can be a real curse as we are then at the whim of our feelings, and feelings, while valuable, are not always right. Feelings can bring us great joy and great pain, neither of which are objective or necessarily brought about by real things.

For instance, we may feel great pain at a story spread by the gossip of a duplicitous individual. The story may be untrue but the pain felt is real. Therefore, it is our thoughts about that story, and not the story itself, that hurt us, since the story spread was untrue. Furthermore, the situation might have been going on for a while before we realised what was happening. Our emotions were changed only when we learnt about the event (the duplicity of our friend), not about the event unfolding. So all the upset and pain we feel is not actually related to the event itself but to our interpretation of this event. Oftentimes, the best action is response rather than reaction. Response means to act thoughtfully, and thought takes time; therefore, to respond implies to delay our reaction. As a friend, we must sometimes be the delay that our friend needs and come between them and their reaction to save them from themselves.

In negotiations, part of the tactics may be to rile an adversary with inflammatory remarks and accusations. But the experienced negotiator knows these tactics well and also the importance of biting his tongue, focusing instead on his goal, and not being prepared to be distracted (see Direction) away from it. There are even times in negotiations when the two protagonists cannot even be allowed to sit in the same room – their cause being so volatile – and a mediator will travel between the two, delaying the eventual meeting of both until such time as common ground has been established and anger has subsided. If you can hold your emotions in check under pressure you can secure great results.

'The greatest remedy for anger is delay.'
Thomas Paine

The Delay Strategy Personally

Breathing Space

Time waits for no man, but sometimes we need a bit of breathing space. Consider those times when we are under pressure, we are in danger of collapse or have an important decision to make but fear making it because the time doesn't feel right, or we have access to insufficient information to make a balanced decision.

At times like these, we can deliberately slow things down until we can make our move with more confidence. To delay takes either courage or confidence (see Faith). As with Patience, delay can be difficult to maintain and choosing the right time to take action could still result in error. The key to calculating delay is to position yourself well, and if that means slowing things down, then so be it. Don't be pushed into decisions that you are not comfortable with making yet. Stick to your guns but also examine your motives. Is your delay a strategic delay or is it just fear of making your decision? There is an important distinction to make between delay and avoidance, so consider this carefully when using delay. Avoidance is the opposite of Fight in 'fight or flight' and its purpose may be to avoid conflict altogether. This can be an intentional decision but it can also be symptomatic of your inability to function (see Function) and reach a decision. You cannot delay for ever and avoid problems altogether. The Delay strategy relies in taking a step back and optimising the time available in order to reach an informed decision on what to do next. It is almost always followed by some form of action. Avoidance means refusing to confront the issue and managing not to make a decision. Both of those can be used efficiently to help us deal with difficult problems but they are not interchangeable and it is important to realise when we're acting either rationally or out of fear.

To delay takes belief in a definite course of action (see Faith) and discipline to carry it out, but the breathing space provided can be invaluable. You will soon find that others who pushed for fast action will, in hindsight, recognise the power of the Delay strategy.

'Indecision and delays are the parents of failure.'
George Canning

The Delay Strategy in Health

No Time like the Present

Taking care of our health is not something to put off until later. Unfortunately, it doesn't work like the Christian idea of deathbed repentance where one can repent one's sins and go straight to heaven redeemed. There is no shortcut, no last minute redemption and no instant magic pill to radiant health.

If we develop a heart condition, cancer, or a stroke, it can be partly a hereditary condition which can't be avoided, but it also might be a condition that is exacerbated by our lifestyle choices. The right amount of exercise keeps our bodies and hearts strong, as does good diet but, let's face it, bad food and a lazy lifestyle is much easier to come by.

Delaying an effective health regime is easy to do because the effects of bad diet and lack of exercise may not be seen for many years. So, if we delay making changes to our poor regime because the effects are only evident over the long term, we end up compounding two dangerous factors. In the short term we can appear to be invincible, but in the long term the effects will become manifest – often at a time in our lives when we are most able to enjoy what we have worked to achieve since we have more time and less stress in our life, yet we are thwarted in enjoying the fruits of our labours by the onset of painful ill-health.

The solution is to use strategic thinking to plan for both the short and the long term. To 'smell the roses as we pass by' is important, but too much time spent on immediate gratification, rather than a healthy mix of both immediate and delayed rewards, can bring unwanted results in later life. This is not to say that we should delay bad habits now to start them again when we retire (some habits should be delayed forever). It is often true that 'a little of what you fancy, does you good' and sometimes thinking as such will still allow us to retain good future health. Think beyond the immediate pleasure of the easy life and, instead, instil discipline to allow you to enjoy the benefits in both the short and the long term. The key is to delay ill-health indefinitely by taking health action immediately.

The good news is that you will soon function better, mentally and physically, today by being fitter, less stressed and sleeping better, so you can benefit at both ends of the spectrum: today and tomorrow.

> **'Procrastination is the thief of time.'**
> Charles Dickens

The Delay Strategy in Wealth

Quick, Quick, Slow

We should always be aware of the duality of the 25 Game Plan strategies, of how they cut both ways, each having their direct opposites as well as their middle ground.

This is a key point to understanding strategy and, by implication, being able to get the life you want. To create wealth, you need both sides of the Delay strategy to work for you:

1. Don't delay building wealth. True wealth accumulation is not a lottery; winning is the application of a system which takes some time and works step by step.
2. Any step that is rushed or missed could result in losses that will set you back, so take action when it is needed.
3. Delay where necessary. Make 'due diligence' your watchword and 'research' your habit; take the steps necessary to study the system and stick to it.
4. Don't delay for too long when there is an opportunity – or you might miss it (see Opportunity and Exploitation).
5. If you do want to rush in because you get emotional or have a hunch, limit your potential losses by limiting your level of investment – in short, don't risk big money (see Risk).

The key to wealth relies on both sides of the Delay strategy, so use it wisely, seeking the balance between the immediate and the eventual; the now and the later. Recognise that some of your wealth actions will pay you now and others will pay you later, and learn to understand when to rush in and when to hold back. As stated before, the key is the control of emotion. No matter how much we might want something to happen straight away, in the long term we learn much more through delay. Sometimes, we are just not ready for the success that we desire. If we were as successful immediately as we felt we deserved, we wouldn't understand the process enough to be able to repeat it again successfully.

Consider also the power of anticipation over participation; anticipation keeps us motivated and excited toward our goals and participation gives us the experience and judgement to be able to appreciate them when they are achieved. The AEGIS Law of Judgement says: 'Good judgement comes through experience, and experience comes through bad judgement.' We often have to get things wrong before we know how to get them right and certainly, in this way, a little delay can do us the world of good.

'Never put off until tomorrow what can be done today.'
Lord Chesterfield

The Delay Strategy in Growth

Take Your Time

Personal growth and development is an on-going and never-ending process; so how does the strategy of Delay fit with this since personal development is not something to delay or to rush, but it is something to pursue and persevere with?

We must persevere through those times where our progress seems delayed (as it often will) and make the most of those times when everything seems to be happening for us quickly. As with so much in life, we sometimes push and push without success for ages and then, suddenly, we break through, like flood gates opening up. It's like a beneficial equivalent of the 'straw that broke the camel's back'. It's easy in these times to think that our last pushes were the ones that counted the most as they were the ones just before the breakthrough, when in fact the breakthrough is an accumulation of all the pushes we've been making from the very beginning.

We are all impatient for success, but it will come in its own time – often, when success comes too early, we waste the opportunity we are offered because in fact we are not ready for it (even though at the time we might think that we are ready). Delay is self-discipline, self-belief and courage (see Faith), especially when it is implemented for the first time in a situation where you don't know what the outcome will be or when you might be seen as weak or procrastinating.

It's easy to rush in – and sometimes that is what is necessary. The Law of Implementation states: 'Nothing happens until something moves', but there are two sides to this law too: action and deliberate inaction. The Taoists have the concept of 'wu wei', which is the action of no action; the decision to act or not to act. Consider the deliberate use of in-action. Is this not the implementation of the Delay strategy? This interaction of action and non-action is a concept that you should apply yourself to with some diligence, as it will reveal both the elemental and spiritual levels that lead to deep understanding of strategy and its application in your life.

However, the difficulty arises when we kid ourselves into thinking we are delaying action, when, in fact, we are simply afraid to act. This is a key difference to identify in yourself if you want to move forward and progress. Beware of your own motivation and also, where applicable, the motives of others. Remember that all motivation is biologically based on the concept of 'fight or flight', either moving towards or moving away from something.

We must use the Delay strategy for the right reasons, when it is necessary and applicable, but never for reasons of unexamined emotions, whether they be fear or desire.

'Fools rush in where angels fear to tread.'
Alexander Pope

Summary

As we study and examine each of the strategies, we can see how they interact and connect with each other. Delay is an important law in that it deals with action, choice (see **Warrior Wisdom** by the author) and judgement. Consider and examine where Delay fits in and supports the other strategies.

Delay Strategy in Brief

1. There are times when we must slow things down so that they move at our pace and not the speed of an enemy or other exterior circumstance.
2. In competition, such as boxing, an opponent may delay his entry into the arena, leaving his adversary waiting to build tension and show disrespect, making him emotional.
3. Response means to act thoughtfully. Thought takes time, therefore, to respond implies to delay one's reaction.
4. To delay takes belief in a specific course of action and the discipline to carry it out. The breathing space provided can be invaluable.
5. Delaying our emotional responses can sometimes be just the right thing to do if we want to keep the peace or consider the best response.
6. Think beyond the immediate pleasure of the easy life and, instead, instil discipline to allow you to enjoy the benefits in both the short and the long term.
7. We often have to get things wrong before we know how to get them right and certainly, in this way, a little delay can do us the world of good.
8. We must use the Delay strategy for the right reasons, when it is necessary and applicable, but never for reasons of unexamined emotions.
9. Delay is an important strategy in that it deals with action, choice and judgement. Consider and examine where Delay fits in and supports the other strategies.
10. If you delay for too long, you might miss your window of opportunity (see Opportunity). Others will accuse you of procrastinating when you delay, but don't react (see Reaction); stay strong and see your plan through till the end.

EXPECTATION STRATEGIES

'You Don't Get What You Want or Wish For. You Only Get What You Confidently Expect' The AEGIS Law of Expectation

Expectation

Expectation strategies deal with both the expected and the unexpected, including the predictable and the unpredictable. In strategy we plan for the expected, but we must also plan for the unexpected. Even though what is unexpected cannot often be predicted exactly, we must expect that what we cannot foresee can and will happen. Expectation teaches us to always have a plan B.

The 5 strategies of Expectation are:

1. *Duplicity* – creating intentionally deceitful expectations
2. *Appearance* – managing how we appear to others
3. *Toughness* – managing the expectation of strength and weakness
4. *Expectation* – managing predictability and expectation
5. *Proximity* – managing expectations of distance in space and time

Expectation strategies deal with what is happening now and what might happen in the future. They teach us to remain vigilant and conscious of appearances, events and of our proximity to them.

STRATEGY NO. 21

The Expectation Strategy of Duplicity

Definition: The Sword Behind the Smile

Overview of Duplicity

There are times when we tell the truth and times when we lie. To mislead someone is usually seen as a bad thing and honesty as a good thing, yet between the two are many shades of grey. We can sometimes lie for good reasons just as we can be honest for wrong reasons. Use duplicity to get what you want, but remember to let your principles guide your motives.

> *'The people to fear are not those who disagree with you, but those who disagree with you and are too cowardly to let you know.'*
>
> Napoleon Bonaparte

The Yin and Yang of Duplicity

The Yang

fraudulence
deception
misrepresentation
deceit
misleading
falsehood
double-dealing
dissimulation
deception
dissembling

The Yin

honesty
candour
straightforwardness
trustworthy
openness
sincerity
frankness
truthfulness

The Duplicity Strategy in Tradition

Having Your Leg Pulled

This phrase, meaning to be the butt of another's joke or jest, has macabre beginnings and, according to Albert Jack's book **Red Herrings and White Elephants** relates back to Scotland in 1867 and a lady known as Old Meg. Meg, it seems, had been wrongfully arrested and tried for a crime she did not commit, being the victim of deceit and treachery. Meg was hanged as a result. In those days, the drop was often insufficient to kill a convicted criminal instantly and consequently, the hanged could suffer a horrible death through slow strangulation. The presiding priest helped innocent Meg on her way by pulling on her legs so that she didn't suffer too much. This practice was quite common at the time. In this instance even a rhyme was composed to commemorate Meg's hastened death:

'He preached and at last pulled the auld body's leg,
sae the Kirk got the gatherins o' our Aunty Meg.'

For ever after, the deceit which Meg suffered and for which she was hanged has been remembered as 'having one's leg pulled.'

'It is discouraging how many people are shocked by honesty and how few by deceit.'

Noel Coward

The Duplicity Strategy in Warfare

All's Fair in Love and War

It is important in conflict to never allow your enemy to know your real intentions, as to do so gives him power over you. Imagine if he knew your plans, your secrets and your weaknesses; what damage could he do? Also, imagine what you could do to him with that same knowledge!

The Duplicity strategy works by appearing to be his friend (see Appearance), smiling to his face while you 'stab him in the back', but hiding your duplicity for as long as you can so you can betray him again. Keep your purpose hidden and work secretly from within his organisation, creating problems and dissension even to the point of directly sabotaging his plans.

Almost every nation in the world has spies in every other country that it either fears or admires. These agents work from within, collecting information that will help their own government. It is dangerous work of course because, whilst we all use spies and admire our own, we hate and despise enemy spies and, when we catch them, we tend to treat them in the worst way possible. Spies are only soldiers, just like those who wear a uniform and carry a gun, but the fact that they build relationships with the adversary and then betray that relationship means they inflict the deepest cut of all.

Chinese Strategy No. 10 – The Sword behind the Smile

The ancient Chinese called this tenth strategy 'the sword behind the smile'. We call it by many names: double crossing, double dealing, spying, lying, cheating and the like. The strategy of 'the sword behind the smile' utilises several of the FLITE strategies, such as Alignment, Recruitment (of information) and, of course, Duplicity. It can use many more still, depending upon the depth and intricacy of the strategy.

Don't be afraid to use Duplicity; it can be a wonderful strategy in combat, business, relationships and war, and always be aware that it might also be being used *against* you. Don't be drawn into paranoia (see Confidence); just exercise a healthy skepticism.

'He who knows how to flatter also knows how to slander.'
Napoleon Bonaparte

The Duplicity Strategy in Combat

Dishonesty is the Best Policy

Combat is conflict and conflict thrives on deception. The greatest deception is duplicity, i.e. saying one thing by either word or deed, when in fact the opposite is true.

You will see examples of Duplicity in the strategies of Reaction and Direction, in Appearance and Toughness, but the main difference is that, in strategy based mainly on Duplicity, you must pretend to be a friend when in fact you really are the enemy.

How do you use Duplicity in combat? It's quite easy actually. For instance, you can tell your opponent a story about how you are feeling unwell, to get him to drop his guard (see Reaction) or fake an injury that prevents you from fighting (see Direction), just before you hit your aggressor right between the eyes. Or you can tell him you don't want any trouble, just before you start it. Work your way around behind him with talks of alliance, and then choke him out. Stamp on his foot to take his focus away from the punch you are going to throw at his head. Offer to shake his hand in apology as you punch his nose. All of this is Duplicity, and whilst it is aggressive and nasty by nature and it seems so morally wrong, it can be used very efficiently in extreme cases when you need to protect yourself and your loved ones (and head-on conflict is a no-go). Even then, make sure that your opponent isn't too badly hurt and act as a responsible individual. In case of serious injury, call an ambulance. Accept his apology if he gives you one, but beware of his motive and entreaties until you are certain that he means what he says.

Remember that combat is conflict, and any combat could have serious consequences, so give yourself the best chance of winning. The theory of 'win/win' can apply when using Duplicity in fighting too: you don't get hurt at all and he doesn't get hurt as much as he could have, had he chosen a less scrupulous opponent. Duplicity in combat is fair as long as you are not the aggressor and it is used as a way to procure you a win (or even just a way out) which would not have been possible otherwise.

> **'The art of living is more like wrestling than dancing.'**
> Marcus Aurelius

The Duplicity Strategy in Relationships

Smell a Rat

In business, the greatest power we can have over our competitors in order to outwit them and beat them is to have inside information. Even though small businesses have smaller budgets to spend on industrial espionage, they can still look to find disgruntled employees who can gather information for them, either for cash or for a better position in their new company.

Trust is a most valued asset in business and is gained through being trustworthy. To be seen as duplicitous is to invite duplicity. Trust your employees and partners, but remember that, at the end of the day, they have to look after their own interests first, which is normal, and even those closest to us can betray us if they have sufficient motivation – and they do not always do so with malicious intent. Keep your guard up at all times and do not take your staff and colleagues for granted.

Trust is at the core of all relationships and duplicity is a great way to ruin all this. Restrict your deceptions to white lies and setting up good surprises. If you are duped, forgive and forget; but learn your lesson. The greater the trust, the greater the hurt, and the extent to which we trust is our decision, so 'if you can't stand the heat, stay out of the kitchen!'

> *'As to the deceit perpetrated upon women, let it pass, for, when love is in the way, men and women as a general rule dupe each other.'*
>
> Giacomo Casanova

The Duplicity Strategy in Friendship

Shed Crocodile Tears

Friendship is about love and trust and if the trust is broken, the love dies. Loyalty is recognised as one of our greatest treasures and disloyalty as one of our greatest crimes. So, is there a place for Duplicity in friendship?

To be a good friend requires more than just always telling the truth and never telling lies. It's never as black and white as that; there are shades of grey between the two opposites. The white lie is permissible to help a friend, but it still can hurt if it is uncovered as a lie. The secret in friendship is to always be ready to listen to an explanation; it's too easy to take on the moral high ground and be self-righteous when we feel we've been wronged. It's easy at that point to cut people off and to believe the worst, and it takes maturity and strength to sit and listen to our friends' explanations when we feel we have been the victim of duplicity.

We all make mistakes. Let's face it; even casinos where we can so easily lose our money only win 52% of the time, and we as individuals can be great successes in life if we are right only that same percentage of times. We usually make decisions based on the outcome we want and with the information available to us at the time, so it's no surprise that we sometimes get things wrong. These mistakes are seen as acceptable whenever they involve catching a ball, making an investment or buying a car, but when it comes to honesty and relationships, we are generally expected to get it right every time.

We take duplicity very hard because it betrays our trust that is not lightly given, and if you have a friend who you feel has betrayed you; make sure you have all the facts before you decide to cut them off. Give them another chance if you can and help them to give their other friends or partners the same chance.

'Half the lies they tell about me aren't true.'

Yogi Berra

The Duplicity Strategy Personally

A Cock and Bull Story

We can lie to others all day long – and some people seem to specialise in this! We can also lie to ourselves, which means we can also be duplicitous with ourselves.

We can lie to ourselves about our reasons for not doing something, or to justify why we do try to achieve things we know we shouldn't. To lie to ourselves is one of the greatest mistakes we can make. There is always a part of us that knows we are lying. This is the part that becomes that 'little voice' inside us that sounds when we go against our true principles. We can lie and steal and cheat and justify it to ourselves: the other person can afford it, we deserve this, they won't notice, they won't be hurt by it. However, deep down, we know that these are only lies we say to ourselves and these things will eventually become our regrets. As the quote above from Marcus Aurelius says: 'Life is more like wrestling than dancing', it rarely runs smoothly or goes as expected unless it is very well planned and executed, and even then, good strategists know that 'the best laid schemes of mice and men gang aft agley (awry)' (Rabbie Burns). Regrets are not the end of the world, but they plague and disturb us. The best way to avoid having any is to do what you know is right and not to beat yourself up when you get things wrong.

The cure for duplicity in your personal life is either forgiveness or expulsion of the guilty party. Forgiveness should be the first resort, if possible, but, if the duplicity continues, you may have to cut that person out of your life. Some people simply cannot be loyal or trustworthy. We expect our friends to speak about us only in positive terms and showcase our qualities to others when we are absent. When the opposite occurs, our ego suffers and we lose trust in that person. Whilst we all do things for self-serving reasons – and should accept that others do too – there are people who just cannot be trusted. Lacking a plan or even a motive, they just go with the flow of a situation without thinking ahead. These types of people are often surprised to learn that they are seen as untrustworthy; all they know is that they changed their mind. The problem is that trust comes from giving your word and sticking to it, even when it hurts – which is why the truly trustworthy don't give their promises carelessly.

In short, don't lie to yourself and don't lie to others if you can avoid it – even if it is in their best interests. If they do find out, they may struggle to forgive you. Life often means that we walk the tightrope between doing right and doing wrong. Just be aware of Duplicity and of how it can work for and against you.

> **'A flow of words is a sure sign of duplicity.'**
> Honoré de Balzac

The Duplicity Strategy in Health

Don't Kid Yourself

Don't be duped by the promises of adverts. Remember: if it sounds too good to be true then it usually is. Health is based on keeping the body active, rested, well-fed and watered, but not to excess.

Avoid eating too many processed and refined foods and favour plenty of that which is natural – and remember that your mind needs to be kept healthy too. The mind directs and controls all that we do and, to optimise our best 'self', we should feed it with positive messages. Examine what you do so that you don't fall in mindlessly with the crowd or into unhelpful thinking.

In health, we should recognise when we are duping ourselves; those times when we chase a quick fix, when inside we know that nothing we have achieved to date in our lives which we consider worthy and lasting has ever come from a magic pill. In the Timing strategies, we learned about discipline, that immediate gratification is an emotional reaction (see Reaction) and from our discussions overall we have learned that emotion is the enemy of strategy and the tool of the strategist. This being said and hopefully understood, then it is easy to see that the promises made by adverts and unscrupulous marketing teams are duplicitous, designed to align with our desires (see Alignment) and focus on our fears (see Faith). They seek to find our weak spot (see Target) and appeal to that part of us that is most vulnerable to their message.

In health, we are bombarded by marketing adverts that promise quick results in a minimum of time and effort. These deceiving marketing ploys seek to raise your expectations (see Expectation) with empty promises and false testimonials, knowing all the while that most customers will try their product and tire of it so quickly that they will not blame the manufacturers, but themselves for it not working. Marketers hide behind the fact that most people who buy on impulse will just as impulsively stop using their product. Thus, those same marketers never have to justify the claims that they make.

Good health is a gradual process that takes time, discipline and breeds conditioning; a regime that develops gradually and becomes trusted, and that we should be wise enough not to be duped out of.

'The greatest deception men suffer is from their own opinions.'
Leonardo da Vinci

The Duplicity Strategy in Wealth

Keep Your Guard Up

An often misquoted verse is 'money is the root of all evil'. This verse has truth in it, but money is not wrong and neither is being rich. How does Duplicity relate to attracting wealth?

We all work to earn money, since it is the only way we can function in our modern society, but we are often taught that too much money is wrong. This conflicted thinking creates internal conflict and stress within us, which can be damaging to both our mental and physical health. How can you be happy doing any work when internally you are ashamed of earning money? This is duplicity aimed at oneself. It is not actually true that money is wrong; it is how people with money sometimes treat others that can come into question. If you have these issues with money, you must examine them closely: are you basing your money issues on simple hearsay conditioned from childhood? On thoughts that have not been properly examined and studied? How do you really feel about money? It is after all only a simple unit of exchange which allows us to buy food and shelter for our family, a piece of paper that represents an agreed value between two individuals. Are you using the strategy of Duplicity against yourself, one part of your psyche working against another creating internal contradiction and stress?

It is how you achieve and maintain wealth, and what you use it for, that can be evil – but money is not evil in and of itself. Some people dupe themselves into believing that money is wrong, in order to justify why they don't have any; they use it as an excuse. You can be sure that anyone who believes money is wrong or evil hasn't got any! In order to achieve your goals, you will find that money is necessary. If you want to run a charity and give it all away to a good cause for instance, you still need to earn it in the first place.

It is a wise thing to have more money than you need to cover for hard times, illness or accidents, and because one day you will want to retire without being a burden on the state or struggling in poverty. It is also wise to take care of your family and loved ones and having money will help you to do this. To think that money is wrong is to think that you are wrong if you have money, to distrust yourself and your motives and that is duplicitous thinking. Clear these negative beliefs out of your system. It's not money that makes people evil; it's what some people do with it and how they obtain it that makes it evil.

Consider how you might be duplicitous against yourself; examine your beliefs, in regard to wealth as well as in all areas of your life.

'For the love of money is the root of all kinds of evil.'
(1 Timothy 6:10)

The Duplicity Strategy in Growth

A Wolf in Sheep's Clothing

Be aware that you can be duped through get-rich-quick schemes, unbelievable products or sometimes just your own personal greed. These schemes usually look too good to be true and they most often are!

Some people use Duplicity to get what they want (and not just as a way to deal with conflict and find a way out of an otherwise impossible situation), but true personal growth is not at the expense of others. Think win/win, rather than win/lose or lose/lose. The concept of win/win might seem at first like some kind of Newspeak, just a way to pacify the nice guys when we all know, 'it's a dog eat dog world'. However, win/win is truly a principle that works; when we strive to get a result that benefits all parties, we really focus on the best of both worlds. In sales, it's easy to believe that the salesman just wants your money, but successful businesses that endure over the long term understand that both the customer and the seller must benefit from every sale. People are not stupid, they will not keep coming back if you con them, and conversely, they will keep coming back time after time if they feel that you are looking out for their best interests. Buying is not all about price, and most of us who have a product to sell actually do care about the quality of what we offer. Most business people are passionate about the service or product that they offer; first they love what they do, and every returning customer becomes a testament to the fact that they are doing it right. As Ken Blanchard said 'profit is the applause we get for doing a good job'. There are, of course, those who are in it for the quick kill and I'm sure we have all been stung once or twice by the duplicitous salesperson, but they are, in the main, a minority.

If you are serious about personal growth, then you must be serious about the quality of any action that gets you there. This means that any duplicity directed at yourself or your customers will become a blockage against actual growth. Growth comes through honesty, not duplicity.

Don't kid yourself that you are travelling the road to success when in reality you are not even trying, or you are trying at the expense of others. However, sometimes, if it will help to kick-start you, you can tell yourself a white lie, e.g. 'it's not the end of the world', even when it really feels like it is. In the final analysis 'honesty is the best policy'.

> *'I pray to God that I shall not live one hour after I have thought of using deception.'*
>
> Elizabeth I

Summary

Duplicity is a powerful weapon but even more powerful is its opposite: honesty. Do your best to be trustworthy, find your core values and stick to them. Examine them carefully to make sure that they are truly your values, and not just those that you have adopted from others – as these will lead you astray and ease you into justifying your actions as right, when they are, in fact, wrong. Your core values need to become your compass that will always guide you down the right path.

Duplicity Strategy in Brief

1. We can lie for good reasons and we can be honest for bad reasons. Use duplicity to get what you want when necessary, but let your principles guide your motives.
2. Combat is conflict and conflict thrives on deception. The greatest deception is duplicity, doing or saying one thing by either word or deed, when in fact the opposite is true.
3. Appear to be his friend, smile to his face while you 'stab him in the back', but hide your duplicity for as long as you can so you can continue to use him.
4. We take duplicity very hard because it betrays our trust which is not lightly given. If you have a friend who has betrayed you, you must have all the facts before you decide to cut them off.
5. Life often means that we walk the tightrope between doing right and doing wrong. Just be aware of Duplicity and of how it can work for and against you.
6. Don't be duped by the promises of adverts. Remember: if it sounds too good to be true then it usually is.
7. Some people dupe themselves into believing that money is wrong in order to justify their reason for not having any.
8. Any duplicity directed at yourself or your customers will become a blockage against actual growth. Growth comes through honesty, not duplicity.
9. Duplicity is a powerful weapon but even more powerful is its opposite, 'honesty'. In friendship and relationships, be trustworthy, find your core values and stick to them.
10. Trust is at the core of all relationships and duplicity is a great way to ruin a good relationship. Restrict your deceptions to white lies and setting up good surprises.

STRATEGY NO. 22

The Expectation Strategy of Appearance

Definition: Never Judge a Book by Its Cover

Overview of Appearance

Each of us has an outward aspect or appearance, yet, what we appear to be is not necessarily a guide to who we really are and we can often use our outward persona to disguise our inner feelings or intended actions. Appearance strategies mean we try not to show who we are, but who we pretend to be, and who we pretend to be can have many different faces. We are judged in the first place by how we appear. It is the easiest way for another person to get a 'handle' on who we are – and it is said we make our minds up on others in less than 17 seconds of any first meeting. But, if we want to discover who someone really is, we must look behind the façade and not always trust the appearance of the people around us.

'Trust not too much to appearances.'

Virgil

The Yin and Yang of Appearance

The Yang
visual aspect
look
image
persona
appearing
show

The Yin
disappearance
hidden
concealment
secret
cover up

The Appearance Strategy in Tradition

A Skeleton in the Cupboard

Up until 1832, it was illegal to perform dissections on corpses. However, doctors wishing to gain knowledge of the structure and function of the human body needed to study anatomy to understand how it worked. Surgeons would pay for corpses and dissect them secretly, but were always in danger of being found out and prosecuted, so they had to carry out their experiments in secret and hide the remains afterwards. The magazine Punch first coined the phrase 'skeleton in the cupboard' as a joke referring to where the bodies were kept and the phrase entered common parlance.

Nowadays, the phrase means to hide a secret from public view and, as such, fits neatly with the strategy of Appearance.

'Judgements prevent us from seeing the good that lies beyond appearances.'

Wayne Dyer

The Appearance Strategy in Warfare

If Looks Could Kill...

If our enemy can foresee our feelings or actions, he has power over us, and he will be able intercept our actions against him. It is important to keep your plans secret and remember that the more people know of your secret plans, the less secret they are. Keep your plans close to your chest for best results. Conversely, if you know your enemy's projects then you have a powerful weapon against him, as you can interrupt his plans, thwart his actions and set the scene to bring about his defeat.

Chinese Strategy No. 1 – Obscure Heaven, Cross the Sea

T'ai Shih-tz'u was an officer in an army whose fortress was under siege by the enemy. With supplies running low and collapse imminent, a messenger was needed to summon reinforcements. T'ai Shih-tz'u volunteered to be that messenger, and he contrived a plan to get past the besiegers by employing an Appearance strategy. He set out from the fortress with 12 men carrying targets. Rather than trying to break through the enemy lines, he had the targets set up close by and began practising archery under the eyes of the enemy – who stood looking on with weapons drawn, ready for trouble. The archers merely did their target practice for a while and re-entered the fortress when they were done. The day after, he did the same again; this time fewer enemy soldiers showed interest, but some still stood guard in anticipation of treachery. On the third day, T'ai Shih-tz'u did the same again and the enemy barely took any notice. At the end of his archery practice, he and his 12 men packed up their targets but this time, instead of riding back into the fortress, they suddenly dropped the targets and galloped through the unsuspecting enemy taking them completely by surprise. He made it through to the reinforcements with the result that the besieging army was defeated by his clever use of the Appearance strategy.

Chinese Strategy No. 21 – The Golden Cicada Sheds Its Skin

This Chinese strategy advises us to maintain an aspect of normality even though there may be hell going on behind the scenes. We recognise this strategy today, more clearly expressed as 'the moonlight flit' where a tenant displays all the signs of normality even though he may be in arrears with his rent or tied into a rental agreement with some time still to go. He keeps up appearances and, if he is in arrears, he makes up an excuse such as 'he's been paid late by his employer but he will pay next week'. The landlord calls to collect the arrears as arranged, only to find the tenant has left secretly, often taking the landlord's fittings and furniture with him. The unscrupulous tenant has made a successful use of the Appearance strategy.

Chinese Strategy No. 27 – Pretend Madness, But Remain Sane

This ancient Chinese strategy recommends creating an air of nonchalance and unconcern in the face of an enemy or getting them accustomed to our extravagant actions so that they see no threat in them. Consider crows at the side of the motorway; they peck away only inches from the cars whizzing past, because, despite their speed and roaring noise, the cars never appear to pose a threat to them. Occasionally, one bird goes too far and gets squashed but, in the main, they have become conditioned to believe that the cars are not a danger.

Another example of this same strategy was used as the basis of the 70s TV show Columbo. Columbo was a scruffy, inadequate, procrastinating detective who worked his way into the trust of his suspects by seeming to be a fool. However, Columbo was no one's fool and his appearance belied a great intelligence which he used to entrap his suspect – Columbo always got his man!

'Appearances are often deceiving.'
Aesop

The Appearance Strategy in Combat

Put on a Brave Face

In combat, our opponent might sometimes 'telegraph' his punches, showing you in advance that he intends to strike and what with. This is a major mistake for him to make and, if he repeats this, he will be easy to beat.

The corollary of the AEGIS Law of Priority states that 'the weapon moves first'. This is important in that it reminds us that nothing should move before we strike. This gives us an element of surprise (see Expectation) which is a major weapon in combat. Also, the appearance of either not being a threat or of being too big a threat (see Pressure and Toughness) are powerful tools in the armoury of the strategist.

The same is true of our feelings. In card playing, we hear the phrase 'poker face' and 'tells' and the best players remain inscrutable even in the face of high pressure. If we can 'see' our enemy's feelings, we can gain a sense of the effect of our actions and, if the enemy can be made emotional (see Reaction and Faith), we can use that against him.

Against any adversary, avoid showing your intention unless the intention you show is not your real one (see Direction, Reaction, Attraction and Faith). Don't telegraph your blows and don't show your pain, unless it is a fake you use as a trap for your opponent. Keep your plans secret and appear to be the opposite of what your opponent expects. Appear ready when you are not and unready when you are, appear friendly when you intend him evil. In short: keep your appearance inscrutable in order to mislead him, and carefully calculate the image you wish to portray.

In competition and self-defence, show no fear unless it's a feint or a draw (see Attraction and Reaction); show no pain and show no disappointment in either winning or losing. Laugh when you're hurting and frown when you're winning; everything you do must be the opposite of how you appear.

'For outward show is a wonderful perverter of the reason.'
Marcus Aurelius

The Appearance Strategy in Relationships

Keeping Up Appearances

The way we look can be the start of a relationship and it can also be the biggest block to starting one. We construct our appearances to suit the kind of people we want to attract, even though judging someone based on their appearance only is foolish and ineffective.

In fact, there can be no relationship based on fascia alone as a relationship is based on anything but an outward façade. However, just because we feel secure in a relationship, we should not either treat that as an excuse to let our appearance go to pot. We can appear more relaxed when we're with family and friends and more formal with people we know less well. In close relationships, we can be ourselves more and let our guard down, not only in our dress but also, and more importantly, be our real selves without any artifice or falseness in our words, actions and opinions.

The core of any relationship is who we are and not only how we appear; we are all familiar with the phrase 'behind closed doors' meaning that an outward look might disguise inward turmoil, like the relationship that seems to be happy on the outside, but behind the scenes, you might find both partners at loggerheads.

In business partnerships, we must show unity (see Alignment) in all meetings with our clients, as to do otherwise may put at risk the trust a client has in the business strength. In private, we might let down our façade, but a customer should only see a show of strength if we want to gain their trust in our company (see Faith and Expectation). Unfortunately, what a person sees first is what they usually believe the longest. 'First impressions last' and they therefore matter. It is for this reason that businesses spend so much on their outer appearance: branding, logos, greetings, livery etc., all designed to create an image that attracts their potential customer. How often have we been let down by a surly staff member with a miserable attitude and poor training and how did this make us feel about the inner values of that company?

The AEGIS law of Base says 'A tall building needs a deep foundation' which tells us that to appear strong is one thing but real strength is often hidden below the surface, like the foundations of a house or the roots of a tree. Similarly, lasting relationships must dig deep roots.

At some point, appearances will begin to fail, just as our looks change from the radiant skin of youth to the wrinkled skin of old age. But behind that skin is still the same person and, in all healthy relationships, we must learn to see past the changeable outer looks and focus on our partner's core values and the core value of the relationship itself.

'In all professions each affects a look and an exterior to appear what he wishes the world to believe that he is. Thus we may say that the whole world is made up of appearances.'
François de La Rochefoucauld

GAME PLAN

The Appearance Strategy in Friendship

Appearances Can Be Deceiving

There are sometimes solid reasons for keeping our turbulent emotions hidden behind an appearance of calm, and, at other times, it is also worth allowing people to see exactly how we feel.

Every strategy cuts both ways. Our skill, if we have any, is to judge when to use either the positive or negative sides of the strategy in any given situation. Our friends are friends because they know and understand us, they forgive us our foibles when we lash out or fail the friendship in some way, just as we do the same for them.

If we have to guide a friend and we have the usual advantage of distance (see Proximity) – i.e. not being directly involved and, therefore, able to see a clearer picture of the situation – we can then advise them using our knowledge of strategy and how to get the best out of it. If they are going for a job interview or an important first meeting for instance, we can help them to wear the appropriate clothes, to know the right questions to ask and how to use their body language to best effect.

If our friends are having relationship problems, we can help there too. Often, in relationship issues, we can adopt an appearance of not caring, in an attempt to protect ourselves from emotional pain. But we sometimes do this at times when we should be ready to expose our feelings; to let our partner know that we are hurt or sorry and that, although we fight or disagree on a subject, we still care. At times we need to show strength and at others we must show our vulnerability (see Target and Toughness). Appearances can be deceptive, and deception is not a healthy ingredient to bring into a relationship.

> *'Gussie, a glutton for punishment, stared at himself in the mirror.'*
> P.G. Wodehouse

The Appearance Strategy Personally

Beauty is Only Skin Deep

We all wear the mask of appearance and we rarely show our true selves to anyone but those closest to us. On the outside, we often try to show who we would like to be rather than who we really are.

This is a kind of mask that we wear. Some of us like wearing the latest fashions, but just take a close look at the fashion industry that produces these trends. Isn't it all just about fascia and falseness? We're assaulted daily with images of beautiful people, assembled by marketers selling their products, but are these images of really happy people or are they a manufactured appearance to tease our senses and desire (see Attraction)?

Young people especially are easily drawn into extravagant fashions in order to fit in with the crowd, in a desire to look like someone who looks like they have got their life together. This allows them to hide how they really feel inside: uncertain, lonely, inadequate or lost… People often work so hard to look cool, as if looking cool will make us cool. We must recognise that the need to look cool means we are not cool to start with. Coolness comes from being comfortable with who we are, with how we feel, and to have the ability to communicate with others without relying on artifice.

These 'cool' behaviours we adopt are intended to make us feel attractive and to be attractive to ourselves and others, especially potential partners and friends. These types of appearances are basically mating rituals – like peacocks sporting their feathers – which, biologically, have their place in human relationship, but emotionally and intellectually say little about the qualities of a person. We use Appearance to draw partners to us (see Attraction and Alignment) initially in the hope that once they get to know us, they will see our real qualities and we can together build a long-lasting deeper relationship.

When we settle with a partner, our need to appear super-sexy diminishes over time as we become more comfortable with each other, even though we hope to still take pride in our appearance. Often, we try to maintain a good level of grooming and cleanliness, but less and less do we require the artifice we first used to make us appear as someone we are not. It is easy to judge people by their appearance, but we must remember that how they look is rarely who they are. We must not be taken in too much by appearances or expect others to be too taken in by ours either.

However, there are times when we must appear to be what people expect (see Expectation) even if it doesn't feel right to us. Business and social culture has over hundreds of years developed distinct mores and folkways that dictate the proper etiquette and protocol for personal appearance, vocabulary and speech. As trivial as it might seem, judging a person by their appearance carries a lot of weight borne out through centuries of expected behaviours (see Expectation). To break the social etiquette is to disrespect the group, which in effect is to insult that same group and to do so will often result in being ostracised from it (see Isolation).

Be conscious that there are times and places when you need to appear in a certain way in order to gain an advantage, and other times when you can just be yourself. Sometimes, it is necessary to hide your feelings and actions and, sometimes, you should put them on show.

'Why do people respect the package rather than the man?'
Michel de Montaigne

The Appearance Strategy in Health

A Picture of Health

How healthy we are inside will show on the outside. How happy and content we feel and our attitude towards others will also show on the outside. There is a saying which goes: 'The face you were born with, you can do nothing about. But the face you have by the age of 40 is the face you deserve.'

It's interesting to see the faces of some people as they get older and how their inner attitude has etched itself upon that face. We've all seen people whose faces reflect disdainful and judgmental attitudes when they are in a relaxed state. The faces of these people seem to reflect their inner pain. They compare others to an ideal of how they should appear and act, and the disappointment that others are not behaving accordingly is written all over their face. These judgemental attitudes are poisonous, literally, as they infect our bodies like a disease that will affect our health in the long term. Holding onto negative emotions wrinkles our skin, depresses our immune system, and increases our production of free radicals. It is also easy to see how people blessed with a great attitude often exude great health and genuine good looks (clear skin, bright eyes, good posture...)

We should seek to keep our bodies healthy which will help keep not only our appearance more attractive but our mind-set too. How we think influences our health, so that a positive and optimistic outlook on life will help keep our bodies fit and strong. It's easy to spot unhappy people, it shows on their faces and how they hold themselves; but what is often forgotten is that we can change how we feel by simply changing our posture. The AEGIS Law of Emotion says: 'Emotion is the fuel that drives motion.' That same motion extends to how we sit, stand, smile, etc. In fact, everything we feel shows in our attitude and affects our health, either positively or negatively. If we let our bodies sag, so will our minds.

If you hold your head high and your shoulders loose and your brow relaxed, your state of mind rises with it, letting your outer appearance reflect your inner feelings – now work to keep those inner feelings healthy ones!

'Fashion is the science of appearances, and it inspires one with the desire to seem rather than to be.'

Edwin Hubbel Chapin

The Appearance Strategy in Wealth

Keeping Up With the Joneses

It is helpful in negotiations to dress for success; only the super-rich can get away with dressing like tramps, since they have the leverage that comes with their wealth.

However, most of us have to conform to specific social mores in order to be accepted. Sometimes, we must dress to impress when the occasion calls for it, to be appropriately attired when attending formal situations such as weddings or funerals where the wrong dress code can be seen as disrespectful. In our careers, if we want to be seen as a winner, we must dress like one. One piece of advice is to dress like the most successful person in the company – provided that they are the best-dressed and not a wealthy tramp!

On the flip side, we should not be tempted into displaying wealth that we don't possess. Many people living big may not be earning big; the car is on finance, as is the private school for their children and the family holidays may be maxing out the credit cards. What is the point of looking wealthy, when you are not? In the short term, it can be a strategy to fit in with the wealthy set; an example of who you aspire to be, but in the long term it can be simply conning yourself. If you want to be wealthy, you have to do much more than just look it, you have to 'walk the walk as well as talk the talk'.

Whilst we might be able to maintain the appearance of wealth, we are actually living beyond our means and we are often the only ones falling for the strategy. Take care not to become a victim of the Appearance strategy by setting up an appearance you can't afford to maintain.

'We are to admit no more causes of natural things than such as are both true and sufficient to explain their appearances.'

Isaac Newton

The Appearance Strategy in Growth

First Impressions Count

Even though we should dress for success, it would be foolish to try to be too far away from who we really are. Match your appearance to the situation. Appearance in terms of fashion is a shallow way to live. Look beyond appearance and recognise that merely looking the part is **not** the part.

True growth, like true health, comes from within. For instance, don't fill your bookshelves with books you haven't read just to impress others; you are the only one who will be the victim of that. Intelligent people will soon see whether you are for real or just a fake, an empty vessel like those people who can say the right things but who are unable to practice what they preach.

In your business, however, bear in mind that you will often be judged by appearances. As shallow as that might seem, it is said that we make up our minds about a person within 7 to 17 seconds and that our first impression lasts, often forever. We only get one chance to make a good first impression and whilst the Appearance strategy can seem pretty shallow in this form, nonetheless, if everyone is living by it then you are going to be subject to it in some form or another.

Don't presume that, just because you have learned not to judge people by their appearance, that they will not judge you by a lesser standard. Use the Appearance strategy to get more from life by having the right look to match the situation, but don't fall for it when that same strategy is used on you.

> *'The way to gain a good reputation is to endeavour to be what you desire to appear.'*
> Socrates

Summary

Appearances might seem shallow, but they do count. Use your appearance to baffle your enemy. Encourage your friends and yourself to understand the appropriate appearance required for any occasion. Be conscious of the fact that everyone is wearing a façade. Be aware of those times when it is necessary to drop the façade and of those when we must maintain it in order to derive optimum benefit from every situation.

Appearance Strategy in Brief

1. The key to our appearance is that it is not who we are but who we pretend to be.
2. Displaying the right appearance helps to keep your plans secret. The more people know of your secret plans, the less secret they are.
3. Maintain an aspect of normality even though there may be hell going on behind the scenes.
4. In competition and self-defence, laugh when you're hurting and frown when you're winning; everything you do must be the opposite of how you appear.
5. There can be no relationship based on fascia alone as a relationship is based on anything but outward superficiality.
6. Appearances can be deceptive, but deception is not a healthy ingredient to bring into a healthy relationship. It should only be kept as a last-resort strategy to help you resolve a conflict.
7. Recognise when you need to appear in a way that gains you an advantage and when there are situations when you can just be yourself, when you need to hide your feelings and when you should put them on show.
8. If you hold your head high, your shoulders loose and your brow relaxed, your state of mind rises with it, letting your outer appearance reflect your inner feelings – now work to keep those inner feelings healthy ones!
9. Match your appearance to the situation. Appearance in terms of fashion is a shallow way to live. Look beyond appearance and recognise that merely looking the part is **not** the part.
10. Appearances might be shallow, but they do count. Manage your appearance to baffle your enemy, and to help your friends and yourself adopt the appropriate appearance required for any occasion.

STRATEGY NO. 23

The Expectation Strategy of Toughness

Definition: An Iron Hand in a Velvet Glove

Overview of Toughness

How tough is tough? And who can judge except in comparison with themselves? We can fake the toughness that we don't have and also display less toughness than we are capable of. The body is the slave of the mind and Toughness resides in the mind. It is strength of body, intellect, spirit and emotion and it is important not to underestimate those who look weak or overestimate those who look strong. Use toughness as a front, an implied threat to avoid conflict. Use weakness, too, to appear too feeble to be a threat and thus you can also avoid conflict, because we tend to avoid fighting with those who look too tough and also with those who look too weak to be a challenge.

'Great leaders don't need to act tough. Their confidence and humility serve to underscore their toughness.'

Simon Sinek

The Yin and Yang of Toughness

The Yang	The Yin
resilient	weakness
hardy	frailty
resolute	timidity
temper	shyness
endurance	feebleness
fortitude	wet

The Toughness Strategy in Tradition

As Bold As Brass

This phrase, meaning 'to be brave enough to tough it out against the odds', dates back to the late 18th Century, and to a judge named Brass Crosby. After dropping the charges against a printer who had illegally reported the proceedings of Parliament, Brass was arrested for treason – a crime which carried the penalty of the death sentence (as did so many crimes in those days). However, Brass stood hard to his judgement. This case created such a public outcry that the Court soon had no choice but to set him free. After that, anyone who was bold enough to stand up for his convictions was said to be as 'bold as Brass'.

'That which does not kill us makes us stronger.'
Friedrich Nietzsche

The Toughness Strategy in Warfare

A Velvet Hand in an Iron Glove

When faced with an enemy, we can avoid direct conflict by putting on a show of strength, which may or may not be the true picture of what we are; just as we can put on a show of weakness, so that we don't appear threatening enough to be of any real challenge. Managing these two extremes effectively means we can avoid many of the injuries involved in physical combat.

The best generals are so described, not because of the battles they survive, but for the battles they manage to avoid. Any fool can charge in and get hurt, but a good fighter keeps his injuries to the absolute minimum, so that he keeps himself strong enough to fight again, if necessary, or healthy enough to enjoy his victory after the war is over.

Chinese Strategy No. 29 – The Empty Fortress

This ancient Chinese strategy is one of the 36 strategies of war; it consists of appearing weak and vulnerable in the face of a more powerful enemy. If we appear weak or vulnerable enough, our adversary may decide not to engage us because we're not worth the effort or they might take it easy on us and let us go more readily. The original example of this strategy was used by a general who was faced with a large enemy making its way toward his position. He had few men in his own force and could not hope to engage his larger foe, not even to try to slow him down. So he opened up the gates of the castle he protected and took away the weapons of his soldiers, instructing them to sit around listlessly and show no interest in the approaching enemy. When the enemy arrived and saw the small force and the unprotected castle, they immediately felt it was a ruse. However, they interpreted it as a trap they were being lured into (see Attraction) and consequently retreated back and around the general's unprotected position. The wise general used his weakness as a bluff which paid off (see Appearance) and so avoided a battle he could not hope to win. He also retained the position of strength he had been ordered to protect so that once reinforcements would arrive, he would have the added strength of his fortified position which he could then defend adequately.

Chinese Strategy No. 32 – Make the Flowers Bloom on the Tree

This strategy is the opposite of the empty fortress; instead of appearing weak and defenceless, we try to appear stronger than we actually are so that our enemy will avoid contact with us. Alexander the Great used this strategy when tying torches to the horns of cattle at night to make it look like his moving army was much larger than it actually was. Chinese generals used the same strategy by lighting many camp fires at night so that their forces appeared much larger than they were in reality.

Nowadays, we can see this strategy used in the recruitment of bodyguards, security personnel and nightclub bouncers, for instance. Because of their build, their posture, the way they dress and present themselves, they all appear tough and well-armed, but how tough are they really? We'll never know for sure unless we decide to test them. And that is the point of the Attitude strategy: they look too tough for us to really want to try. So, it doesn't matter how tough we really are as long as we look tough enough to deter any potential attack (or too weak to be worth the hassle).

> *'I am sometimes a fox and sometimes a lion. The whole secret of government lies in knowing when to be the one or the other.'*
> Napoleon Bonaparte

The Toughness Strategy in Combat

Brass Neck

The use of the Toughness strategy in its 'tough' sense is to avoid combat by appearing too tough, and we have seen above how this can be applied. It might be enough to have the reputation of being tough to create a 'rep' as they say (short for 'reputation for toughness'), as in Al Capone's reputation for violence, for instance. On the other hand, the weakness side of the toughness strategy can be equally effective if we can reconcile it with our own ego because to appear weak and non-threatening can be difficult for those who struggle with their ego and need to always appear tough in front of others.

In competition combat, fighters can often be seen complaining to their potential opponents that they are suffering from flu and shouldn't even be fighting, in the hope that appearing too weakened might afford them some advantage – as well as being able to justify later why they lost. Or they give their opponent the impression that they will be a push-over, so that when their adversary drops his guard (see Reaction), they come out fighting like a tiger. It sometimes also works by appealing to their opponent's softer side, in an attempt to get him to go easy on them. Whatever the reason, it is an effective strategy if it is convincing enough in its delivery.

It's worth mentioning that poor combat strategists often boast the toughness of their fighters. The only strategy they use is the 'face first' strategy based purely on how much punishment their fighter is capable of taking and giving. However, by needing their fighters to be the toughest or strongest is a weak strategy. We cannot always be the toughest but that doesn't mean we can't win. The best fighters throughout history were not always the biggest toughest or strongest. Those lesser skilled coaches who lack a thorough knowledge of strategy therefore limit their fighters to the junior ranks and, often, they get no further than that because every fight they have turns into a 'war' in which their fighter takes heavy punishment. Even when the fighter wins, the scars of both physical and mental injury stay with him, every new contest sapping his strength and resolve (see Energy) a little more than the last. This is not what the Toughness strategy is about. An intelligent fighter avoids injury as much as possible and uses a variety of strategies in order to overcome his opponent, not just trying to be tough and withstand whatever is thrown at him.

The whole point of this book and its examination of strategy are based on the fact that pure strength is not enough to win. Often, when only strength is used, the victory it brings does so at such a high cost that we are left with a Pyrrhic victory. If you are a fight coach or trainer, you will gain more longevity for your fighter plus a greater reputation and higher world ranking by focusing on his mental toughness as well as his physical strength, but even more importantly, focus on helping him develop his strategic skills as covered in this book. For physical strategies, work on the Focus strategies; teach your fighter how to feint, fake, draw, clinch, (plus grapples where applicable), plus help him build confidence in his skills. Also, for personal skills, teach your fighter the Vulnerability strategies (Manoeuvre, Exploitation, Target, Risk and Example) and Timing strategies (Pace, Opportunity, Interruption, Patience and Delay). Teach him the skills of Distance, Space and Reach (see Proximity) as well as how to hit hard (see Energy, Recruitment, Isolation, and Alignment) and how to apply pressure (see Pressure) in his training so that he builds a variety of skills gradually in order that they become second nature. A trainer who does not have a deep understanding of the FLITE strategies but merely uses pre-prepared drills has no right to put any fighter into the ring, and merely risks his fighter's safety.

The best fighters in history were tough, but their achievements did not rely solely on toughness; the best fighters are masters of strategy, in and out of the ring, working in partnership with their coaches who care for the longevity and safety of their fighter.

> **'Brave men are all vertebrates; they have their softness on the surface and their toughness in the middle.'**
>
> Gilbert K. Chesterton

The Toughness Strategy in Relationships

Take it on the Chin

How would we apply the Toughness strategy in relationships? As in friendship, one would hope that any kind of façade would be unnecessary in a close relationship, but not all of our relationships are close or even friendly; consider the uneasy peace between two competitors in business, or even business partners with different goals for their own business.

In the workplace, a boss may appear very tough and ruthless at work, only to be meek and timid at home. A few years back, a known tactic to help a young man placed in a junior management position was for him to answer questions from his staff by responding with a very impatient 'What!?' This way, they always feared approaching him! In our days of more enlightened business practice, we would like to think that this tactic was dead, but that is sadly not the case and many people still approach their boss with trepidation, especially middle management who are newly risen from the ranks and have not mastered the art of managing people without needing to impose their superior position. Experienced managers gain respect through allowing their staff to disagree and express their opinions, knowing that even the most intelligent of us does not know all the answers. The skills of a good leader come from not having to pretend to be tough to make their presence felt and, instead, empowering their people to harness their ideas and support.

Recognise in relationships that you have to be tough enough to say what you really think and also be tough enough to be subject to your partner's opinions. Emotionally, we are often sensitive to criticism and judgement, especially from those close to us, but any improvement we can make in ourselves can only come through a comparative relationship with others. In life, we must learn to 'take it on the chin' that is, to be resilient enough to take the knocks as well as to give them. This is a key to the Toughness strategy.

'Out of suffering have emerged the strongest souls; the most massive characters are seared with scars.'

Khalil Gibran

//GAME PLAN//

The Toughness Strategy in Friendship

Let Your Guard Down

We all have within us some elements of toughness, and often we exhibit or portray our toughness as part of an image we construct so can fit in with a specific crowd, or as a source of defiance.

In men, we call this *machismo* or acting 'macho'. This usually derives from a sense of ego, which itself derives from a feeling of inadequacy or fearfulness. Men assume an aura of toughness, which may well serve to protect their fragile ego or even construct a sufficient front to keep them out of unnecessary fights. We can often see young men swaggering down the street exhibiting an air of toughness, and we might wonder why they feel the need to display themselves this way. Is it because they feel a sense of lacking in their personality, or are they truly fearful? Or is it, perhaps, the equivalent of the peacock's tail feathers, a display to attract (see Attraction) a certain type of mate?

In friendship, we should expect to be able to drop those façades of toughness and weakness, and just be ourselves. The quality of any friendship is defined by the lack of façade, and it should only be in the presence of false friends that we feel the need to try to be anything but ourselves. With our friends, shouldn't we be able to be at our most vulnerable and have no sense of fear? If we cannot lower our guard sufficiently, perhaps we should question whether this is because we do not feel genuinely comfortable with this friend or whether we are carrying a general sense of fear around with us in our lives.

When in need, a friend may try to 'put on a brave face' so as not to seem or feel too weak or helpless in the face of adversity. We may need to remind them to 'keep their chin up' – which is a method of changing their mental state in order to feel tougher – and encourage them with the belief that things will get better, that they are tough enough to see this thing through. Imagine a friend who has suffered a loss of face (or faith), and suddenly feels vulnerable. We can try to build their confidence back up or be the temporary crutch that they can lean on. Perhaps you know an adult or child who is being bullied or intimidated (see Pressure, Isolation and Faith). If they are afraid to face their aggressor alone, you could stand at their side while they confront their threat, or even stand up to the bully yourself if your friend or family member is too weak or frightened.

The strength of the Toughness strategy lies in being perceived as either too big or too small a threat, both of which can be used to avoid physical combat, and, therefore, avoid the cause of injury or loss on either side.

> ***'A lot of people are afraid to tell the truth, to say no.***
> ***That's where toughness comes into play.***
> ***Toughness is not being a bully. It's having backbone.'***
> Robert T. Kiyosaki

The Toughness Strategy Personally

Be Yourself

The Toughness strategy is concerned with using the appearance of Toughness as a tool to achieve a result, to get something that we want, and it can be duplicitous in its nature as it disguises our real level of toughness. We can appear stronger than we are, or weaker, or (without duplicity) as tough as we are.

But how tough are you? The answer is as tough as you need to be or can be. For instance, there is physical toughness, emotional toughness, mental toughness and spiritual toughness. In the face of bereavement, our emotional toughness is put to the test. Some people can pull themselves together quickly and others may never fully recover. Physically, we might look to those who are strong and think that because they can lift heavy things or have extraordinary endurance, that they are physically tough. Yet some of the toughest people of the last century such as Gandhi, Winston Churchill, Mother Teresa, Nelson Mandela, Martin Luther King and the like did not rely on big muscles or the ability to lift weight as part of their toughness. They displayed mental and spiritual toughness.

Where is real toughness? In their muscles, their emotions, their minds or their spirit? The answer is probably a combination of all 4 of these intelligences with their spiritual toughness being the driver. Spiritual toughness is driven by borne of powerful beliefs and values.

If we have this power of belief, we can harness our other areas of toughness and, if necessary, we can also learn to override them. This kind of toughness is not often necessary in our daily life except in those areas where our core beliefs are sorely challenged, like when we are pushed around, bullied or simply underestimated.

True toughness comes from the power of our core beliefs and it is important to discover what these are and to challenge them to see if they are truly core beliefs, or whether you are just following a fad or fashion. This is what makes the difference between people who achieve great things and others who achieve only trivial things. Of course, who is to say that one thing is trivial and another is not? The answer is you are the one who is qualified to judge, by simply asking yourself 'what is important in my life, and what is my purpose or goal toward that thing of importance?'

Once you discover what is important, what your core beliefs are, and pursue these things with passion, you will immediately become tough. Not just as in Appearance or Duplicity, but in reality, because you will pursue a course that means more to you than even your own life. Something that is bigger than you are and which will be your legacy for others to follow.

When you discover your core beliefs, learn about them, study them and begin to pursue them, your life will change forever and you will reveal what you are truly made of.

'*Anyone who has a continuous smile on his face conceals a toughness that is almost frightening.*'
Greta Garbo

The Toughness Strategy in Health

Tough it Out

We all have at our core a degree of toughness, and sometimes we are tougher than we look, and at other times we are weaker. Toughness can be developed through regular mental and physical training which is why the martial artist often has the reputation (at least) of being tough.

How tough we are depends entirely on how tough we are prepared to be, which implies demonstrating an attitude of mind that overrides any pain the body might suffer. In order to be able to, at least, match or better any challenge we might face, we must keep our bodies strong through regular exercise, conditioning ourselves to work through the pain barriers with progressively more difficult tasks. We can also feed ourselves on a well-planned diet, full of the right nutrients, vitamins and minerals, drink plenty of water, and so on, to keep our bodies resistant to ill-health.

But, regarding our own health, we cannot really use the Toughness strategy against ourselves in all good conscience because the Toughness strategy is a ploy used to achieve an aim without fighting. We can con those around us into believing that we are tough or weak, but we cannot con ourselves. Or, rather, we can – and many do – but we shouldn't as this is completely counter-productive, pretending we are something we are not.

Having broad shoulders and a six-pack may make you look tough, but what is the reality? Are you genetically pre-disposed to this look or have you built this through determined and prolonged discipline? The question is: Are you really tough or do you just appear to be?

'Toughness is in the soul and spirit, not in muscles.'
Alex Karras

The Toughness Strategy in Wealth

Call His Bluff

Achieving wealth can be done in many ways, and often requires that we learn how to negotiate. The 25 Game Plan strategies are invaluable in this respect and the Toughness strategy is no different.

There will be times when we have to bluff our hand. Imagine, for instance, negotiating the price of an investment property; we might 'tough' out our stance, holding at our price to get the other side to accept our offer, while inside we are quivering because we want the deal so much. Will the strategy work? Who knows? Certainly, sometimes it will, sometimes it won't, but we'll never know for definite until we try. On the other hand, we might present ourselves as the weak side, trying to get the other side to drop their guard and better their price.

The key to negotiating is to understand exactly what you want and what your opposite negotiator wants also. In negotiating, there is a concept known as a BATNA which stands for the 'best alternative to a negotiated agreement'. The BATNA is that point where you exit the negotiations because either you cannot agree, or to agree would mean getting too a bad deal. To back out of a deal that you really want takes toughness and emotional control and you should be tough with yourself and your opponent to ensure that you never agree to a deal that doesn't take you forward.

When you enter into negotiations, you must identify your BATNA as this will tell you when to push hard and be tough, or when to back off (see Proximity) and seek another deal.

Recognise also that your opponent has his own BATNA. He too must try to achieve the best result for himself, as it's no use doing a business deal if it doesn't make you a profit, either financially or otherwise. Sometimes both of you will bluff and sometimes you will be honest. The skill in negotiations is to choose the right response at the right time. To be too tough is to be inflexible and to be too soft is to be too flexible and, therefore, be manipulated into an agreement that weakens your position more than it strengthens it.

As in all strategy, we must first decide what we want and what we are willing to pay to get it, which is why we often have to stick to our decisions and refuse compromises. This is the pain we have to endure in order to get what we want. Sometimes, real toughness comes from saying 'no' and being able to walk away from something we desire when the terms are not agreeable.

'Concentration and mental toughness are the margins of victory.'
Bill Russell

The Toughness Strategy in Growth

No Pain, No Gain

As you have no doubt seen by now, the Toughness strategy is about bluff as well as honesty, about creating in our target the expectation that we are either too tough to mess, or too weak to be bothered with, and somewhere in the middle is our real toughness.

So how does this apply to our growth? Just as we can bluff others, we can also bluff ourselves. We can use the Toughness strategy, by acting out that we are tough enough to make it, when in fact we don't feel we are at the time. Having the right attitude is one thing, but having experience and a good education is necessary too. This is why it is important that we challenge our own position often. We must be honest with ourselves: 'Am I ready for this challenge right now or do I have some more work to do first?' Although you must also be careful that this does not lead you to unnecessary procrastination (see Delay).

Most people are motivated by their emotions and act according to how they feel. But to run your life emotionally is to court disaster because emotions are transient, they shift as quickly as the breeze and we must therefore recognise that they are not the truth. How often have we said or done something when emotional that we have regretted later? The toughness found in people is not like the toughness of diamonds. Diamonds are consistently tough, the toughest thing on Earth actually, but people have many different levels of toughness, often depending on their situation or motivation. For instance, a mother may be weak and passive, but threaten her child or family, and you will see her with the ferocity of a lioness. People also have the ability to decide on how tough they want to be and, with sufficient motivation, they can be almost as tough as diamonds.

The key to toughness lies in the strength of belief in the thing we are being tough about. Is it worth the risk or not (see Risk)? Is it real toughness or is it just a show? Or is a pretence of weakness required to get what we want?

To achieve great things in life, to become the person you desire to become, you will have to master all sides of the Toughness strategy, to understand how tough you are, and how tough you can be when the need arises.

> **'Mental toughness is to physical as 4 is to one.'**
> Bobby Knight

Summary

So, how tough are you really? Can you take physical pain but not mental stress, or vice versa? Are you conning yourself that you are tougher than you are, or that you are weaker than you are? Can you identify when the Toughness strategy is being used for or against you? And can you look for when you can apply it to get the result that you want?

Toughness Strategy in Brief

1. How tough is tough and who can judge except in comparison with themselves? We can fake more toughness than we actually have or more weakness than we feel.
2. Any fool can charge in and get hurt but a good fighter keeps his injuries to the absolute minimum, so that he is strong enough to fight again.
3. The point of the Toughness strategy is that it doesn't matter how tough we really are as long as we look tough enough to deter any potential attack.
4. The best fighters in history were tough, but their achievements did not rely solely on toughness; the best fighters were and are masters of strategy, in and out of the ring.
5. In life, we must learn to 'take it on the chin', to be resilient enough to take the knocks as well as to give them.
6. We all have some element of toughness, and often we exhibit or portray our toughness as part of an image we construct in order to fit in with a specific crowd or as a source of defiance.
7. Finding what we want in life and recognising who we are at our core requires that we identify what we believe so that we are tough for the right reasons.
8. Having broad shoulders and a six-pack may make you look tough, but what is the reality? Are you really tough or do you just appear to be?
9. We must first decide what we want and what we are willing to pay, what we might call the pain we have to endure, in order to get what we want. This way, we can assess how tough we need to be to get what we want.
10. The Toughness strategy is about bluff, creating in our target an expectation of us being either too tough to mess with or too weak to be bothered with.

STRATEGY NO. 24

The Expectation Strategy of Expectation

Definition: Expect the Unexpected

Overview of Expectation

We all have expectations of every situation, whether optimistic or pessimistic, realistic or not. These expectations tend to colour how we perceive things and determine how we behave at any given time. The strategy of Expectation also covers the unexpected and unpredicted which is why it is a powerful weapon in strategy. Lead your opponent into the unexpected and your friends away from it. Gain trust and loyalty through the fulfilment of expectations and gain respect and fear from your enemies through your ability to be predictably dangerous. In war, never do the expected, and in friendship always do it when applicable (so you appear strong, reliable and constant) but do not be afraid to behave unexpectedly when it helps create positive energy in those around you.

'The best thing about the future is that it comes one day at a time.'

Abraham Lincoln

The Yin & Yang of Expectation

The Yang

prospect
anticipation
hope
outlook
projection
belief
presumption
prediction

The Yin

unexpected
surprise
disbelief
unpredictable
unlikelihood
distrust

The Expectation Strategy in Tradition

Come Up to Scratch

This common phrase dates back to the early prize fighting ring when fighters fought bare knuckled and each round lasted until a fighter was knocked down. In those days, the ring was formed by the crowd and a line was scratched in the middle of the ring where both fighters were called. When the fight began and a fighter was knocked to the ground, he had 30 seconds in which to come up to the scratch line. If he failed to 'come up to scratch', the match was awarded to the last man standing. Today, this phrase relates to the standard or expectation placed upon an individual or organisation in the performance of a task or attainment of a standard.

'High expectations are the key to everything.'
Sam Walton

The Expectation Strategy in Warfare

Expect the Unexpected

As every good strategist from Sun Tzu to Clauswitz has stated before, all warfare is about deceit. In warfare, you can never do the expected unless it is a ruse used to lull your enemy into a false sense of security. The goal of every general is to create the unexpected; the unexpected gives them open targets, time, leverage and opportunity (to name but a few of the Game Plan strategies) whereas the expected in war only serves to create difficulties by removing all the advantages that the unexpected provides us with. If our enemy can predict our actions, then we have no advantage, but when our actions cannot be successfully predicted then our enemy is at our mercy.

Chinese Strategy No.13 – Beat the Grass Surprise the Snake

This strategy also fits with the feint (see Reaction) but it also has a strong use of the Expectation strategy which is why it appears here also. Expectation is what the strategist calculates will be the predictable response of the victim who falls for the ploy which he did not expect. The whole point of the Yang strategy is to work against another person or situation because all strategy is based on deception and all deception creates surprise.

When we know our enemy might attack but don't know where or when, we know we should expect an attack but we do not know exactly what to expect (or when and where). The enemy is close but his intentions are unclear and unpredictable. This is when it might be necessary to be pre-emptive and therefore use this strategy to make his next move more predictable.

The Suez Crisis of 1956

The Suez Canal was the fastest shipping route between the Mediterranean and Indian Ocean, and the British and French relied upon it heavily for trade and commerce. In 1956, Egypt nationalised the Suez Canal, creating a lot of upset and anger in Europe. Were the Egyptians creating a bluff or were they ready to go to war against the British and French in order to keep them from using the Canal? The British and French had a declared enemy but did not know how he would defend his claims, with what, from where and with what amount of force. This was truly a case of expecting the unexpected, which was when Britain and France used the strategy of 'Beat the grass to surprise the snake'. They placed forces close to the canal as a show of force ready to take control if the Egyptians didn't back down. The Egyptians launched attacks on the Anglo-French forces, revealing where their forces were and how they would attack. The Europeans had beaten the grass and surprised the snake. The next phase was to focus their attack on Egypt's now revealed forces (see Direction and Target strategies). The Anglo-French forces launched their own attacks quickly on and over land and nullified the Egyptian forces. Anthony Eden, the British Premier, was convinced that finding out early what the Egyptian plan was and the quick action of the Anglo-French forces prevented the crisis escalating into a potentially much larger war.

> **'If you align expectations with reality, you will never be disappointed.'**
> Terrell Owens

The Expectation Strategy in Combat

Surprise, Surprise!!

Create expectations and turn them into the unexpected, the unpredictable; create in your enemy the prospect of success and then break their expectations into pieces.

Be what they don't expect when they think they have you 'sussed' and when they don't know what to do for the best, you can be obvious and surprise them once gain. Do not let the expectations of your enemies affect you negatively; examine yourself deeply and trust yourself to know what is really right. The skill in all strategy is as much about applying it yourself as it is in recognising when it is aimed at you.

The only time an enemy should be able to predict what you do is when it is your intention that he would do so. Our enemies will use knowledge of our actions to create victories against us, so we must guard our movements, intentions and information carefully. Take care over who you share your secrets with, and remember that, if lots of people know a secret, then it's no longer a secret.

In self-defence, the unexpected is a powerful tool, especially painful if we are the victim of it, so we must recognise those times when we are at risk (see Risk). Opening the door to strangers, walking alone through isolated areas, entering into high crime areas are all situations where we should raise our guard. For this purpose, we should consider the 5 levels of threat which are:

1. *Aware*
2. *Surprised*
3. *Expected*
4. *Mutual*
5. *Attack*

'***Aware***' involves consciousness, which is to recognise that danger can arise quickly and unexpectedly. The AEGIS Law of recognition states: 'We can only respond to a challenge or opportunity if we recognise that there is one' meaning we must be conscious always of our surroundings in order to get the most out of any situation. '***Surprised***' is the opposite of expectation;

it is something we hope to be in control of and not controlled by, especially when danger lurks by. *'Expected'* is the knowledge that danger is impending but the timing (see Timing strategies) is uncertain. *'Mutual'* is an agreed combat such as we find in tournament competition fighting which we have trained and prepared for. The final level of threat, *'Attack'* is where we become the threat and the controller of the situation; our actions are predictable only to us (if we have planned strategically) and unpredictable to our adversary; we control the expectation. This is the most powerful position to be in, as it is fully in our control. To define the threat level we are in, in this way, should help us make the most of our situation at all times, in combat as well as in life.

Expectation deals with outcomes and goals; it deals with predictability and unpredictability. It deals also with trust and distrust; our actions, if they are to be used against an adversary, must appear to have a different outcome than what he perceives and yet, even if we have defeated him before, they must appear (see Appearance) to be the truth. Consider carefully what your enemy expects and remember to compile a convincing strategy using those tactics that will thwart his expectations, such as Reaction, Attraction, Direction, Function, Confidence and Duplicity.

> **'The best things in life are unexpected –
> because there were no expectations.'**
> Eli Khamarov

The Expectation Strategy in Relationships

Be the Real McCoy

Be trustworthy and predictable for your friends. Don't let them down if you can help it and don't build them up if you know you cannot fulfil your obligations. Friends, colleagues and family can be great assets and sources of joy, but only if you cultivate them and look after them.

The strategy of Expectation is controlled by, as well as being named after, the AEGIS Law of Expectation which states: 'You don't get what you want or wish for, you only get what you confidently expect'. Expectations can be consciously created but also they can be created unconsciously through actions which arise through habits. Some habits are deliberately chosen by us, such as getting fit or eating a structured diet, but others are chosen unconsciously from childhood conditioning that we now take as the norm. In relationships, we have expectations placed upon us, and we also place them upon others. We must strive to place realistic expectations on others if we want the relationship to thrive, and we must also fulfil the reasonable expectations of others.

Find out who is worthy of your trust and be the same to them. Find out who is not to be trusted, and eliminate them from your circle of influence. In a romantic relationship, the ability to fulfil your partner's expectations is a great way to build a relationship of trust, and the inability to be trusted will break even the strongest of relationships. The only type of surprise that should be allowed in a loving relationship is the ability to positively surprise your spouse either through an unexpected gift, action or a facet of your personality that has hitherto been concealed.

How do we create expectations in a relationship? One way which is unavoidable is through experience; through trial and error. We can never hope to get our behaviour right every time, as we don't always know what our partner will expect and whether that expectation is thoughtfully chosen or the result of some skewed mind-set that is unreasonable. Another way is to choose our expectation through thoughtful study, by considering and constructing our behaviours through examination of past situations, social mores and basing our behaviours on how we would like to be treated ourselves.

The same rules apply in business relationships too. Always strive to know the expectations which your business places upon you. Each relationship places upon us an expectation of trust to keep the joint secrets, perform the duties involved and fulfil the required obligations. If you can maintain this standard, then your part of the relationship has been upheld and, providing your partners do the same, then your relationship will be the real McCoy.

**'Never idealize others.
They will never live up to your expectations.'**
Leo Buscaglia

The Expectation Strategy in Friendship

You Can Bank on Me

The word 'bank' comes from the Italian word 'banco' which means 'bench' and the medieval bench men in Venice who were trusted to hold other people's money safely when they were away on a voyage or expedition. Therefore, 'to bank on someone' means to place an expectation of trust in them.

One of the greatest gifts you can give a friend is your trust in them and the ability to be trusted by them. We all have expectations of behaviour in a relationship and only through experience can we clearly define and calculate what we can expect from one another. We come to every relationship with a set of expectations, and we think we know what they are. However, this is not necessarily true, as many of our expectations have been conditioned into us without our realising, so when we face something that goes against our expectations, we may feel it is wrong but not quite know why. What has happened is that they have broken some of the rules we have set for them unconsciously, yet we are not always aware of it. So, if we don't fully understand our own expectations, we should go kindly with those we have for our friends, family and colleagues. If your friend is messy and you're tidy, you must recognise that their messy state is no more right or wrong than your tidy state. Friendship is based on acceptance, love, cooperation and compromises, and to be a good friend, you must first give your acceptance before you can expect to receive theirs.

Help friends in need, be their support, but not so much that your own life suffers for too long. Remember that you don't always get back what you give out and sometimes you give your all and get nothing in return (that can be seen in the short-term anyway). At other times, you give out your worst and your friend still stands there in support of you. Reciprocity – that is, give and take – is the oil that lubricates a good relationship.

There can come a time when you recognise that you are giving too much for no return and, at other times, you are not giving enough. Consider carefully what you can give and what you should expect in return.

'The best way to keep one's word is not to give it.'
Napoleon Bonaparte

The Expectation Strategy Personally

It's On the Cards

Consider your own expectations in your personal life: what do you want from them and what are you prepared to give in exchange?

To achieve your life goals you must set goals that motivate you; it's no good trying to achieve things that you only think you should achieve or that others expect you to achieve. Because anything that you don't really want will not turn you on for long enough for you to fully commit to it. Certainly, you will be able to achieve shorter term goals like a degree or new job, but it won't be long before what you REALLY want pushes its way into your psyche. By achieving short-terms goals because you think you should, either to impress friends or family, or even through being temporarily infatuated with that goal, you will find yourself climbing the wrong tree or heading into a dead end. The secret to managing your own expectations is to discover, through personal examination, meditation and study, what it is that you REALLY want in life. This involves judgement and, as the Law of Judgement states: 'Good judgement comes from experience and experience comes from bad judgement'.

One way to find out what you want is to try various things, gradually eliminating the things you don't want until you come to the point where you recognise what you really want. This can sometimes take many years but it doesn't have to. All it needs is for you to have the courage (see Faith) to listen to the advice of those around you and to NOT take their advice if you feel deep down that it is not what you want. You also have to listen to yourself; study your life and look at those things that keep drawing you back, or those things that are consistent in your life, and examine your motivations deeply; consider how you can use them to make your life worthwhile.

Trust yourself to make the right choices, if not immediately, then eventually. Recruit to your cause (see Recruitment) others whom you can trust; trust them and be trustworthy to them. Be consistent in the way you behave, even if it sometimes takes some effort. Being a good friend is not always an easy thing, to fulfil your greatest expectations is most often a team effort but, with the right strategy, your positive result is on the cards.

'If it is not right, do not do it; if it is not true, do not say it.'
Marcus Aurelius

The Expectation Strategy in Health

Pie in the Sky

Mark Twain once said: 'There are only two certainties: death and taxes.' We are all going to shuffle off this mortal coil eventually, but the quality of our lives and the legacy we leave behind is important. Match your actions to your expectations and remember there is a price to pay, both good and bad, for the actions you take. If you drink, smoke, use drugs, eat poorly, take little exercise and don't manage your stress, you can end up not living long enough to make your mark on the world. Treat yourself well – and that doesn't mean just doing what you want, it means doing what is right and necessary, which includes taking a balanced view of your personal health and managing your future expectations by dealing with your present ones to the best of your abilities.

Be wary of setting unrealistic expectations for your health, for instance expecting to get a six pack whilst still eating too many calories and simple sugars, or planning to run a marathon without getting the necessary miles in to condition your heart, lungs and muscles to be ready for the test.

Unrealistic goals won't be taken seriously by the mind and will not stir our emotions enough to motivate us toward the task. Consider carefully what you want for your health goals and make sure that your goals are not just pie in the sky.

> **'Winners make a habit of manufacturing their own positive expectations in advance of the event.'**
> Brian Tracy

The Expectation Strategy in Wealth

It's in the Bag

Discover what your expectation of wealth is: Do you expect to ever get rich or do you feel that it will never happen to you? Do you secretly fear wealth? Or perhaps despise those who have it? These are all factors that will colour your expectations. If you feel that you will never acquire wealth, then you create a negative expectation for yourself. To create wealth, you must create the positive expectation that it can happen to you.

Every self-made millionaire started out poor, possibly poorer than you are now, but if you can't imagine being wealthy, try this: can you imagine having £100 more than you have now? The answer is probably 'yes'... Can you imagine having £1 million more than you have now? No…? That's because the jump from where you are to where you need to be is too big for you to visualise. Manage your expectations by taking small steps toward wealth; for £100 try adding a zero to make it a £1000. Build wealth gradually, step by step – as Lao Tzu said: 'A journey of 1,000 leagues begins with a single step'. Take your wealth step by step.

Wealth takes time, a plan, a system and the discipline to stick with it, and whilst we would all like to win the lottery and become wealthy overnight, if we did, what lessons would we have learned on the way? Like those lottery winners we read about who win a fortune, only to have spent it all within a few short years. Anything worth having takes time, effort and realistic expectations, which includes patience and discipline. Imagine you had £10 million today... How would you manage it? Where would you keep it? How much would you spend and how much would you save for yourself and your family's future? Can you answer simple questions such as 'What is the difference between saving and investing?' What is your attitude to risk? If you bank the cash, will you earn enough interest to outstrip inflation, and if you invest your money, how will you check the safety of your fund managers or business managers? The novice rich are faced with all these problems and here's something to consider: if you can't manage what you have now, then how will you manage thousands or millions? Managing bigger amounts is exponentially more difficult than managing smaller amounts.

If you take your wealth-building step by step and set goals for what you can truly visualise and expect, learn how to manage your money and stick to your plan, your creation of wealth is in the bag.

> **'The only thing that should surprise us is that there are still some things that can surprise us.'**
> François de La Rochefoucauld

The Expectation Strategy in Growth

Pipe Dreams

Our personal growth relies on the strategy of Expectation, as it deals with managing the expectations we have for our personal future. If you feel you can't achieve what you set out to do, it is probably because you are setting your goals too high.

Some people are motivated by setting step by step goals and others by huge outcome-based goals. Either way, find goals that you believe in and that motivate you. The way to recognise a good goal is to test your adrenaline factor: if your goal starts a little flutter of 'butterflies' in your belly, which is the secretion of adrenalin, then you have chosen a good goal. If it doesn't start that little buzz then the chances are that the goal is too small to challenge you or too big for your subconscious to take seriously. Either way, you won't get far with it.

Manage your successes and failures; expect both on your journey of growth and, in doing so, you can deal with both more realistically. Success and failure are merely concepts, as Rudyard Kipling said, 'If you can meet with triumph and disaster and treat those two imposters just the same…' The difference lies between what you expect and what you get. As a minimum, set worthy, well thought-out goals and also create a Plan B, in case you achieve either more or less than you expected to. This is the secret to achievement in all areas of your life, but if your expectations are too high, you will welcome failure and if they are not high enough, you will welcome apathy toward that goal.

A well thought-out goal, which is beyond your immediate reach but not so far that it is just a pipe dream, is the kind of goal you need and, with practice in setting goals of the right expectation, you will get better and better at achieving them, and be more motivated to keep setting and achieving more goals in order to get the life you feel you deserve.

'Success consists of going from failure to failure without loss of enthusiasm.'
Winston Churchill

Summary

In combat, do the unexpected. With friends, do the expected. In wealth, create realistic step-by-step expectations and do the same in personal growth. Manage what you expect and recognise what is expected and necessary for you to achieve your goals. Since you cannot always predict your outcome, then you must also expect and plan for the unexpected.

Expectation Strategy in Brief

1. We all have expectations of every situation, whether optimistic or pessimistic, realistic or otherwise.
2. As every good strategist has said, all warfare is about deception. In warfare, we can never do the expected unless it is part of a ruse to use against our enemy.
3. Create expectations and turn them into the unexpected, the unpredictable; create in your adversary a prospect of success and then break their expectations into pieces.
4. Be trustworthy and predictable for your friends. Don't let them down if you can help it and don't build them up if you know you cannot fulfil your obligations.
5. There can come a time when you recognise that you are giving too much for no return and, at other times, you are not giving enough. Consider carefully what you can give and what you should expect in return.
6. To fulfil your greatest expectations is most often a team effort but, with the right strategy, your positive result is on the cards.
7. Match your actions to your expectations and remember there is a price to pay, both good and bad, for the actions you take.
8. If you take your wealth building step by step and set goals for what you can truly visualise and expect, manage your money and stick to your plan, your wealth is in the bag.
9. A well thought-out goal, which is beyond your immediate reach but not so far that it is just a pipe dream, is the kind of goal you need and, with practice, you will learn how to set goals of the right expectation.
10. Since you cannot always predict your outcome, then you must also expect and plan for the unexpected.

STRATEGY NO. 25

The Expectation Strategy of Proximity

Definition: Keep Your Distance

Overview of Proximity

The distance between where we are and where we want to be is one of the most crucial areas of achievement. Knowing where we are and how to get to where we want to be is an invaluable skill of the master strategist. Consider Proximity in terms of distance in 4 different dimensions if you want to achieve true mastery of this strategy. These are:

1. *forwards and backwards*
2. *sideways*
3. *up and down*
4. *time/duration*

How far away should you be from an enemy and how close should you be to a friend? As the Definition of the Aegis Law of Proximity says: 'The fighter who controls the distance is the fighter who controls the fight'. This includes the distance in terms of what you can reach with or without taking a step and/or how many steps will be necessary to take you to your target, how long it will take you to get there, or to move away, and which angle of approach is best at the time.

'Between stimulus and response there is a space. In that space is our power to choose our response. In our response lies our growth and our freedom.'

Viktor E. Frankl

The Yin and Yang of Proximity

The Yang

retreat
departure
move out
avoidance
escape
exit
retire

The Yin

distance
gap
space
reach
close
move in

The Proximity Strategy in Tradition

Cut and Run

This phrase meaning 'to quickly escape from a potentially dangerous situation' is a marine term first recorded in 1704. The sailing ships of old had only the wind to manoeuvre with (see Manoeuvre) so their acceleration (see Pace) was totally governed by the speed and direction of the wind. Their turning circle, too, was dictated by the wind. If a warship was caught unawares by an enemy vessel, it would have no time to wind in its anchor if it was to escape safely. So, to avoid wasting the time it would take to bring the anchor up, the crew would cut through the anchor rope so that the ship was free to run before the wind and make its escape, putting a safe distance between themselves and their threat. By 1867 the phrase had entered popular parlance.

> *'How you think when you lose determines how long it will be until you win.'*
> Gilbert K. Chesterton

The Proximity Strategy in Warfare

One Step Beyond

The Law of Proximity deals with the importance of distance needed between yourself and an enemy. We should always consider our reasons for moving in or moving away from our target and what motivates this movement. If we close on an enemy for emotional reasons, we must be pretty sure that we can outgun him (see Recruitment and Pressure). If we fear retreat for emotional reasons, we are also failing to act strategically – retreat is not always a loss, it is sometimes the wisest course of action.

Chinese Strategy No. 36 – Retreat is Considered Best

In the West, we have ideas about retreat being cowardly, but tacticians in ancient China understood the benefit of running away when they could not win. There is no point in fighting on when the day is lost, unless it is a tactical decision (see Example) made to sacrifice the few to save the many. Also, it is possible to attack as you retreat, as expressed by the adage: 'Discretion is the better part of valour' meaning that you can retreat, re-gather your forces and come back to try again. Retreat is considered a failure only by those who do not understand that it can be an efficient strategy allowing us to control the distance and time between ourselves and our enemy.

Accurate perception and control of distance are major skills in battle. Throughout the ages, warlords have sought to control distance with boundaries and territories; to create weapons that can hit their target from increasingly greater distances, to the extent that today we can launch missiles that can travel thousands of miles to their destination.

There are many places you can be in relation to your enemy, not just at a great distance or close up. Consider the spy (see Duplicity and Alignment) who stands so close to his target that he appears not to be an enemy, or the suicide bomber who lives amongst his enemies and behaves as a completely normal and integrated member of that society.

The spy Kim Philby, an Englishman working for the Russians, was supposedly recruited by the NKVD (the predecessor of the KGB) when he was just 22. Philby was eventually appointed head of MI6, even after he was incriminated in the defection of two other spy friends of his (Burgess and McLean). He was also employed by a newspaper as a political correspondent based near the

British Embassy in Beirut. Eventually, in 1963, things became too hot for Philby and he jumped aboard a Russian Freighter headed for Moscow. Philby had been privy to some of Britain's most sensitive and secret information without ever being caught, and so successful was he as a double agent that even the Russians didn't fully trust him when he arrived on their shores. Philby defected just before he was caught, apparently tipped off by another spy, suspected to be Anthony Blunt, a close confident of the Royal household who was himself exposed in 1979. Philby made great use of the Proximity strategy, staying physically close to Britain whilst being emotionally and intellectually closer to the Soviets.

In combat, we must strive to be close enough to strike whilst too distant to be hit. To be safe, you need to be at the range that your opponent cannot deal with; if you have longer arms, then stay out of his reach using your greater reach to strike safely. If you are shorter, then slip, left and right, dip underneath or combine the two movements into a bob and weave, evading his strikes even as you close in on him.

It is a great skill to know when to move in and when to retreat, and to have the skill to do either, without sustaining injury or loss, is the sign of a true master. Disguise both the close and the retreat so that your enemy cannot recognise what you are doing until it is too late (see Appearance). Learn how to use your range as one of the most important strategies of all.

Examine how you can be close frontally but out of his line of sight laterally or horizontally, and how to avoid (retreat), how to evade (laterally) and how to attack (close) your opponent. Consider also, how your ability to use Proximity relates and connects with Manoeuvrability (see Manoeuvre).

'He that fights and runs away may turn and fight another day; but he that is in battle slain will never rise to fight again.'

Tacitus

The Proximity Strategy in Combat

'They couldn't hit an elephant at this di...' General John Sedgwick

These were the final words of General John Sedgwick, the highest ranking Union officer to be killed in the American Civil War. After uttering his final words to his men, he fell dead, killed by a sniper's bullet at over 1000 yards.

If you work no other skill in combat, you must work to master your distance because when to move in, when to move out, when to duck, sidestep and slip are the key skills of combat. If you have mastery of these skills and your opponent does not, you can make him look foolish, creating doubt (see Faith) in him. You will be able to use more power if you use the correct range in your attacks and you should soon win the fight.

There are 5 ranges in unarmed combat which must be studied by every fighter who wants to understand the strength and power of Proximity. Briefly, these distances are:

Distance 5 is the range of kicks which outreach hand strikes

Distance 4 is the reach of the open and closed hands

Distance 3 is the range of hook punches

Distance 2 is the range of uppercut punches

Distance 1 is the range of the clinch

We call this 'Bull's Eye' distancing (think of it like a huge archery target laid flat on the ground, where each range is one of the coloured circles.) Within each range there are subsections, subtle changes in proximity which can mean the difference between hitting lightly and heavily, between being grabbed and avoiding the grab.

Knowledge of these ranges and how they are affected by the distance we can reach with, and without having to step, are essential knowledge for a fighter who wants to win through good strategy.

Consider your opponent's strengths and weaknesses. Kickers struggle to kick at close range; grapplers struggle at long range; a good kick boxer will be comfortable at all 5 ranges, but in the clinch will be at the mercy of the wrestler. One false move can place a fighter into the wrong range, so make sure your fight game is complete at all ranges. The wrestler must close the gap on a striker and the striker must learn to keep his distance. A boxer must close on a kicker and a kicker must keep a boxer as far as possible. Each style of combat has its strength at given distances, and some have many strengths, while some have few. The master of combat knows he cannot easily master all distances, which is why most have specialities and use strategies to get their opponent into their preferred distance.

Some of the most important martial arts training you can practise is bettering your ability to move (see also Manoeuvre) in and out of danger at both fast and slow speeds (see Pace), over and under and alongside your opponent. If you can keep your opponent at bay and yet close enough to strike, then you are the victor. Learn when to retreat and when to advance in all 4 dimensions, master your distance and you will master the fight.

'Part of the happiness of life consists not in fighting battles, but in avoiding them. A masterly retreat is in itself a victory.'

Norman Vincent Peale

The Proximity Strategy in Relationships

Sling Your Hook

Often we fail to make the move toward a potential partner for fear of rebuttal and the pain it might cause us emotionally. Instead, we retreat and fail to act, in order to protect ourselves from hurt.

Some of us care too much at the outset and end up building a wall between ourselves and a potential mate who might have been interested in us, had we but made the first move. If they're not interested in the first place, then it might hurt us, but only to the extent of how much we dwell on that failure. Remember: 'Faint heart never won fair lady'. You must learn to develop rhino skin against hurts like this or you will miss many opportunities and end up incapable of bridging the gap between you and the people you want to have in your life. Sometimes, you need to 'man up' and create strategies where you can make yourself a more attractive prospect (see Attraction) by choosing people with similar interests; don't just choose your potential partners based solely on looks, as those who spend the most time on their appearance are often shallow and trivial. Create situations where you can develop a relationship before you leap in and ask for a date. Test the water (see Risk); if you see signs of interest, then develop them, and if you see none, retreat and move on.

Remember that a direct attack is often the one that gets the worst response. Use subtle, cautious and well-planned strategies to come closer to the people you like and, if it becomes obvious that you cannot win, then (and only then) it might be time to sling your hook.

> **'Woman begins by resisting a man's advances and ends by blocking his retreat.'**
>
> Oscar Wilde

The Proximity Strategy in Friendship

Keep Your Friends Close and Your Enemies Closer

Proximity links closely to both the law and strategy of Timing, as to move in or out takes time, and every strike, block or interception (see Interruption) relies on timing your movement correctly so that you are at the optimum distance at the optimum time.

There are times when you should give your friends space to move and think, and there are times when you need to be close and supportive. Sometimes, you need to be behind them and sometimes you must stand by their side. Help your allies to recognise when they should close (move in) and when they should avoid (move out) and make sure that your choice is dictated by logic rather than motivated by out-of-control emotions. We must also guide our friends when they let go of their goals and start to drop back when they should move in, or move in when they should retreat (for reasons of ego, for instance). Don't allow your allies to be drawn into danger whether it be physical, financial or emotional.

Keep shallow and trivial friends at a distance when you know that what you need is the support of a serious friend. Confine 'fair weather' friends to light fun social events, keep them at 'arm's length' in times of crisis, and recognise the difference between an acquaintance and a real friend. Learn who your real friends are, and who is just pretending (see Alignment, Appearance and Duplicity) - and remember that not everyone has your best interests at heart. There are people who just want to leverage your money, time or relationships. Others want to hurt you – in fact most dangerous psychopaths get close to their victims through friendship before they reveal (see Appearance) their dangerous intent.

Remember the Law of Proximity – 'the fighter who controls the distance is the fighter who controls the fight' – and a good strategist will use his skill in distance management to maximise his impact on anyone who makes a threatening advance.

'The longest absence is less perilous to love than the terrible trials of incessant proximity.'

Edna St. Vincent Millay

The Proximity Strategy Personally

By Hook or By Crook

Few realise that this phrase refers originally to what we can reach from a tree using a (bale) hook or a (shepherd's) crook and deals with what is and is not within our immediate reach. Similarly, you decide, when you set your goal, at what distance it is placed, in both time and space, and you decide on how far you are ready to go to get what you want.

Once a goal is set, quantified and dated, it begins to move inexorably toward you (if you are working properly) or away from you (if you aren't working for it) and your ability to manage the distance between you and that goal is a masterly skill. Achieving the same type of goal over and over gives us the judgment necessary to plan our tasks to meet it and beat it. But every goal that is completely new to us has within it that element which is totally unknown – the X factor – which can be assessed or experienced in relation to something similar, but never the actual thing itself. This is when it can get very hard to plan how to reach that goal. Start by assessing the distance between you and your desired outcome (whether it be physical, financial, temporal, etc…) and what you can do to bridge that gap. Consider your goals as if they were an enemy that must be defeated, but which is moving inexorably toward you all the time, or like a friend planning to meet you, and you need to get everything ready in time for his arrival. Either way, know that once the date is set, that day is approaching and cannot be stopped, and you must act every day if you want to reach your target on time.

Every target (goal) you aim for will resist you to a certain extent, but it will become more achievable in direct proportion to the quality of your planning and task completion. Always be conscious of where you are in relation to your important goals and, if you know when to move in, to stay or move out, you will be able to achieve great things. Conversely, if you procrastinate too much you will achieve nothing.

'We are not retreating – we are advancing in another direction.'
Douglas MacArthur

The Proximity Strategy in Health

An Apple a Day Keeps the Doctor Away

We can do many things which adversely affect our health, such as drinking alcohol, smoking or taking recreational drugs, etc. We use these damaging substances because, in the short term, they seem to have only pleasant effects on how we feel and how we relate to those around us.

However, in the long term, they are harming us silently and irreparably and we never know how much damage they are actually causing us until it is too late. If you smoked a cigarette and immediately collapsed in the same agony as a late stage cancer victim, it is doubtful whether you would ever smoke again. But this doesn't happen; cigarettes eat away gradually at your insides, unseen, unfelt and unknown, yet one thing is certain: if you keep on smoking, the effects of that smoke will get you eventually, in a small or big way. Many things that seem harmless when we use them can be damaging in the long term.

Consider your health in terms of distance: close in on the positives of good diet, exercise, meditation and the like, and retreat from those things that you know will do you no good. Fend off those emotions that demand to be satisfied with quick fixes and embrace the good feelings that your discipline has given you.

Learn to recognise that, often, what is easy now brings hardship later, and what is challenging today reaps long term benefits tomorrow.

> **'I take rejection as someone blowing a bugle in my ear to wake me up and get going, rather than retreat.'**
>
> Sylvester Stallone

The Proximity Strategy in Wealth

Tempus Fugit (Time Flies)

We often start out in our teens and early 20s expecting to be rich and successful and, by the time we hit our 30s, these dreams are often crushed by our experience.

Our education and conditioning can be to blame as so often this does nothing to prepare us for the real world. The advice to get a good education is sound, but which education you get is vital. We are taught maths at school, but not how to save, invest, manage credit or read a balance sheet. Many people are in jobs they don't like because their education has taught them how to be employed by others and to be trapped in so-called career paths, which from the outside look no better than cages. Many careers are so demanding that they destroy our family life and health, whilst never bringing that promise of wealth that attracted us to them in the first place. Imagine the joy experienced by those of us who are able to pursue a career doing something we love, whilst also being able to spend quality time with our loved ones and build our net worth quickly; able to retire young, free to do what we want without having the heavy worries of mortgages, loans, or a petty boss to please.

Too often people end up in dead-end jobs that they hate, in relationships that are not supportive, and they resort to complaining, blaming and waiting eagerly for each weekend to escape from their life's reality by drinking and partying. Why do so many over 30s live like this? Part of the reason people get trapped in the rat race is their education and expectations (see Expectation), but the strategy of Proximity is even more relevant to this aspect of our lives.

A big part of the problem is the lack of distance appreciation. In our teens, we think we have forever to achieve our dreams and, consequently, we fail to appreciate the passing of time. We waste our time partying at university or school instead of working, studying and learning skills that will release us from the 'rat race'. We study subjects based on how much we enjoy them (which is a good thing in itself) but we do not consider how we will use that skill when we get our degree. We push away thoughts of 'how' and 'when' and instead we live on hope; hope that we'll find a job, hope that it will pay well, hope that it will be secure.

Suddenly, we are faced with having a degree in a subject that employers don't want anymore because times have moved on more quickly than we expected. So we get a job in a different industry earning less because we have no relevant qualification in it, biding our time until a better opportunity comes along. By the time we hit our 30s and have kids, alongside mortgages and debts, and that job never did materialise, we feel that wealth will always elude us and we remove it from our dream list.

Don't we all know people who have done just this? Don't we also know people who are about to? Hey, it may even be you! Can you see now how knowledge of the strategy of Proximity could teach these people how to manage their past, present and future better? Can you see that time is passing and never stops? So why waste it going in the wrong direction or procrastinating, when, with a little study of how life works and knowledge of what others have achieved and what we want to achieve, we could live a life that is free of the rat race and, instead, put us on the fast track to wealth and freedom.

We must have a proper understanding of the strategy of Proximity and understand how it works in terms of physical distance and chronological distance. Make distance in time and space your focus and your friend, and you will understand a key part of a strategy and implementation which will, when used in the right direction (see Direction), bring wealth and success back into your sights.

> **'The human voice can never reach the distance that is covered by the still small voice of conscience.'**
> Mahatma Gandhi

The Proximity Strategy in Growth

Time and Tide Wait for No Man

Personal growth takes planning, which itself requires a deep understanding of Proximity. In order to draw an effective plan, it is essential for you to know where you are in relation to your goals.

Are you close or distant? Are you in the line of fire, under it, over it or have you sidestepped it? Are you procrastinating and avoiding the action you must take to achieve your goals or are you rushing in blindly and sustaining too many injuries as you advance? The clock is ticking on all your goals and dreams; the time frames you have set are moving towards you constantly and, if you fail to complete the tasks necessary to achieve your goals (because you get side tracked by the unimportant or retreat because of fear of injuries sustained by charging in without a plan, for example), then you are failing to apply the strategy of Proximity efficiently. Consider Proximity in all its forms, including retirement, which is the point when you decide to step out of the game and put your feet up. In order to be able to do this, you must have set good, worthy, helpful goals (for yourself and others) that will eventually put you in a place where you can afford to pass over the reins to the next generation, whilst you take a well-earned retirement living on the passive income that you have built up – allowing you to still earn without having to go to work anymore.

If you can learn nothing else from the 25 Game Plan strategies, at least learn this message: 'Time waits for no one' and, if you want to achieve your dreams before you are too old or too sick to enjoy them, then you must become a master of Proximity.

> *'Always be closing… That doesn't mean you're always closing the deal, but it does mean that you need to be always closing on the next step in the process.'*
>
> Shane Gibson

Summary

By now, you should understand why Proximity is so important to what we want to achieve in life. Sometimes, we have to move in and, at other times we have to retreat; sometimes we have to sidestep issues and, conversely, sometimes we do all of these things when we should simply hold our ground and wait. The management of distance is one of the greatest skills you can possess because it deals with positioning in both space and time.

Proximity Strategy in Brief

1. Consider Proximity in terms of 4 dimensions: forwards and backwards, sideways, up and down, and the passing of time
2. Consider your reasons for moving in or moving away. If we close in, or retreat from an enemy for emotional reasons, we are failing to act strategically.
3. In the West, we have ideas about retreat being cowardly, but tacticians in ancient China understood the benefit of running away when they could not win. There is no point in fighting on when the day is lost.
4. If you can keep your opponent at bay yet close enough to strike, then you can be the victor. Learn when to retreat and when to advance in all dimensions; master your distance and you will master the fight.
5. Remember that a direct attack is often the one that gets the worst response. Be subtle, cautious and well planned and, if it becomes obvious that you cannot win, then (and only then), sling your hook.
6. Consider those times when you should give your friends space to move and think, and other times when you should be close and supportive.
7. You have power over the distance between you and your goal; when you set your goal, you decide at what distance to place it in both time and space.
8. Consider your health in terms of distance: close in on the positives of good diet, exercise, meditation and the like, and retreat from those things that you know will do you no good.
9. Make distance in time and space your focus and you'll understand a key part of success which will, when used in the right direction, bring wealth and success into your sights.
10. If you want to achieve your dreams before you are too old or too sick to enjoy them, then you must become a master of the strategy of Proximity.

Epilogue

We have covered the 25 FLITE stratagems in detail, from definition to folk tradition to warfare, relationships, health, wealth and personal growth. I have tried to provide an understanding of each stratagem from several angles so that each appears obvious, which is as it should be, as we have all used them at some point in our lives, even if we have not been aware of doing so at the time.

Now we have now seen examples of how they can work with us and against us, and are aware that we are often the author of their direction in either instance, and that they are not always affected by an individual alone, but by life itself. The strategies are elemental, just like the laws that govern them, which means they are older than time and constant. They are not designed by man, but can be manipulated by him if he understands them well enough.

So, what next? The extent to which you are committed to learning about strategy and how much of its use you have grasped so far will affect how comfortable you feel in applying what you know. Personally, I find it useful to look at different strategy sets and to examine the behaviour of those I interact with, to identify and analyse the strategies they employ in our meetings or discussions.

For the most part, people are using strategy without realising it. Since our behaviour has been conditioned in us from a young age, it is advisable to re-examine our own behaviour closely, to identify which strategies we habitually use, the reasons why we use them, and whether we can improve our results by changing or refining them.

The results we've had in life so far are the results of the strategies we have applied so far. Since this happened without a very clear understanding of what they were or how they work, it follows that the majority of the results we have had up to now have been the result of chance rather than design.

Think of the things you tried and failed or those things that stand out in your mind as mistakes; how would they have turned out if you had known what you know now about the laws governing strategy? Then imagine how those things could have turned out if you had studied and mastered the FLITE strategies, so that you had been well-prepared for the situations.

Understanding the strategies has changed my life and made me very aware of every action I take, conscious of strategies that are available to me and those that I face. I consider more carefully my actions and motivations, and those of others with whom I come into contact. Motivation is generally quite simple: we are either drawn to something because we want it or we are repelled by something and seek to escape it. However, our motivation, whether toward or away from something, stems from deeply held beliefs and conditioning, most of which we have never examined nor questioned their origins to discover whether what drives us is rational or emotional, and helping or hindering us.

With the FLITE strategies at our disposal, we can gain deeper knowledge of what drives us, by examining our needs, wants and desires (and their opposites) and, in so doing, we can discover those needs and wants that will bring us what will help us in the short and long term. However, we can only truly do this if we apply ourselves to understanding our own nature and the nature of our life. The 25 strategies will help us to achieve this understanding if we study them well.

Good Strategising!

Tony Higo

Bibliography

The following books have been invaluable in helping me to define the FLITE strategies and to help me write this book. I would like to acknowledge and thank the following authors and to recommend their books, all of which are available on Amazon.com.

The 36 Strategies of War – Robert Green

The 48 Laws of Power – Robert Green

36 Secret Strategies of the Martial Arts – William Scott Wilson

Red Herrings and White Elephants – Albert Jack

The Art of War – Sun Tzu

Brutal Wisdom – Master 'Dutch' Hinkle

36 Strategies for Executives – Donald G. Krause and Jeff Carter

The Book of 5 Rings – Miyamoto Musashi

The Life-Giving Sword – Yagya Munenori

Warrior Wisdom – Tony Higo

Acknowledgements

Thank you to my wife Amaya for listening to my ideas on this book and helping me to explore and examine how they work, for reading through the book (many times), proofreading and editing and, as ever, for her support in getting this project to completion.